EVERYBODY'S AUTOBIOGRAPHY

EVERYBODY'S AUTOBIOGRAPHY

Gertrude Stein

VINTAGE BOOKS
A DIVISION OF RANDOM HOUSE
NEW YORK

VINTAGE BOOKS EDITION, March 1973

Library of Congress Cataloging in Publication Data
Stein, Gertrude, 1874–1946.
    Everybody's autobiography.

    Reprint of the 1937 ed.
    I. Title.
[PS3537.T323Z53   1973]   818'.5'209 [B]
ISBN 0–384–71826–7   72–8694

The index for this edition was compiled by Patricia
Meyerowitz.

Contents

EVERYBODY'S AUTOBIOGRAPHY

Alice B. Toklas did hers and now everybody will do theirs.

Alice B. Toklas says and if they are all going to do theirs the way she did hers.

In the first place she did not want it to be Alice B. Toklas, if it has to be at all it should be Alice Toklas and in the French translation it was Alice Toklas in French it just could not be Alice B. Toklas but in America and in England too Alice B. Toklas was more than Alice Toklas. Alice Toklas never thought so and always said so.

That is the way any autobiography has to be written which reminds me of Dashiell Hammett.

But before I am reminded of Dashiell Hammett I want to say that just today I met Miss Hennessy and she was carrying, she did not have it with her, but she usually carried a wooden umbrella. This wooden umbrella is carved out of wood and looks exactly like a real one even to the little button and the rubber string that holds it together. It is all right except when it rains. When it rains it does not open and so Miss Hennessy looks a little foolish but she does not mind because after all it is the only wooden umbrella in Paris. And even if there were lots of others it would not make any difference.

Which does remind me of David Edstrom but I have been reminded of him after I was reminded of Dashiell Hammett.

It is very nice being a celebrity a real celebrity who can decide who they want to meet and say so and they come or do not come as you want them. I never imagined that would happen to me to be a celebrity like that but it did and when it did I liked it but all that will come much later. Anyway I was a celebrity and when I was at Pasadena Mrs. Ehrman whom I had met at Carl Van Vechten's in New York asked us to come over to Beverly Hills and dine with her. Whom did we want to meet. Anybody she liked, she said she would get Charlie Chaplin and the Emersons and some others not more than twelve in all would that do. Yes and Alice Toklas hung up.

Later on in the day I never get up early I get up as late as possible I like not to get up in the morning and no one ever wakes me anyway I was told about it and was pleased, then suddenly the next day I said but I did want to meet Dashiell Hammett and somebody in New York said he was in California.

I never was interested in cross word puzzles or any kind of puzzles but I do like detective stories. I never try to guess who has done the crime and if I did I would be sure to guess wrong but I like somebody being dead and how it moves along and Dashiell Hammett was all that and more. So Alice Toklas rang up Mrs. Ehrman and said we wanted to meet Dashiell Hammett.

She said yes what is his name. Dashiell Hammett said Miss Toklas. And how do you spell it. Alice Toklas spelt it. Yes and where does he live. Ah that said Alice Toklas we do not know, we asked in New York and Knopf his editor said he could not give his address. Ah yes said Mrs. Ehrman now what is he. Dashiell Hammett you know The Thin Man said Alice Toklas. Oh yes said Mrs. Ehrman yes and they both hung up.

We went to dinner that evening and there was Dashiell Hammett and we had an interesting talk about autobiography, but first how did he get there I mean at Mrs. Ehrman's for dinner. Between them they told it.

Mrs. Ehrman called up an office he had at Hollywood and asked for his address, she was told he was in San Francisco, then she called up the producer of The Thin Man he said Hammett was in New York. So said Mrs. Ehrman to herself he must be in Hollywood. So she called up the man who had wanted to produce The Thin Man and had failed to get it and he gave Hammett's address. Mrs. Ehrman telegraphed to Hammett saying would he come that evening and dine with her to meet Gertrude Stein. It was April Fool's Day and he did nothing and then he looked up Ehrman and it was a furrier and no Mrs. Ehrman and then he asked everybody and heard that it was all true and telegraphed and said if he might bring who was to be his hostess he could come and Mrs. Ehrman said of course come and they came. His hostess but all that will come when the dinner happens later.

Anything is an autobiography but this was a conversation.

I said to Hammett there is something that is puzzling. In the nineteenth century the men when they were writing did invent all kinds and a great number of men. The women on the other hand never could invent women they always made the women be themselves seen splendidly or sadly or heroically or beautifully or desparingly or gently, and they never could make any other kind of woman. From Charlotte Brontë to George Eliot and many years later this was true. Now in the twentieth century it is the men who do it. The men all write about themselves, they are always themselves as strong or weak or mysterious or passionate or drunk or controlled but always themselves as the women used to do in the nineteenth century. Now you yourself always do it now why is it. He said it's simple. In the nineteenth century men were confident, the women were not but in the twentieth century the men have no confidence and so they have to make themselves as you say more beautiful more intriguing more everything and they cannot make any other man because they have to hold on to themselves not having any confidence. Now I he went on have even thought of doing a father and a son to see if in that way I could make another one. That's interesting I said.

Anyway autobiography is easy like it or not autobiography is easy for any one and so this is to be everybody's autobiography.

As I said after I was reminded of Dashiell Hammett I was reminded of David Edstrom. And that happened in Los Angeles too.

David Edstrom was the big Swede who was a sculptor and was thin when I first knew him and then enormously fat and married the head of the Paris Christian Science Church, and then well and then she was dead but so he says that has nothing to do with him.

I had not seen him for years and never expected to see him again.

When we were at Pasadena there he was on the telephone. One of the things that was funny about being in America was that so little of my past came up. I went to school with lots of them and to college at Radcliffe and Medical school and knew lots in Paris, but not a great many turned up. However Edstrom did. He telephoned and said will you come. We came. He was as fat as ever a little older and now was doing a statue of some benefactor was it Jenny Lind, or Grace Darling or Florence Nightingale, well anyway he wanted us to be photographed together. Being photographed together reminds me of another one. However. We were not photographed together. But what reminded me of David Edstrom was that he used to complain so that I liked everybody in character.

In those comparatively young days I did. I thought everybody had a character and I knew it and I liked them to be in character. Now, well they are in character I suppose so but I would like it just as well if they were not anyway if they are or if they are not is not exciting to me now. Anything that is is quite enough if it is. What is it Helen says, our old servant who has come back to us, there is too much of nothing or there is never enough of anything, well anyway.

Being photographed together reminds me of another thing and then chapter one will begin.

In New York a great many places wanted us to come that was

natural enough but we did not go, we did not go at all because in that way it was easy to say so but Alice Toklas felt that when the women writers asked us to tea we had to go, she feels that way from time to time so she said yes we would come. Max White and Lindley Hubbell had come to see us and we took them along. Lindley Hubbell had been for many years a comfort to me, he read all I wrote and he always told me so warmly that he had. I had thought that he would be a tallish pale and sympathetic New Englander. Not at all, he was short and dark and neat and prim and he attends to all the maps in the Astor library. Well however we went to tea and there were a great many writers and others there. I drifted around and then I saw a short little woman with a large head and there were curls but I did not notice them. We were asked to meet each other, Mary Pickford and I. She said she wished she knew more French and I said I talked it all right but I never read it I did not care about it as a written language she said she did wish she did know more French, and then, I do not quite know how it happened, she said and suppose we should be photographed together. Wonderful idea I said. We were by this time standing near a couch where Belle Greene was seated. I had never met Belle Greene before although everybody I knew knew her. It is funny about meeting and not meeting not that it makes any difference if you don't you don't if you do you do. Nathalie Barney was just telling me that her mother often asked her to come in and meet Whistler. Even if you do not care about his pictures he will amuse you, she said, but Nathalie Barney was always busy writing a letter whenever her mother happened to ask her and so she never met him. Mary Pickford said it would be easy to get the Journal photographer to come over, yes I will telephone said some one rushing off, yes I said it would be wonderful we might be taken shaking hands. You are not going to do it, said Belle Greene excitedly behind me, of course I am going to I said, nothing would please me better of course we are said I turning to Mary Pickford, Mary Pickford said perhaps I will not be able to stay and she began to back away, Oh yes you must I said it will not be long now, no no she said I think I had better not and she melted away. I knew you would not do it, said Belle Greene behind me. And then I asked every one because I was interested just what it was that went on inside Mary Pickford. It was her idea and then when I was enthusiastic she melted away. They all said that what she thought was if I were enthusiastic it meant that I thought that it would do me more good than it would do her and so she melted away or others said perhaps after all it would not be good for her audience that we should be photographed together, anyway I was very much interested to know just what they know about what is good publicity and what is not. Harcourt was very surprised when I said to him on first meeting him in New York remember this extraordinary welcome that I am having does not come from the books of mine that they do understand like the Autobiography but the books of mine that they did not understand and he called his partner and said listen to what she says and perhaps after all she is right.

Well anyway we all went away and as we came downstairs there was an elderly colored man and he came up to me and said Miss Gertrude Stein and I said yes and he said I am (I have forgotten the name), I was the first music teacher of Mr. Matthews who sang the Saint Ignatius and I wanted to say how do you do to you and I was very touched. And then we four Max White and Lindley Hubbell and Alice Toklas and I walked down Fifth Avenue together and my book Portraits and Prayers was just to come out that day and on the cover was to be a photograph of me by Carl Van Vechten and as we were walking down Fifth Avenue together, a young colored woman smiled and slowly pointed and there it was a copy of the book in a shop window and she smiled and went away. That was what New York was and all that will come later but before all that we had stayed in France.

CHAPTER I

What happened
after The Autobiography of Alice B. Toklas

I always remembered that Victor Hugo said that if it had not rained on the night of the 17th of June, 1815, the fate of Europe would have been changed. Of course it is not so, if you win you do not lose and if you lose you do not win, at least if you win or if you lose it seems so. Well anyway, there are floods, when one reads about them in the paper they seem worse than they are, and yet they often are worse than they seem in the newspaper only those there are busy and so they do not worry and so it is not as bad as it reads. Well anyway Alice Toklas' father during the war sent with great bother to himself and to us who received it, dried provisions because the papers said we were starving in France well we were not, not at all and still in a kind of a way the war was worse than that. In short floods or no floods things pretty much do happen and they used to say it will be all the same a hundred years hence but really it will not. And so I said. If there had not been a beautiful and unusually dry October at Bilignin in France in nineteen thirty two followed by an unusually dry and beautiful first two weeks of November would The Autobiography of Alice B. Toklas have been written. Possibly but probably not then. And still one does not, no one does not in one's heart believe in mute inglorious Miltons. If one has succeeded in doing anything one is certain that anybody who really has it in them to really do anything will really do that thing. Anyway I have done something and anyway I did write The Autobiography of Alice B. Toklas and since then a great many things happened, and the first thing that

9

happened was that we came back to Paris, we generally almost always do do that.

When we came back and with everything that has happened in between we are here now, the first thing I did was to telephone to Pablo Picasso and tell him what I had done. I want to hear it he said and he came and I began to translate it to him. Picasso's name originally was well anyway his father's name was Ruiz and his mother's name was Picasso. In Spain you take your father's and your mother's name like Ruiz y Picasso like Merry y del Val, del Val was Spanish and Merry was Irish and finally the names pile up and you take your choice.

I used to think the name of anybody was very important and the name made you and I have often said so. Perhaps I still think so but still there are so many names and anybody nowadays can call anybody any name they like. We have Chinese servants now and sometimes the name they say they are has nothing to do with what they are they may have borrowed or gambled away their reference and they seem to be there or not there as well with any name and anyway the Oriental, and perhaps a name there is not a name, is invading the Western world. It is the peaceful penetration that is important not wars. You may think this has nothing to do with Pablo Picasso and with me but wait and you will see. Any Oriental can wait and any Oriental is supposed to be able to see well we will see. Peaceful penetration, nice words and quiet words and long but not too long words. I was out walking, we have to be out walking what else can we do we do not like sitting or standing at least not too long so we have to be out walking. We have a Chinese servant now because alas the French servants and their cooking is not what it was. It is curious very curious and yet not at all unreasonable that when there is a great deal of unemployment and misery you can never find anybody to work for you. It is funny that but that is the way it is.

For peaceful penetration there may be pacific defence. When I was walking the other day I saw some workmen digging up the street, that happens very often and I always ask them what they are doing and why they are doing it. It is a way I have, and means nothing except that while I am walking I like to stop and say a few words to some one. They said they were preparing the pacific defence of Paris. Pacific defence of Paris I said, what is that. Oh that they said is preparing a larger flow of water and the more frequent placing of openings for large rubber hose. Oh yes I said.

Alice B. Toklas is always forethoughtful which is what is pleasant for me so she said she would make copies of all my writing not yet published and send it to Carl Van Vechten for safe keeping. In spite of everything and everything means a fair amount printed there still is a good deal unpublished.

Well anyway she worked at it very hard and she sent it to Carl explaining that it was in case of any trouble in Paris. Carl wrote back that it was all carefully put away and he would take the best of care of it, but said Carl perhaps it will be here first. Well you never can tell about it. The other day this is March nineteen thirty-six my brother in California that is another story a rather nice story. My brother had lived in France almost as long as I have, he is ten years my senior, I am the youngest of the family, it is nice being the youngest or the oldest, and I am the youngest and this brother was the oldest. It does not make so much difference now but it made a lot when we were younger, well anyway, he cabled advise send over pictures and drawings to America. And I wrote back and said no there is no use in being too forethoughtful. We might have decided to live in the Connecticut valley and now it is all flooded or so the newspapers say. Everybody knows if you are too careful you are so occupied in being careful that you are sure to stumble over something. But all this still has something to do with being oriental and the oriental peaceful penetration of the West and why it is reasonable.

When I was young the most awful moment of my life was when

I really realized that the stars are worlds and when I really realized that there were civilizations that had completely disappeared from this earth. And now it happens again. Then I was frightened badly frightened, now well now being frightened is something less frightening than it was. There are a great many things about that but that will come gradually in Everybody's Autobiography. Now I am still out walking. I like walking.

Yesterday when I went out walking I met some one. I used to say one of the things about Paris was that you never met any one you know when you were out walking. But now everything is changing and you that is I well now any one often meets them people you know or people who know you.

Anyway I did yesterday and he was an Egyptian.

When I said I was frightened when I really knew that the stars were worlds that was before everybody was certain that there are men only on this earth and that being men is therefore a very difficult thing to be. But more of this as we go on.

The Egyptian is a young fellow I had only met him once before when he was with a young Frenchman who had just written a nice little book about Proust. I had only met him twice the young Frenchman once when he was very amusing and once when he was too drunk to be amusing and wanted everybody to eat something and he had to be put out from where he was. Well anyway the young Frenchman was walking along with this other one that was another day and I met them. Then on this day which was yesterday I met the Egyptian. I did not recognize him because I had not known he was an Egyptian but he told me who he was. And we talked and we both said we liked to walk alone but we walked on together and he told me about the Egyptian language and that is what I want to tell about before I go on with Picasso because it has a great deal to do with everything.

He said now in Egypt there was a written language and a spoken one but that many people his mother and father for example know French better than they know either although they the family had from the beginning of time been Egyptian. Gradually we made it all clear to ourselves and to each other.

The Egyptians in the old days only had one language, that is to say everybody used only a little of any language in the ordinary life but when they were in love or talked to their hero or were moved or told tales then they spoke in an exalted and fanciful language that has now become a written language because nowadays in talking they are not exalted any more and they use just ordinary language all the time and so they have forgotten the language of exaltation and that is now only written but never spoken.

That is very interesting I said, now the English language I said has gone just the other way, they always tried to write like anybody talked and it is only comparatively lately that it is true that the written language knows that that is of no interest and cannot be done that is to write as anybody talks because what anybody talks because everybody talks as the newspapers and movies and radios tell them to talk the spoken language is no longer interesting and so gradually the written language says something and says it differently than the spoken language. I was very much interested in what I said when I gradually said these things, and it is very important all this is just now. So soon we will come to have a written language that is a thing apart in English. If you begin one place you always end at another. Let me tell you about my brother.

As I said he had lived in France as long as I had he had a son he had a grandson here, he had his wife and friends he seemed reasonably content and happy. And about five years ago he said he wanted to go back to California but why I said what's the matter you've lived here so long what's the matter, oh he said you don't understand, he said I want to say in English to the man who brings the letters and does the gardening I want to say things to them and have them say it to me in American. But Mike, I said, yes yes I know he said but I can't help it, I must go and hear them say these things in American, I must go back there to live that is all there is about it I must. And he has sold his house, it was a bad time to sell and nobody could sell anything but he wandered around until he saw a man who looked as if he was looking for a house and he was and my brother said why not buy mine and he did and in a week they were gone, all except the son who had been married in France and liked to talk to everybody in French because that is what he likes to do.

Well that is a true story.

And Picasso came with his wife when we came back to Paris after having written The Autobiography of Alice B. Toklas.

I began reading it to him in French, he and I were on the couch together and his wife was sitting on a chair and was talking to Alice Toklas and then they all listened as I began.

I talk French badly and write it worse but so does Pablo he says we write and talk our French but that is a later story.

So I began at the beginning with the description of the room as it was and the description of our servant Helen. You made one mistake said Pablo you left out something there were three swords that hung on that wall one underneath the other and he said it was very exciting. Then I went on and Fernande came in.

I was reading he was listening and his eyes were wide open and then suddenly his wife Olga Picasso got up and said she would not listen she would go away she said. What's the matter, we said, I do not know that woman she said and left. Pablo said go on reading, I said no you must go after your wife, he said oh I said oh, and he left and until this year and that was two years in between we did not see each other again but now he has left his wife and we have seen each other again.

When I saw him again I said how did you ever make the decision and keep it of leaving your wife. Yes he said you and I we have weak characters and no initiative and if I had died before I did it

14

you never would have thought that I had a strong enough character to do this thing. No I said I did not think you ever could really do a thing like that, hitherto when you changed anything somebody always took you away and this time nobody did and how did it happen. I suppose he said when a thing is where there is no life left then you either die or go on living, well he said that is what happened to me.

When he got rid of his wife he stopped painting and took to writing poetry. Everything does something I suppose and this is what that did and about this poetry it is a very curious story.

He told me about this poetry I had already heard about it, he said he was not going to paint any more perhaps never, he was going to write poetry would I come some evening and listen. I said I would yes and I said I would bring some one who was here now, and I brought along Thornton Wilder. I will tell later all about Thornton Wilder but now it is about Pablo and his writing and his living.

When I first heard that he was writing poetry I had a funny feeling. It was Henry Kahnweiler the dealer who first told me about it. What kind of poetry is it I said, why just poetry he said you know poetry like everybody writes. Oh I said.

Well as I say when I first heard he was writing I had a funny feeling one does you know. Things belong to you and writing belonged to me, there is no doubt about it writing belonged to me. I know writing belongs to me, I am quite certain and nobody no matter how certain you are about anything about anything belonging to you if you hear that somebody says it belongs to them it gives you a funny feeling. You are certain but it does give you a funny feeling. So that was the kind of feeling I had when I heard that Picasso was writing and that was the kind of feeling I had when I went over to listen.

You know perfectly well the miracle never does happen the one that cannot do a thing does not do it but it always gives you a

15

funny feeling because although you know the miracle never can happen nevertheless anything does give you that funny feeling. Just recently it was like that.

Meraude Guiness Guevara I mentioned her in Alice B. Toklas it was through her I actually first met Francis Rose. Meraude is like not a great many but some who are like her. Meraude has technic and some facility and she has to be a painter. There is no reason not and there is no reason to but she has to be a painter and so she falls in love with a painter, whether to paint as he paints or because she is in love she paints as he paints but anyway she is never in love with anybody who is not a painter.

And now she was in love with a painter again only nobody really knew whether he was a painter, nor does anybody really know now. He came from Aix that is where Cezanne came from and that is the way people are they feel that if they come from there they perhaps do share in what did come from there. Of course it is true that lightning never strikes twice in the same place and that is because the particular combination that makes lightning come there has so many things make it that all those things are not likely to come together again, they might but they do not. As Edwin Dodge used to say the lives of great men all remind us we should leave no sons behind us. Well anyway Meraude was in love with a young man from Aix, a very good-looking and very big young man. In the first place most people that do anything in painting are not very tall and broad, there may be exceptions but generally speaking you have to be small. Well anyway he came to Paris and he was impressive and he was painting and we wondered was it interesting and we wondered so much that it seemed so. It is not, said Picabia but any one always does have the feeling that the miracle can happen, that somebody who is not a painter may paint something if he has that way about him but he never does said Picabia sadly, you have to have always been painting and to paint just as you always have been painting to paint anything.

And so the painting of the painter who was not a painter was nothing. We will all see him again, but that is after all all there is to that.

And so I went over and we all went over Alice B. Toklas and Thornton Wilder and we left Basket and Pépé in the car but we all went over to listen all evening to Pablo Picasso's poetry.

The room everybody sits in is a dining room with a large table in it, you either do or do not like sitting in a dining room but a large table is always in it. We talked a little and then I asked him where his writing was, he said I will show it to you in a minute and then he gradually went to get it. His hand-writing is very interesting and whenever it puts itself down he makes a picture of it and I was a little nervous and I sat beside him and he was not so nervous and he began reading.

The poems were in French and Spanish and first he read a French one and then a Spanish one that he turned into French and then he read on and on and then he looked at me and I drew a long breath and I said it is very interesting. We both had put on our glasses to do this reading he to read and I to look on while he was reading. In France they always read everything aloud they read more with their ears than with their eyes but in reading English we read more with our eyes than with our ears. I am often wondering what is going to happen now. I think what is going to happen is that a written language is going to be existing like it did in old civilizations where it is read with the eyes and then another language which only says what everybody knows and therefore is not really interesting which is read with the ears. However. Pablo went on reading and he looked up and said to Thornton Wilder did you follow and Thornton said yes and might he look at it and Picasso passed it to him. Thornton said yes he was not nervous he said yes yes it is very interesting and then we talked about how beautiful words look when they are written and how one can have one language and how Spanish is Spanish and then after a little while we said good night and left. I had a funny feeling the miracle had not come the poetry was not poetry it was well Thornton said like the school of Jean Cocteau and I said for heaven's sake do not tell him. And then I said but after all why should it not be he never felt anything in words and he never read anything unless it was written by a friend and after all he had been brought up in the school of Apollinaire and later Jean Cocteau well of course there was Max. Max was saying just the other day why should he bark at me, I am a sad and happy little old man why should he. And I said everything is troubling him, and Max said but he has everything yes I said but everything is troubling him. Well anyway said Max there was no use in saying to me, you who were a poet, yes I was a poet, whatever I am I was a poet, and I had not asked him to come.

Well anyway.

And a few days after he came over and I was alone and we were talking, and I did not say anything about his writing. That American he said the one that came he looks interesting what did he say about my writing. He said it was interesting. Yes but did he not say anything more, yes I said he said that certain descriptions that you make have the same quality as your painting. Oh yes said Picasso and he did find it interesting. Yes I said and he did find it interesting. And then we talked some more. And you Gertrude he said you do not say much of anything. Well you see Pablo I said you see the egotism of a painter is an entirely different egotism than the egotism of a writer. What do you mean he said well I said I will read you my lecture on painting so I translated it to him, that is very interesting he said. I said well go on writing. Yes he said that is what I am doing. I will never paint again very likely not I like the life of a literary man, I go to cafes and I think and I make poetry and I like it. It is most interesting I said and then for a little time we did not see each other again.

He did not look at the pictures much he said he understood that

Francis Rose had not come to anything, I said not just now but everybody was kind of stopping just now, I still thought he would go on and Picabia he said, I had some Picabias in the room one big one and two little ones, after all he is the worst painter of any one said Picasso. Tell me why I said, because he cannot paint at all, he said, well I said his writing does not interest me and he did not answer.

Then for a little while we did not meet and then he called me up and said he wanted to bring Dali over and I said yes and we arranged an evening.

But before that there was an amusing evening. He said Sarbates, that is a Spaniard whom he had known all his life and now he was knowing again and now Sarbates and his wife had come to live with him. Sarbates said that his life had been a long life of permanently installing himself somewhere but these permanent installations never last long. He said if he could only make up his mind to install himself somewhere temporarily he might stay forever but he never had he always asked himself or was asked to take up a permanent residence somewhere and nothing is so impermanent as a permanent residence, well anyway now that Picasso was living all alone they all lived with him.

And Sarbates had taught at a Berlitz school of languages and he knew a good many different kinds of men and there was an American and could he bring him and so they all came. Nobody had been invited but everybody came it always happens like that or it sometimes happens like that and when it does well it does. The Picabias came and I have forgotten who else was there oh yes Marcel Duchamp and Georges Maratier and everybody would have been just as well pleased not to meet everybody but then one cannot bother about that. They were all there.

Picabia and Picasso are about the same height which is not a high one and they are about the same weight which is a fair one. And they would not be what they are as each one is never the other one. And yet sometimes they call Picasso a French painter and Picabia a Spanish one. Well anyway it does happen, they do wear without knowing it the same tie and this time they had exactly the same kind of shoes and everybody noticed so they mentioned it to one another and I made them get up and stand together and they were the same height and they had the same shoes but they do not look like one another no they do not. Well in the meantime it was getting difficult so I got the American started, I got him started, he had been telling me about it, he was a college professor I got him started telling about thumbing his way all the summer, everywhere in America and he told how he did it. It was most interesting and everybody listened.

He told about how you had to know that you should never stop before a red light signal, anybody in an automobile is too impatient not to lose any time starting if the lights should change to take anybody up so you want to stop beyond the crossing because then having made the start anybody is good natured and willing to take you up, you should also always think about hills in the same way, you should never stand with any one and above all not with a woman, some one might take up a woman alone but they would never take a young man with any kind of a woman, and as he went on and he made those long roads so real Picasso got scared, it is a funny thing but knowing so much about what people are going to do on the part of anybody always scares people who are occupied in creating they like to analyze and talk about what people are going to do but they never like that anybody can know what anybody will do, really know and act successfully act upon what people are going to do. As this American went on and on I saw that Picasso was getting terrified it was all so real, oh said he terror stricken he who has been through poverty and starvation and Montmartre and everything I would never let my chauffeur stop never he said. And it was not because he was afraid of the man who would get in except insofar as the man who would get in knew too much about how to bring it about. Picabia had soon stopped listening, nothing is real to him that is not painting and so knowing anything can not frighten him.

Well as I was saying Picasso had said to me that he wanted to bring Dali to see me. I said certainly and we arranged an evening and Dali and his wife came but Picasso did not bring him and soon you will see why I did not know why then.

Dali like many Spanish painters has married a Russian. I once asked a Russian woman why Spaniards married Russians when after all they were the least likely to like each other and the marriages always were unhappy. Well she said you see it is because superficially they are alike and that is attracting and gradually then they come to the part where they are not alike and then it is hopeless because all that is alike is in the covering. And then I thought about it and it is true Spaniards have no sense of time that is to say the night is the day and the day is the night to them, then they are very brutal not brutal but callous to human emotion and they also never listen. They do not hear what you say nor do they listen but they use for the thing they want to do the thing they are not hearing.

And then it came to me it is perfectly simple, the Russian and the Spaniard are oriental, and there is the same mixing. Scratch a Russian and you find a Tartar. Scratch a Spaniard and you find a Saracen.

And all this is very important with what I have been saying about the peaceful Oriental penetration into European culture or rather the tendency for this generation that is for the twentieth century to be no longer European because perhaps Europe is finished.

Painting in the nineteenth century was French at the end of the nineteenth century it had become Spanish Spanish in France but still Spanish, and philosophy and literature had the same tendency, Einstein was the creative philosophic mind of the century and I have been the creative literary mind of the century also with the Oriental mixing with the European.

However here is Dali waiting to come and his Russian wife with him.

Dali has the most beautiful mustache of any European but and that mustache is Saracen there is no doubt about that and it is a most beautiful mustache there is no doubt about that.

Dali was a notary's son, in Europe the role in the arts played by sons of notaries is a very interesting one. They take the place of ministers' sons in America. Notaries are what in England are called solicitors and with us in America I do not believe there is anything that quite does it all. A notary is something that always makes one think of the novels of Balzac because notaries are just like that.

They do everything they in the smaller towns run the auctions they make out all legal papers they act in all sales and in all disputes about inheritances that do not actually come to law, they administer estates they keep everybody's papers they give endless advice and they can only charge for legal papers. I know a lot about them because they have been awfully good to me when we were having trouble with the tenant who was subletting Bilignin to us, and I spent all my time rushing down and telling him my troubles while the Captain who was the tenant sat in the other room waiting to tell him his troubles and finally he straightened us all out.

It is really a nice story of French life.

I told in Alice B. Toklas how we found the house where we spend the summers across a valley and they said we could have it when the present tenant left it. The present tenant was a lieutenant in the army and as he was stationed at the garrison in Belley, they have a battalion of Moroccan troops there, it is always strange to see in a mountain French village these native troops. It is queer the use of that word, native always means people who belong somewhere else, because they had once belonged somewhere. That shows that the white race does not really think they belong anywhere because they think of everybody else as native. Anyway the lieutenant who was in the house that we had seen across the valley and that we had had to have was stationed in the garrison at Belley. We had never seen the house inside because they were still going on being there. Why said everybody do you not get him made captain, then he would have to leave as there is no room for another captain there in the garrison. We thought that an excellent idea.

It is remarkable how much influence one has to accomplish anything in France that is if you never expect anybody who is important to do anything for you. We found that out during the war. A general is no good he can only listen to you and make speeches to you he has no power to do anything for you because if he did every one would know about it and then everything would be all over, so the person to do it for you is a pleasant female clerk or an amiable sergeant. They can get anything done for you from extra essence to a decoration if you want it. As I explained when we wanted the red ribbon for Mildred Aldrich all the important people said they would but nothing happened but it was a woman secretary in an office who did get it for her.

Well we know a man he is a nice man his name is George, it is not for nothing that anybody calls anybody whom they want to do anything for them George. There is something in a name. I said I was no longer sure that there is but there is something in the name of George. In any case we told our troubles to this one. When he was doing his military service he was clerk in the war office. He used to tell how every one even a general would come in and ask him if he could not get something done a little quicker for him. Well sometimes he did and sometimes he did not, it all means slipping the cards to bring one before another one, the way librarians do with renewal cards, the way anybody does with anything.

George said let me see you want him to become a captain tell me more about him. George by this time was a business man and had nothing further to do with the war office or anything military, however he said tell me what you want me to do. That is what George always says and sometimes he does do something. He tells us when we should take enough money out of the bank to take us to the country for a month if there is going to be a revolution, so far there has not been any but if there was to be he would know. The only curious thing about him is that he believes in the Napoleonic dynasty. That is one of the queer things about France, you never know what anybody has as their loyalty, they just go on being republican but even so a very considerable number of them go on contributing to the king coming again or the emperor or something. George believes in the Bonapartists, I do not know why it does seem very foolish as the Bonapartists never did anything except bring disaster upon France and George loves France and does not love disaster. However we did tell him that we wanted the lieutenant to become a captain.

George went off and after some months of waiting in which you look anxious but ask no questions and he mysteriously said wait he came and said I have had news for you, they say at the war office that he is not much good as a lieutenant, he is a war lieutenant, and cannot pass any further examinations but as a captain he would not do at all and then besides when he retired he would have to be paid a pension as a captain and now in two or three years he retires and they only have to pay his pension as a lieutenant, but said George perhaps he could go to Morocco that would be good for him he would get more money for active service and he would leave the house free. No no said we as good Americans and George went off and said nothing. A month after the proprietor wrote and said the lieutenant was going to Morocco and was ready to sublet the house to us with his furniture for the two years he would be away, would we take it would we, we did and it was then we first saw the notary, who too has a son and in this way we came to discover that a notary's son in France is like a minister's son in America and whether the lieutenant's going to Morocco was George's doing or a coincidence we never knew, he never would tell and so we never knew.

So the notary drew up the lease and we had the house and about six months after war broke out in Morocco and the news came to Belley that the lieutenant was a prisoner. Alice Toklas' conscience troubled her, mine did not trouble me but hers troubled her and then later came the news that he was not a prisoner and nothing happened to him and Alice B. Toklas was very relieved about him but later considerably later she would not have been sorry if he had been taken forever, and this when we came to know all about what a notary does.

We had been very peaceful in Bilignin for two years and then the lieutenant came back, and he wanted to sell us the next piece of his lease that he had not got because we had taken the end of his and yet he said he wanted to take as much furniture out as he wanted to furnish the house he was to take elsewhere because he was no longer to be stationed in Belley, and he wanted the piano and I like to improvise on a piano I like to play sonatinas followed by another always on the white keys I do not like black keys and never two notes struck by the same hand at the same time because I do not like chords, but most of the time I have no piano and I do very nicely without it and I was not there when the lieutenant and his wife demanded the piano which was part of the furnishing for which we were paying, and Alice Toklas refused the piano to them and everything else to them for which we were paying and then they said that in that case they would take the house back. When I came back I had been out walking with the dogs every-thing was in confusion and I said I will rush to the notary, his office was closed but I made him see me any way and after I told him everything he said the lieutenant was waiting to see him too and tell him everything. Monsieur Saint Pierre the notary is a large fair man whose family like many of the notary families in France and particularly near Lyon have papers to show that they have been notaries or something like that since the eleventh century so they know all about what a notary should do. He calmed me and he calmed him although there was a wall between and he the lieutenant was in the wrong because as an officer in the army he could not rent two houses in France, he could own two but he could not rent two so if he was going to rent another one he could not continue to rent Bilignin so there we were, and if we would give him his furniture sooner our landlord would give us other furniture and make out a lease for us and everything and slowly everything calmed down and we had the furniture out of the home of Brillat-Savarin because our landlord had inherited that house from the heirs of Brillat-Savarin and after a great deal of excitement everything was calm, the notary loaned us his clerk so that the lieutenant and his wife would be peaceful about the inventory and finally they left behind them a cavalry saber, and that is there yet and there is another piano that was left over not from Brillat-Savarin but from very nearly Brillat-Savarin and does very nicely to play sonatinas followed by another on.

So that is what a notary is and his sons there is always one as there are ministers' sons remember Cummings is one, but anyway there is always a notary's son they have a violence in freedom but they are never free, that is what it is to be a notary's son. Jean Cocteau is one, Foch was one, Bernard Faÿ is one and the other day a lot of people were here and Marcel Duchamp and somebody said or he did that Marcel Duchamp was a notary's son oh said I that explains everything. Everything said Marcel and everybody burst out laughing but it is true it does, and Dali is a notary's son and this is a history of him.

26

...t the most important surrealist and yes yes in

...Paris quite young from the north of Spain. As I ...since the twentieth century painting has been Spanish, as Picasso says he likes Dali because Dali, like himself, and that is Spanish bases everything on his own ignorance, they receive a wonderful inspiration and it is based oh yes it is based on ignorance, on their own ignorance because of course a Spanish notary does not know anything and has had no means of learning.

Now alas it is changing they could go and learn just like any one but until then a Spaniard was naturally ignorant. There was one exception and that was Juan Gris he had no natural ignorance, he complained bitterly when his son came up from Spain where he had been raised and had the ignorance that was natural to any one who was a Spaniard, but Juan had none, and yet he was an exception, but I suppose naturally among all the millions of Spaniards there must be once in a while an exception. The South Americans have something of the same thing only with them ignorance tends to soften and so make as Guevara says of all Chileans a soft center inside them, but the Spanish ignorance may dry up as the center but it never goes soft or rotten.

Anyway Dali as a young one came from Spain and very soon everybody was excited about him, and the surrealists had known about him before he came and before him had come Miró. However Miró was nice and excited every one by his painting but he had nothing to follow up his painting more than just the natural center of ignorance that any Spaniard has inside him but Dali had a special one and so he kept on being more exciting.

They knew about him in Paris before he came, surrealists had heard of him. He was the son of a notary and he had the feeling in him of painting like Picasso and like surrealism and he did and some of these early pictures enormous and with big shapes are full of energy, and then he came to Paris and soon everybody heard of him. He painted a picture and on it he wrote I spit upon the face of my mother, he was very fond of his mother who had been a long time dead and so of course this was a symbolism. He knew about Freud and he had the revolt of having a notary for his father and having his mother dead since he was a child. And so painting this picture with this motto was a natural thing and it made of him the most important of the painters who were surrealists. Masson's wandering line had stopped wandering and he was lost just then, Miró had found out what he was to paint and he was continuing painting the same thing, and so Dali came and everybody knew about him. It is awfully hard to go on painting. I often think about this thing. It is awfully hard for any one to go on doing anything because everybody is troubled by everything. Having done anything you naturally want to do it again and if you do it again then you know you are doing it again and it is not interesting. That is what worries everybody, anybody having done anything naturally does it again, whether it is a crime or a work of art or a daily occupation or anything like eating and sleeping and dancing and war. Well there you are having done it you do it again and knowing you are doing it again spoils its having been existing even as much as it spoils its going to be existing. A painter has more trouble about it than any one. Most people at least do not see what they have just done a writer does not see what he has just written, a musician does not hear what he has just played, but a painter has constantly in front of him what he has just painted, his walls are covered with it, when he comes back to his picture to go on there just under his eyes is what he has just done. An actor a cook nobody else has so continually before him what he has just done. And so a painter has more and less trouble going on than any one. I am often sorry for them. I know that I am the most important writer writing today but I never have any of my books before me naturally not, but they have all the time naturally everything they have just done right in front of them.

And like it or not that is the way they are and have to be. Now in the old days when they were so they said copying nature after all there was something there anyway even if their pictures did not resemble what they were copying, but since Picasso no painter uses a model at least no painter whose painting interests anybody and so they paint with what is inside them as it is in them and the only thing that is outside them is the painting they have just been painting and all the others which of course are always around them. Even if they sell a good many there are still a good many there and they see them. A writer as I say never looks at his writing, once it is a finished thing, but a painter well he sees it because his room is full of it, and there is nothing really nothing else to do about it except to have it there and to see it.

It is funny I was just thinking about it the other day. I remember so well showing in the old days the Picasso drawings and the great thing to say about them was that they were all drawn without a model. And then always there was complete astonishment. Matisse always had a model Picasso never had one, that was where French painting ended and Spanish painting began.

My brother once was bothered because Picasso never had and never had had a model to look at and it worried finally worried my brother. He liked it but it finally did worry him, this was some years later after Picasso had done my portrait there he had had me to be a model why this was an exception I do not know and as there was never any question there was never any answer. Anyway my brother was worried, he had commenced to paint himself and he had a model so he wanted Picasso to have one. He bothered him so much about it that finally one afternoon Picasso went with him to the model class and drew two drawings while he was looking at the model, and he said what do I want to look at them for, I know what they look like so much that looking is not necessary, and if I do not then looking does not tell anything. I guess that is true, when you are going to hire a servant you look at them very hard but they are never at all what you think they are going to be so why look. The best we ever had we never saw at all until she was everything we could want. Well anyway.

It is strange when you remember that models were everything until the beginning of the twentieth century and now hardly any painter who interests anybody really has any realization that everybody used to have a model. It is an interesting thing this, it began with Picasso and now everybody is doing it. But this has a great deal to do with everything and later when I tell about the Seurat exhibition and how I found out everything I will tell all about this thing but now to go on with Dali and how everybody knew about him.

So Dali was beginning to be well known, at that time I did not meet him I was not interested in him, surrealism never did interest me, because after all it all came from Chirico and he was not a surrealist he is very fanciful and his eye is caught by it and he has no distinction between the real and the unreal because everything is alike to him, he says so, but the rest of them nothing is alike to them and so they do not say so, and that is the trouble with them and so they are dead before they go again. However, I did see Dali when he painted his big picture about William Tell. He said it showed the power of the father and child complex but said some one William Tell did not shoot the apple off his child's head because he wanted to he did not practice it every day in the garden as a form of sadism, Dali did not hear anything of this he was listening to himself tell about Freud and the feeling a father had about his children. And it was true enough that Dali's father had a feeling about his son and would not see him. But Dali is very earnest and does not go on hearing anything. Well anyway he came with his wife and Picasso did not come. We talked a great deal together but we neither of us listened very much to one another. We talked about the writing of painters, Dali had just brought me a poem he had written about Picasso, and I said I was bored with the hopelessness of painters and poetry. That in a way was the trouble with the painters they did not know what poetry was. Dali said that if it were not for the titles of Chirico's pictures and his own nobody would understand him, he himself would not understand the paintings of Chirico if he did not know their titles and as for Picasso's poems, they had finally made possible for him to understand Picasso's paintings. Oh dear I said.

Well we went on and I said I would go and see him which I since have done, by the way some of his early painting is very large and full of emotion, there has just been recently an exhibition of Spanish painting here and a good deal of Spanish painting done in Spain, they do do more than can be done, which carries them so far that they are not there, but certainly twentieth century painting is Spanish, they do it but it is never begun. That is what makes the painting today Spanish.

Well anyway the Dalis left and I did not see Picasso for some time and then one day I happened to go in to Rosenberg's Gallery and they were hanging a show of Braque and Rosenberg said did I want to come in and there were Picasso and Braque and we said how do you do you.

It was funny about The Autobiography of Alice B. Toklas, writers well I suppose it is because writers write but anyway writers did not really mind anything any one said about them, they might have minded something or liked something but since writing is writing and writers know that writing is writing they do not really suffer very much about anything that has been written. Besides writers have an endless curiosity about themselves and anything that is written about them helps to help them know something about themselves or about what anybody else says about them. Anything interests anybody who is writing but not so a painter oh no not at all. As I told Picasso the egotism of a writer is not at all the same egotism as the egotism of a painter and all the painters felt that way about The Autobiography of Alice B. Toklas, Braque and

31

Marie Laurencin and Matisse they did not like it and they did not get used to it.

The first to feel that way about it was Braque or Matisse or Marie Laurencin. Matisse had pieces translated to him so did Braque, Marie Laurencin had pieces translated to her but not by me. Matisse I never saw again but Braque yes twice and Marie Laurencin once.

Henry McBride wrote to me that he had seen Matisse in New York, he said all the painters should be delighted because I had re-vivified them at a moment when everybody was not thinking about painting. Henry McBride wrote that as he said these words Matisse shuddered. Later on they wrote in English it was written in English in transition it never was written in French, Matisse said that Picasso was not the great painter of the period that his wife did not look like a horse and that he was certain that the omelette had been an omelette or something. Braque said that he had invented cubism, he did not say this but at any rate if what he said was so then that was so. And Marie Laurencin, Marie Laurencin is always Marie Laurencin, we had not met for many a year.

This was a long time after.

In later years perhaps it had to do with the Autobiography and how it affected me but anyway there has been a tendency to go out more and see different kinds of people. In the older days mostly they came to see me but then we began to go out to see them. I had never been to any literary salons in Paris, and now well I did not go to many of them but I did go to some.

It is natural that if anybody asks you to go anywhere, once you have the habit of going anywhere, that you go anywhere once. If you go again you go again but if you have a lot of interest in seeing anything you will go anywhere once. Anyway I will.

René Crevel used to tell us about Marie Louise Bousquet and her salon. She had all the old men and then at the same time she would have the young men. She liked the young men to upset the old men and she liked to upset the young men to please the old men and besides she was very gay and very lively and very kind to every one and it was a literary salon and of course we had never been.

And now after the Autobiography and Bernard Faÿ had translated it and they all had read it we began to naturally be going out more to meet French literary people and one day we went to André Germain's.

André Germain is a very funny man, he is the son of the Credit Lyonnais the most important bank in France and the son of a banker is not the same as a son of a notary. In the first place he is always rich and that makes that difference and he is always careful and he always is taken care of, but he can like revolutions and he very often does. André Germain did.

That afternoon I was talking to a very pleasant man and finally he said he was Monsieur Bousquet and his wife would so want me to come. I said yes of course and he went off and telephoned and then we went. Then we went again and there we met Marie Laurencin.

Marie Laurencin had been in Paris ever since the war was over, and sometimes everything went well with her and sometimes everything did not go so well but she always went on pretty well. She was not one of the painters who made an extraordinarily large amount of money during the period that was called the epoch roughly from twenty-three to thirty-three she made less then than any of them and finally she took to teaching and all her pupils found her very amusing. She had grown stout by then but not too stout to be amusing. The French women always used to say a woman's silhouette should change every ten years. It should not grow less it should grow more and mostly it does. Marie Laurencin's had but it made her just that more pleasing. She used to play the harmonium and René Crevel and all the others described her doing so and it was very pleasing. Her pupils later were pleased

33

that when they could not draw a foot she would tell them that she herself when she could not do anything always did it in profile, that was an easier way to do everything.

We had met from time to time not often but from time to time during this period, always by accident and we were always pleased to see each other and had embraced each other and said Chère Gertrude and Chère Marie, and now we once again met accidentally. I knew that Marie had not been pleased that I had spoken of all of them and of the old days but then I knew painters were like that so when we met there at Marie Louise's salon we embraced as we had always done and then she told me just how she felt about everything that I had done and this is what she said.

She said of course no painter could be pleased the past of a painter was not a past because a painter lived in what he saw and he could not see his past and if his past was not his past then it was nobody's past and so nobody could say what that past was. And Apollinaire belonged to the painters they had all loved him and as they had all loved him nobody could describe him nobody could describe anybody whom all the painters had loved because the painters could no longer see him and Picasso had no past because he had a son and if one had a son one had no past and so nobody could dare to describe anything and that well that was the way she felt about it and we could embrace again but that was the way it was and it was that way and that is what she had to say.

It was interesting, she stated what they felt they the men could not say this thing because as they said it it would have sounded foolish to them but that is the way they did feel, I imagine Marie Laurencin was right painters feel that way about anything and as painters they are right that is the way they should feel about anything.

After all anybody creating anything has to have it as a present thing, the writer can include a great deal into that present thing

34

and make it all present but the painter can only include what he sees and he has so to speak only one surface and that is a flat surface which he has to see and so whether he will or not he must see it in that way. They can include as much as they can but it has to be seen, Marie Laurencin said it and she saw it and it has to be seen.

Braque was another thing. Braque was a man who had a gift of singing and like all who sing he could mistake what he sang as being something that he had said but it is not the same thing. When I say he sang I mean he sang in paint, I do not believe he sang otherwise but he might have, he had the voice and the looks of a great baritone.

In mistaking what he sang as something that he had said he lived his life and he was always hoping that the time would come that he could be sure that he was the one that had said what he could only sing and it never came although he sometimes felt that it had come. Like all singers he was very seductive, Juan Gris used to say of him he seduces me and then he seduces me again and I know he is just singing but he seduces me again.

Well anyway he always had been on the point of seducing himself and Juan and Picasso and occasionally any one to believe that he was the one that had all the ideas that made cubism and modern painting. And when the Autobiography was written considerable time after there was written what he signed as written by him but it was never in French but in English and he never read or wrote English of course not and it said that there was no sense in the Autobiography because it was written by one who did not understand and who said that Picasso had invented everything. Well anyway. When I came back from America I went into Kahnweiler's one day and somebody was hidden in the back. Who is in there I asked Kahnweiler I always like to know who is anywhere and I always ask. Braque said Kahnweiler, oh I must speak to him. I went in Braque was very old looking and he was very

35

pale and he sat and was looking in front of him. How do you do I said to him and I shook hands with him. He shook hands but he did not get up, shaking hands in France is funny, no matter how mad you are with any one you shake hands if you are French an American or an Englishman can refuse to shake hands but a Frenchman cannot, when a hand is there it has to be shaken, and so we shook hands. I asked him how his wife was and we said a few words and then we left and I had not seen him again until I met him when they were hanging the pictures and Picasso was there. I said hello to each one and shook hands with each one and we did not look at the pictures of Braque but we began talking. I asked Pablo what he had been doing and he said he was not painting he was leading a poet's life still and here he was with Braque who was still painting. Well I said and Picasso said well you did see Dali, sure I said but you did not come no said Pablo you see I knew you would tell him what you thought of my poetry and you would not tell me. Sure I did I said and that was easy, why said he, why I said because you see one discusses things with stupid people but not with sensible ones, you know that very well I said getting a little angry, one never discusses anything with anybody who can understand one discusses things with people who cannot understand and that is the reason I discussed with Dali and I do not discuss with you. What he said Dali cannot understand anything, of course he can't I said you know that as well as I do, he looked a little sheepish yes I guess that is true, he said and then he got excited but you said that painters can't write poetry, well they can't I said, look at you, my poetry is good he said Breton says so, Breton I said Breton admires anything to which he can sign his name and you know as well as I do that a hundred years hence nobody will remember his name you know that perfectly well, oh well he muttered they say he can write, yes said I you do not take their word for whether somebody can paint, don't he an ass I said, Braque spoke up, a painter can write he said I have written all my life, well I said I only saw one thing of yours that was written and that in a language that you cannot understand and I did not think much of it that is all I can say, and he said but that I did not write he said, oh didn't you I said well anyway you signed it I said and I have never seen any other writing of yours so you do not count, and anyway we are talking about Pablo's poetry, and even Michael Angelo did not make much of a success of it. Rosenberg the dealer murmured although nobody heard him and then there was Fromentin. You see I said continuing to Pablo you can't stand looking at Jean Cocteau's drawings, it does something to you, they are more offensive than drawings that are just bad drawings now that's the way it is with your poetry it is more offensive than just bad poetry I do not know why but it just is, somebody who can really do something very well when he does something else which he cannot do and in which he cannot live it is particularly repellent, now you I said to him, you never read a book in your life that was not written by a friend and then not then and you never had any feelings about any words, words annoy you more than they do anything else so how can you write you know better you yourself know better, well he said getting truculent, you yourself always said I was an extraordinary person well then an extraordinary person can do anything, ah I said catching him by the lapels of his coat and shaking him, you are extraordinary within your limits but your limits are extraordinarily there and I said shaking him hard, you know it, you know it as well as I know it, it is all right you are doing this to get rid of everything that has been too much for you all right all right go on doing it but don't go on trying to make me tell you it is poetry and I shook him again, well he said supposing I do know it, what will I do, what will you do said I and I kissed him, you will go on until you are more cheerful or less dismal and then you will, yes he said, and then you will paint a very beautiful picture and then more of them, and I kissed him again, yes said he.

Rosenberg went out with me, oh thank you thank you, he said, he must paint again oh thank you thank you said he.

I did not see him often again practically not. He was going out and staying out all evening until the morning and drinking Vichy water and then he went away with his dog to Cannes and we went away for six months to Bilignin but before that he did have a show of the pictures he had painted before he stopped painting and it was a great success the show and he said he was not going to commence painting but he did not talk much about poetry or anything and as I said he went away with no one but his dog an Airedale terrier called Elf which he had once bought in Switzerland.

CHAPTER II

What was the effect upon me of the Autobiography

Before one is successful that is before any one is ready to pay money for anything you do then you are certain that every word you have written is an important word to have written and that any word you have written is as important as any other word and you keep everything you have written with great care. And then it happens sometimes sooner and sometimes later that it has a money value I had mine very much later and it is upsetting because when nothing had any commercial value everything was important and when something began having a commercial value it was upsetting, I imagine this is true of any one.

Before anything you write had commercial value you could not change anything that you had written but once it had commercial value well then changing or not changing was not so important. All this is true and now I will tell how it all happened to me as it did.

I was getting older when I wrote the Autobiography, not that it makes much difference how old you are because the only thing that is any different is the historical fact that you are older or younger. One thing is certain the only thing that makes you younger or older is that nothing can happen that is different from what you expected and when that happens and it mostly does happen everything is different from what you expected then there is no difference between being younger or older. Just the other day they thought well anyway America thought that there was going to be war again in Europe and they called me up on the telephone to ask me what I thought about it. I said I do not believe that there is going to be another European war just now but as I am most generally always wrong perhaps there is. When I was very small we always used to say let us toss up a coin to decide and then as it came down we always said and now let's do the other way. That is a natural way and if you are that way then anything is a surprise and if anything is a surprise then there is not much difference between older or younger because the only thing that does make anybody older is that they cannot be surprised. I suppose there are some people who get so that they cannot be surprised so that things happen as they think they will happen. It always has been a game with me to think if something is going to happen just all the possible ways a thing is going to happen and then when it does happen it always does happen in a way I had never thought of. That is why I like detective stories, I never know ever how they are going to happen and anybody ought to yes I realize that anybody really ought to.

Well anyway it was a beautiful autumn in Bilignin and in six weeks I wrote The Autobiography of Alice B. Toklas and it was published and it became a best seller and first it was printed in the Atlantic Monthly and there is a nice story about that but first I bought myself a new eight cylinder Ford car and the most expensive coat made to order by Hermes and fitted by the man who makes horse covers for race horses for Basket the white poodle and two collars studded for Basket. I had never made any money before in my life and I was most excited.

When I was a child I used to be fascinated with the stories of how everybody had earned their first dollar. I always wanted to have earned my first dollar but I never had. I know a lot about money just because I never had earned my first dollar and now I have. We were all amused during the war there was an American over here and he once said he had just made five hundred thousand dollars and he added all honestly earned. Well that is the way I felt there it was and all honestly earned. I have been writing a lot about money lately, it is a fascinating subject, it is really the difference between men and animals, most of the things men feel animals feel and vice versa, but animals do not know about money, money is purely a human conception and that is very important to know very very important.

About every once in so often there is a movement to do away with money. Roosevelt tries to spend so much that perhaps money will not exist, communists try to live without money but it never lasts because if you live without money you have to do as the animals do live on what you find each day to eat and that is just the difference the minute you do not do that you have to have money and so everybody has to make up their mind if money is money or if money isn't money and sooner or later they always do decide that money is money.

The Jews and once more we have the orientalizing of Europe being always certain that money is money finally decide and that makes a Marxian state that money is not money. That is the way it is if you believe in anything deeply enough it turns into something else and so money turns into not money. That is what mysticism is but I will tell all about that when I tell about Saint Therese and the Four Saints and what they did. Then later not money turns into money. Well anyway the earth turns and it is almost certain that there are no men anywhere except here on this earth and so being men is not an easy thing to be and men because they are like animals in everything except in having money always have to have what they do not have, and so I wrote the Autobiography.

One of the things that interested me most is all the conversations I had after I wrote the Autobiography.

There is always something that everybody tells you about anybody that you did not know before. Marcoussis told me about Picasso and Guillaume Apollinaire and Max Jacob. He told me he said he knew about it at the time and yet he was very much younger anyway he said that in those early days Picasso had conceived the series production exactly as in America they were doing it. He said that each one of the poets had to write a poem every day just as he had to paint a picture every day and if they each wrote a poem every day and he painted a picture every day there would be such an accumulation that it would completely force a market for the poems and the pictures and this is what would happen. Every day he said they had to bring their poem to him and of course he would have a picture ready to show to them and he did and they did. Certainly they did not make so many poems but he did make as many pictures as one every day.

All this so Marcoussis said happened just before we knew them, perhaps yes. Max Jacob then told me all about his knowing them before I knew them. Max Jacob does discover everybody before anybody does that is quite certain. Everybody comes to him he is always there and so he always sees them and they are always there and so they always see him.

He was older than they were and he had already had a little reputation for writing literary criticism and somebody told him about a young Spaniard who had just come from Barcelona and he went to see him and immediately was excited about him and was the first to mention him in writing. Just about that time Max Jacob found Apollinaire, Max says that he Max at that time wore a coat and a high hat and was very much a gentleman. Well anyway he found Apollinaire and was very excited about him and took Apollinaire to see Picasso and then and that was about the time we met them Apollinaire and Picasso did not care about him. Well that always happens, later on money has something to do with it but in the beginning anything has something to do with it and it always happens. Max Jacob goes on finding every one before anybody else knows anything about them but that does not make him find any one more than he always finds them.

Then Picabia I was beginning to see a good deal of Picabia then and he told me something. He said that the show that I described where my brother first saw Picassos to which Sagot had sent him and where Picasso and another Spaniard showed together the other Spaniard whose name everybody has forgotten, Picabia says there were three Spaniards there not two and that he was the third one. They were to have a show together again and then they did not because we began to buy from Picasso. In those days I never heard anything about a third one. It was not until nineteen ten that I knew anything about Picabia.

And now I will tell all about both of them. But first to go back to what writing the Autobiography did to me.

It seems very long ago and it is long ago because at that time I had never made any money and since then I have made some and I feel differently now about everything, so it is a long time ago four years ago that I wrote The Autobiography of Alice B. Toklas. I had commenced having an agent then, I do not know that literary agents are anything, that is to say I have had them but they have never been able to sell anything of mine, they do not seem to be able to even now although about once in so often I have one, I had one years ago way back in the time of Three Lives and then I tried to have another one only he did not want to have me. Janet Scudder tried arranging that for me and then about a year before I wrote the Autobiography I had another one William Aspinwall Bradley.

So he was excited and I had to have a telephone put in first at twenty seven rue de Fleurus and then here at Bilignin. I had always before that not had a telephone but now that I was going to be an author whose agent could place something I had of course to have a telephone. We are just now putting in an electric stove but that is because it is difficult if not impossible to get coal that will burn and besides the coal stove does not heat the oven and anyway France is getting so that French cooks do not like to cook on a coal stove. To be sure cooking with coal is like lighting with gas it is an intermediate stage which is a mistake. It would seem that cooking should be done with wood, charcoal or electricity and I guess they are right, just as lighting should be done by candles or electricity, coal and gas are a mistake, like railroad trains, it should be horses or automobiles or airplanes, coal, gas and railroads are a mistake and that has perhaps a great deal to do with politics and government and the nineteenth century and everything however to come back to my agent and to my success.

It is funny about money.

If you have earned money it is not the same thing as if you have not earned money. And now the time had come that I was beginning to earn some and that was a fortunate thing because now nobody unless they are really rich can live on an income. Even the French and they until now most of them have always lived on an income even they are beginning to realize that nobody any longer if they are not very rich can live on an income, well I did not know that I couldn't but things do happen like that, when the time comes when you do earn money the time has come when you could not any longer live on your income. That is politics and superstition it is a cuckoo coming to sing to you when you have money in your pocket or even a green spider coming to you at sunset, a spider at night makes everything bright a spider in the morning is a warning.

Well anyway my success did begin.

And so Mr. Bradley telephoned every morning and they gradually decided about everything and slowly everything changed inside me. Yes of course it did because suddenly it was all different, what I did had a value that made people ready to pay, up to that time everything I did had a value because nobody was ready to pay. It is funny about money. And it is funny about identity. You are you because your little dog knows you, but when your public knows you and does not want to pay for you and when your public

44

knows you and does want to pay for you, you are not the same you.

Anyway life in Paris began but it was less Paris than it had been and so it was natural that sooner or later I should go to America again.

It was less Paris than it had been. And in a way it is natural as the world is getting all filled up with people and they all do the same thing it is natural that countries need to be bigger. And in Europe they are not, the countries are smaller, and so there is not much use in anything. Anyway when they asked me just now is there going to be war in Europe I said no I don't think so, although as I am always wrong perhaps there is. But anyway Europe is not big enough for a war any more, it really is not, for a war countries should be bigger. Well anyway I did go to America but before that some few things did happen. Other things change inside me but I still did have to quarrel and this is the way it happened that I quarreled with my agent. It was all about going to America.

As I say Paris was very pleasant, the crisis was beginning the time of big spending was over, and I began to like the streets again. You could hear people talking, anybody could talk to you and you could talk to them. Spending money does not agree with French people. One of the things that used to strike anyone coming to France from America was that the women's faces never had any worry lines on them. That was because Frenchmen and French-women in general lived on last year's income and not on this one. So much so that one woman never used today's milk, she always used yesterday's milk. Some day, so she said, there will be no milk but I will have some. And it did happen, war came and there was no milk but she had some. Nobody in France no matter how poor or how rich ever thought of living on current earnings, they always lived on last year's earnings and that made the French live their unworried living, the only thing that ever troubled them was the possibility of war or the possibility of changing the regime,

45

that is a revolution, but otherwise there was nothing to worry them except family quarrels and family quarrels are exciting but not really worrisome, so Frenchwomen never had worry lines in their faces. And now they had because they were spending this year's earnings. But even so they were beginning to hope not going on doing this thing and they were beginning economizing.

And so gradually Paris was beginning to be as it had been. They had had their war, and now perhaps they are going to have their revolution, well anyway, I was liking Paris but it was not very exciting, as Paris, but it was very exciting as myself selling The Autobiography of Alice B. Toklas.

While I was writing it I used to ask Alice B. Toklas if she thought it was going to be a best seller and she said no she did not think so because it was not sentimental enough and then later on when it was a best seller she said well after all it was sentimental enough.

As I had said I always wanted two things to happen to be printed in the Atlantic Monthly and in the Saturday Evening Post and so I told Mr. Bradley that I wanted him to try the Atlantic Monthly.

I do wish Mildred Aldrich had lived to see it, she would have liked it, for they did print it, but after all I do want them to print something else to prove that it was not only that that they wanted but of course they do not. I can be accepted more than I was but I can be refused almost as often. After all if nobody refuses what you offer there must be something the matter, I do not quite know why this is so but it is so. It was not so in the nineteenth century but it is so in the twentieth century. And that is because talking and writing have gotten more and more separated. Talking is not thinking or feeling at all any more, it used to be but it is not now but writing is, and so writing naturally needs more refusing.

So Aspinwall Bradley made these arrangements and we were all of us very happy, and fan letters began to pour in and also money.

46

Henry McBride always said that success spoils one and he always used to say to me that he hoped that I would not have any and now I was having some. He was very sweet about it and said it pleased him as much as it did me and it did not spoil me but even so it did change me.

The thing is like this, it is all the question of identity. It is all a question of the outside being outside and the inside being inside. As long as the outside does not put a value on you it remains outside but when it does put a value on you then it gets inside or rather if the outside puts a value on you then all your inside gets to be outside. I used to tell all the men who were being successful young how bad this was for them and then I who was no longer young was having it happen.

But there was the spending of money and there is no doubt about it there is no pleasure like it, the sudden splendid spending of money and we spent it.

We had always lived so very simply, we had a home in the country but we lived in that just as simply as we did in the city. It was always a surprise to every one to really know how little we lived on. We lived very comfortably but we lived very simply and we had no expenses, we had a car but we made it cost as little as possible and for many years it was well it still is a little old Ford car. But now I bought an eight cylinder one and we gave up just having one servant we had a couple, a man and woman, and we spent a very hectic summer with them. I like detective stories and I have always been going to write one and about the summer we had with them.

We did not meet many new men or women who were interesting.

So this is what happened, we came back to Paris very late in the autumn and we installed a telephone and we talked over the telephone every morning Mr. Bradley and I and decided who was to publish the book because there was no doubt that everybody would be ready to publish this one.

We considered American publishers and Mr. Bradley said he thought Harcourt Brace would be the right one and I said I wanted in England to have the Bodley Head for sentimental reasons, after all John Lane was the only real publisher who had really ever thought of publishing a book for me, and you have to be loyal to every one if you do quarrel with any one. And so everything was settled we had advance royalties from every one and everything began.

In the meantime it is not to be not remembered that I had quarreled with Virgil Thomson and I had heard nothing from him, he had gone to America and the opera with him. The Four Saints in Three Acts that I had written for him and that he had written. He took it to America with him and played it to any one who would listen to him and quite a few did listen. And now there was a chance that somebody would undertake to perform it, that is to give some especial performance in Hartford Connecticut of it and so we had to have a contract. We quarreled a little about that but finally it was all settled and I had really no very great hope that anything would come of it. I do never really think that anything good is going to happen, it mostly does, but I never expect it.

Well anyway as I say Paris was a peaceful place but not so interesting as it had been, there were a great many young there but anyway they seemed fairly old that is to say nothing was really inspiring to them or to any of us just then. But then as I say I did hear a great many conversations and I began to get interested in Picabia's painting and then we lost Byron.

Everything changes I had never had any life with dogs and now I had more life with dogs than with any one.

Everything changes it is extraordinary how everything does change.

Byron was a little Mexican dog given to us by Picabia. Once about ten years ago a Mexican was much interested in his paintings, she was a rich woman and she bought several of them and one day she said to him, would you like a pair of Mexican dogs you are fond of dogs and he said yes, everybody always does say yes, I do not suppose that if anybody offers to give you anything whether you want it or not you ever say no, certainly not if you are a writer or a painter so he said yes. It was almost a year after and a captain of a ship at Havre sent him notice that a man on board had some dogs for him. He went to see and there was a native Mexican servant who spoke only Mexican and who had a hand-made cage and on one side was one little Mexican dog and on the other side was another little Mexican dog, and having delivered the cage and the little dogs the man went back on the boat to Mexico.

So they called the two little Mexican dogs Monsieur and Madame and Byron was a son and a grandson. We called him Byron because he was to have as a wife his sister or his mother and so we called him Byron. Poor little Byron his name gave him a strange and feverish nature, he was very fierce and tender and he danced strange little war dances and frightened Basket. Basket was always frightened of Byron. And then Byron died suddenly one night of typhus.

Picabia was in Paris and he said we should have another one immediately have another one, and Basket was happy that Byron was dead and gone and then we had Pépé and as he had feared and dreaded Byron Basket loved Pépé. Pépé was named after Francis Picabia and perhaps that made the difference anyway Pépé was and is a nice little dog but not at all like Byron although in a picture of him you can never tell which one is which one.

So then spending money and the arranging for the publication of The Autobiography of Alice B. Toklas and the losing Byron was almost all that did happen that winter and then we prepared to go to the country and it was a lively summer. There was another thing that did happen that winter. Mr. Bradley was very pleased with everything and he had a man who came every winter to find people to go to America and lecture and he brought him to see me.

49

He was different from anything I had ever seen. He was a solemn man and he published religious books and school books and when he came to Europe on business he also acted as agent for and looked for people to lecture. He had just found the Princess Bibesco and now he was brought to me. Bradley said to him that I would be a very popular lecturer because there was a book of mine that was coming out in the autumn that was going to be a best seller. The man listened solemnly to Mr. Bradley's enthusiasm and then said very solemnly, interesting if true.

And then he said what would I want if I went over. Well I said of course Miss Toklas would have to go over and the two dogs. Oh he said. Yes I said but I said I do not think that any of us will really go over. Oh he said. I decided that if lecture agents were like that that certainly I would not go over and so I told him not to bother. And Mr. Bradley said I was making a mistake but I said no, Jo Davidson always said one should sell one's personality and I always said only insofar as that personality expressed itself in work. It always did bother me that the American public were more interested in me than in my work. And after all there is no sense in it because if it were not for my work they would not be interested in me so why should they not be more interested in my work than in me. That is one of the things one has to worry about in America, and later I learned a lot more about that.

So the winter was over, the winter of the beginning of making money and the summer came.

I said we had given up having only one servant and living simply, we had gotten an Italian couple Mario and Pia. It was most exciting. Mario was a very big man and we had to take him to the Belle Jardiniere to buy him clothes to work in and to wait on us in, and it was most exciting.

He had to have all the biggest sizes and then the two of them began to clean. They were clean. They washed down the little pavilion inside and outside and they insisted that the atelier had to

50

have a coat of paint put on. So we had it done. And they even took down the doors to wash and they made it as they said very coquet. It had not been that since nineteen fourteen.

And then we went to the country and then the trouble began. They thought the house was too large for only two servants and perhaps it is but we had always lived in it with one. They thought that having completely cleaned one house and that a little one they did not want to begin on another and that a big one.

And then they got sadder. They did not like lighting fires and he did not like cutting up kindling wood to light them so he moved about and picked up what he could find. It rained it always does just then, it is doing so now, that is what makes this country lovely and green with clouds and a blue sky, and the sticks he found on the ground were wet and he had to put them on the stove to dry them and even then they were not very many of them. They were sad then. They had been deceived about everything.

Never having seen them before they become your servants and live in the house they are just as intimate as if they were your parents or your children. It is funny that because there naturally is just as much need as possible of always having known everybody you know and they come in answer to an advertisement and you never saw them before and you live in the house with them. And then they go away and you never ever see them again.

It was a funny thing that summer so many things happened and they had nothing to do with me or writing. I have so often wanted to make a story of them a detective story of everything happening that summer and here I am trying to do it again. I never have wanted to write about any other summer because every other summer was a natural one for me to be living, but that summer that first summer after the Autobiography was not a natural summer and so it is a thing to be written once more and yet again.

There was the Hotel Pernollet and its tragedy, there was the family who came to succeed the Italians and we did not know it was to be a family and then there was the death of the English-woman and it did not end with that, Seabrook came and after that it happened again, differently but it did happen again.

It is funny about how often I have tried to tell the story of that summer, I have tried to tell it again and again.

The Hotel Pernollet is a typical French hotel the husband does the cooking and the wife manages everything and they never go out. They are very rich and they have four children. The children went out a little oftener but later when they will succeed to the hotel they will be married and they will not go out. Perhaps they will not be as rich as their father.

It was this hotel keeper who said what it is said I said that the war generation was a lost generation. And he said it in this way. He said that every man becomes civilized between the ages of eighteen and twenty-five. If he does not go through a civilizing experience at that time in his life he will not be a civilized man. And the men who went to the war at eighteen missed the period of civilizing, and they could never be civilized. They were a lost generation. Naturally if they are at war they do not have the influences of women of parents and of preparation.

Everybody says something, certainly everybody here does.

Now it is revolution, and this time it is going to be a revolution. After every great war there is a time of spending and having everything and then there is nothing and everybody talks about revolution and France having the habit of revolution is pretty sure to have one. After all revolutions are a matter of habit.

Everything is a habit.

I said all this to an old French lady Madame Pierlot, she is eighty-four and remembers everything and she says, yes of course but knowing it is no consolation.

She might have been important that summer when everything was different, what else does she say yes it is nature but that does not make it natural. She says also that whenever she is comfortably seated she is not comfortable unless everybody else is comfortably sitting, but after all she never is sitting comfortably so perhaps quite naturally everybody else is not comfortably sitting.

Well anyhow. We did know Madame Pernollet and her husband and they were interesting.

He had been a cook for four generations, his father and his grandfather and his great grandfather and when the war came and they wanted him to cook he said no he wanted to fight and though he was a very little man he did fight for four years and during these four years his wife bore him two children there had already been two born and she managed everything. She came from poorer people than he did, indeed, as they kept a very small and poor hardware store, her people did, it could not have been considered a good marriage for him and it was not but she was as small as he was and she was very pretty and he married her. She managed everything while he was away and had the children and every now and then everything was overwhelming.

Then the war was over and he came home again and he organized everything and from a little hotel it became a big one, not in size but in business and they never went out, they never had gone out, his mother never had before him, and he cooked and organized his cooking and she managed the young girls from the country whom she taught to do everything and she would gently push them forward and then back until she made good waitresses of them and she looked after all the fruit and the cake and chose the right one for every one and they made a great deal of money everybody did of course just then but they made more than any of them. Once in a while she said to us, well she did not say it, but once in a while she did say it as if it was, not the work, but something was overwhelming, not the not going out, that was not overwhelming not her children, she had three boys and a little girl, well anyway they did go on as they always had done. Then they decided and it was a little late because the time for making money was almost over, they decided to add another building and build a new kitchen and a new refrigerator and having everything electric. It began just as they were not earning as much as they had been and that is worrisome but anyway they went on. Then the second son was to come and help his father and succeed him. Then this boy had tuberculosis and they had to send him to the mountains and now for the first time they went out because they had to go and visit him. Then one day, it was that summer, she was found early in the morning on the cement where she had fallen, and they picked her up and took her to the hospital and no one staying in the hotel knew anything had happened to her and then she was very religious she always had been and then she was dead and I went to the church, and in the French way went up to shake hands with the husband and the father and the two sons and the hotel keeper who had been a very fat little man became a very thin one and his son was cured and all his sons came to be with him in the hotel business and he went out from time to time and whether they will pay for the new piece of hotel or not is not anybody's business. Anyway he is courageous enough to fly a flag just now when communism has commenced and the national flag is particularly forbidden.

As I say it was a queer summer and our Italian servants were gone and we had someone find us another man and wife to replace them.

It is undoubtedly a very strange thing that when there is a great deal of unemployment you can never get anybody to do any work. But that is natural enough because if everybody is unemployed everybody loses the habit of work, and work like revolutions is a habit it just naturally is.

So Georges Maratier put an advertisement in the paper and saw a great many couples who were not worth anything and finally he said he had found an excellent one and was sending them. He did not tell us they had a child with them, however they had and it was quite a pretty one and she went up the stairs and down again very prettily indeed but that was not surprising as her mother was a Portuguese and had been and still was a very pretty woman. The husband was an Alsatian and like many Alsatians he felt he could do everything even if he had never done anything and he mostly had not. Also as do most Alsatians he admired writing and he said to me, Madame, I have a great deal of pleasure in telling you that my wife and myself and my daughter are going to dedicate our lives to you as long as you are living, all that I ask of you is that if anything happens to me you will undertake their care for their future life. Yes yes I said, and that pleased him. Soon we found that she cooked beautifully but she only had one kidney and if you only have one kidney and you cook beautifully and have a husband who does nothing it is very tiring. And it was, and she could not sleep and so the Alsatian thought they would all sleep under the trees. You can not very well do that in the mountains particularly if you have one kidney missing, it is cold and there is dew under the trees and besides country people do not like to see it, not here. All this excited the Alsatian.

Everything excited the Alsatian until the people in the village became afraid of him and the lack of a kidney troubled his pretty Portuguese wife who could cook everything and whom he had converted to protestantism, more and more until we had the country doctor to see her. He said she had better quit working and they had nothing except themselves but finally they separately left and the Alsatian was left behind in the village and was even more frightening to them and so we once more had to find another couple as we were expecting guests just then, and the Alsatian finally disappeared too.

I never get over the fact that you are very likely to know everybody a long time and the difference between knowing them a long time and not knowing them at all is really nothing. Anyway nobody can get lost any more because the earth is all so covered with everybody and everybody is always moving around and you always see everybody and nevertheless very often you never see any of them again. This is what happened then.

Some one said that there were a couple somewhere on the mountains so we went to see them. They were there, the priest not the priest there but the priest elsewhere recommended them and we took them. They were not a couple that is they had not been then when the priest recommended them and were they now, they did not seem to be one. She had everything the matter so the doctor said whom we finally called in to see her and he took her to the hospital and he said they never have enough patients in the hospital so they would keep her and he the husband went out in to the hallway and fell and so he decided he would leave us and her. So once more we were without a couple and we went to Lyon to get one. This time we got a Polish woman and a Czechoslovak husband and that seemed better. She was a very good cook and said she hoped she would be happy although she never had been and he said he liked to be a mechanic but he did not like to lie under a car with his legs sticking out and if you were an automobile mechanic this is what you had to do so he decided that he would be a valet de chambre but he had been and was a pretty good mechanic.

The Picabias came.

We had just had a bathroom and a water closet put in and running water. Up to this time we had bathed in a rubber tub and had the water brought in from the fountain. In France you do not have a pump you have a fountain.

And then the Picabias came and Picabïa has now a Swiss wife well anyway the water closet was stopped up it was late at night and it was flooded. I called Jean who woke up and immediately he manipulated something and stopped the flow of water and stopped the flood. Now we all can do it but he was the first one to manage it and we were pleased with him.

As I said I had been finding Francis Picabia more and more interesting. I had known him many years and had not cared for him

56

he was too brilliant and he talked too much and he was too fatiguing, besides that I had not cared for his painting. I did not care for the way it resembled Picasso and I did not care for the way it did not resemble him. But now I was changing. Perhaps he was changing that however I do not quite believe.

In a way it was Francis Rose who first interested me in Picabia's painting and that was because I found Francis Rose the only interesting one among the young men painting and insofar as he had learned anything he had learned it from Picabia and not from Picasso.

One might say they were both called Francis and anybody called Francis is elegant, unbalanced and intelligent and certain to be right not about everything but about themselves. At least such has been true of any Francis as Francis in history or as I have known them. Francis Rose was all that and Picabia was coming to be all that.

Picabia objects to Cezanne is it because he is jealous of that painting or is it because he is right about it. Everybody of that period was influenced by Cezanne but he says he was not and was not.

Picabia's father was a Spaniard born in Cuba and his mother was the daughter of a French scientist and one of the inventors of photography. So Picabia was brought up on photography not on taking photographs but on the science of photography and he when he was a boy and his grandfather used to go on trips and visit museums and his grandfather photographed and Picabia was not interested as no one is if another one does it. But and so he thinks that is the reason he was not influenced by Cezanne. Then his grandfather died and it had been a household of men his grandfather and his father and his uncle and when his grandfather was dead or even before the household of men bored him and he ran away and with a little girl he loved then he ran away to Switzerland. He was seventeen years old then and to support them he painted picture postal cards in Switzerland and they got along.

After that he went back to Paris and other places and painted and he knew Pissaro and his children and perhaps Pissaro influenced him. But he was worried so he said about painting not being painting he did not think about photography but he did think about painting not being painting. Just then he met Gabrielle who was studying music and she suggested to him that since painting should not be painting perhaps it should be music. He agreed that perhaps it should. And it was that for quite some time for him perhaps for too long a time. Anyway he was certain that anything should not look like anything even if it did and that really it did not. That was the influence of photography upon him it certainly was.

That is where photography is different from painting, painting looks like something and photography does not.

And Cezanne and Picasso have nothing to do with photography but Picabia has. Well.

The only reason why people work or run around, and naturally everybody does all of one or the other of them is that they will not know that time is something and that time can pass. That is the only reason for working or for running around.

And this too has to do with photography and modern painting.

I begin to see what Picabia means about Cezanne. Not that I do not like Cezanne best but I begin to see what he means.

This winter they had a Seurat show and that was interesting. They talk about mechanics and science but the only thing about mechanics and science is that it works, anything moving around makes another thing move around and so there is satisfaction. But and it is very important, anything that is alive if it moves around can fail to make something else move around as well as make it move around and so there is not complete satisfaction. Now what has art got to do with all this. Art is a little of both and until now it has gone on being something of both. It does make something move around by coming in contact with that thing but also it fails

58

to do so that is it has failed to do so and so it has to do with something living.

Now then came the domination of mechanical things and art which always has to see what the contemporary sees had to see in this way, that is to say had to see that a thing moving automatically made another thing move exactly in the way it did move and it could not fail as before insofar as it had been living it had had to fail.

Well then what happened. It is still happening. Only now it is not any longer very interesting. Perhaps government which is neither mechanics nor life will begin and be something. Well anyway that is not for me to worry about. Not that I was ever worried or disturbed, how could I be when after all the question is after all does it do something and any something is or is not everything because it does look like it.

I thought I understood all about what we had done and now understanding Picabia made me start all over again. And suddenly with the Seurat show it came. Besides then there is the question of photography in painting.

Well anyway the Picabias stayed for several days and then they went away.

That is the trouble with a distraction. A distraction is to avoid the consciousness of the passage of time. That is the trouble with any Utopia, any system, as soon as it is a system it is not a distraction and so it does not any longer make it possible not to know the passage of time. Picabia is fond of saying there should in painting be no distraction, that is why he hates the following of Cezanne and if as he says Cezanne was not so real then his reality would not be a distraction. He likes to tell how when he was a young man some Japanese painters whom he knew were all excited when they were to see a Cezanne for the first time and then they said but it looks like the thing he painted and we hoped well we hoped it would not and anybody can do that can make it look like the thing

59

from which it is painted. Well anyway Picabia likes to say this and he keeps on painting which is more just now than anybody else does. So he says and it is. He came to see us again but just now after he had been there a few days and made drawings of us they went away the Picabias went away.

The couple we had the Polish woman and the Czechoslovak man stayed on, he wanted to drive my car but I like to drive my own car, and she went on cooking and she did cook very well and she had been wonderful with horses she had come to France to work on a farm the way lots of Poles did after the war was over. They liked her on the farm but they did not like him. Janet Scudder always says how is it possible that a couple a husband and wife can be good for anything. It is hard to find one person in this world both useful and pleasant but what chance is there that that one person could marry another person useful and pleasant. Better give it up, says Janet.

We were very quiet that is were living in the country and that is very occupying. Madame Pierlot says that in the country you do not have to get ready to go out, in the city if you want to go out you have to get ready to go out but in the country if you go out you are out and you do not have to get ready. For some weeks nothing happened and then Janet Scudder announced that she was coming with a friend and that they would stay a few days. Janet always has a friend anybody always has a friend. As the earth is covered all over with people and they all do the same thing in the same way anybody can and does have a friend.

So Janet and her friend were to come and they came later than they were expected, however they did come.

They were very tired because I had told them to take two days to come and they had come in one. It is not a very long drive and still they had better not have come in one. Blood on the dining room floor and they had better not have come in one.

We had a late dinner and then everybody went to bed.

The Polish woman cook did not look as happy as she had hoped to look and everybody went to bed.

The next morning was very busy, it is like that. Janet wanted to paint, she wanted to paint the house with Basket the dog. We wanted to have her paint. She wanted to have her car fixed at least her friend did because the car needed fixing. We had asked two women living in the country to come to lunch. They were the ones that were to have the tragedy one was English and one was French. They both wore trousers and raised chickens and turkeys. The home they lived in belonged to the Frenchwoman, it had belonged to her father and we had known him, she bought it from her sister and her step-mother and now some knew her. She had a friend who was the mother of four children when we first knew her, she herself had two. Anyway she and the Englishwoman were to come together as they lived together. It was a lively day.

Then Janet's friend called me, she could not start the car. It was a Ford car and I ought to know how to start any Ford car but this one did not start. All right I said I will go with mine and get Mr. Humbert who fixes my car I said. I started to start mine. It did not start. Mine is a Ford car too and it should start but it did not start. I said I would telephone to the garage man. The telephone would not telephone. Then I went out to speak to every one. The Polish woman was there and I said well and she said yes and she said Jean is always like that when anything like that can happen. What I said. Blood on the dining room floor she said. Well I said I will go out and telephone. Luckily in the village is another telephone, but nobody in the house had known about that so I went to telephone and I asked the garage man to come and I asked the telephone people to come. In the meanwhile every one was there Janet was not painting, Alice Toklas was not arranging anything and Janet's friend was there and Jean was there and the Polish woman. The garage man came with two cars. First he looked at Janet's. Well he said there is water in the reservoir he said. Water in the reservoir

61

water in the reservoir he said. And now I will look at yours he looked and he found a piece of cloth in the distributor and dirt in it besides. Well he said well I said, and the spark plugs of my car were broken, well he said, well I said I wonder, who is that man, he said, I said he is our valet de chambre, call him over he said, the garage man is a big fat man and he looked at Jean who is a small man. Well he said, and Jean did not say anything, I guess you better get rid of him and say no more about it was all the garage man said. Just then, our friends came and just then and that was what happened then I went into the dining room and there was Francis Rose with a picture in his hand. I kissed him, I said where did you come from. He said I came on the way from Cannes to Paris to bring you this thing. It is very lovely I said, but everything is in confusion. We had had a quarrel and I was not expecting to see him, it was very easy seeing him everything being in confusion, I said and how did you come, oh Carley is outside in the car, we were of course not seeing him, we had completely quarreled with him, so I went outside the gate and once more kissed Francis and thanked him and shook hands with Carley but did not stop not seeing him, and then we had lunch and then we sent Jean and the Polish woman away, she said she had not come to be as happy as she hoped to have been but then she was certain it never could happen that she could come to be happy again and then Janet and her friend left Janet never does believe in staying, and the other two the Frenchwoman and the Englishwoman left and there we were once more looking for servants to have come and live in the house without our knowing anything about them.

The thing about it all that is puzzling is that really nothing is frightening. Anything scares me, anything scares any one but really after all considering how dangerous everything is nothing is really very frightening.

Having exhausted Paris and the country we again tried Lyon and a very serious old pair came out of Lyon, he was an old soldier and she was an old French cook and he was a valet de chambre and he did not care about the clothes we had and he wanted different ones, well he did not get them and his brother had been a carpenter, so he did know how to polish furniture.

Any country is pretty but the country here is very lovely. Any sky is lively but the sky here is very lively very tiny clouds and enormous big ones.

The land is not too far away and the hills are high. I like it here.

William Aspinwall Bradley our agent came to stay. After a little while I asked him to go away, not because he was not a pleasant guest because he was but I do not like any one to stay, not because they are in the way but because after a time they are part of the way we live every day or they are not and I prefer them to be not.

While Bradley was with us Madame de Clermont-Tonnerre came to see us. She had been persuaded to go to America and lecture under the auspices that Bradley had tried to get me to accept but I had said no and she had said yes. She came and lunched with us, and then after lunch we sat in a circle and she was to read to us what she was to say in America. I am very found of Madame de Clermont Tonnerre, she has what always charms us in the mixture of peasant and duchess. The earth is the earth as a peasant sees it, the world is the world as a duchess sees it, and anyway a duchess would be nothing if the earth was not there as the peasant tills it. I suppose that is the reason why the French country is so occupying, any peasant sees the earth as any other class can see it and they all see it as any peasant sees it, and they never stop seeing it. That is what worries any one when they think that anything else can happen. Now instead of letting everybody go and do a little digging they are organizing them to have a vacation. Well nobody can let anybody alone. The eighteenth century began the passion for individual freedom, the end of the nineteenth century by conceiving organization began the beginning of a passion for being enslaved not so much for enslaving but for being enslaved. Any detective story in America says of

63

course crime has to be organized you got to have somebody to do your thinking, and a very able young man Donald Vestal wants Roosevelt because he is ready to do their thinking for them and after all what is the use of thinking if after all there is to be organization. Of course the war which made so many things come to be more definite, things that had already come to exist made organization have so much more meaning. We used to be pleased when Mrs. Lathrop said organization, she made each syllable in it a separate thing to be organized into one. And the French soldiers said war was comfortable nobody had to worry about anything. Of course as soon as one is enslaved why then they will begin to pine for freedom, of course it all has to do with changing so that nobody will really feel inside them that time is passing. However Madame de Clermont-Tonnerre was to read her lecture to us and we all sat around to listen. Just then Basket found his ball. Basket loves his little red ball next best after eating but I took it away from him, And Madame de Clermont-Tonnerre began reading and Basket in the middle of all of us sat up and begged to have his ball given to him. Poodles are circus dogs they have no sense of home and no sense of being a dog, they do not realize danger nor ordinary life because in a circus there is no such thing. Well anyway, Madame de Clermont-Tonnerre went to America to lecture and she came back and she was no longer friends with our agent Bradley.

All this time I did no writing. I had written and was writing nothing. Nothing inside me needed to be written. Nothing needed any word and there was no word inside me that could not be spoken and so there was no word inside me. And I was not writing. I began to worry about identity. I had always been I because I had words that had to be written inside me and now any word I had inside could be spoken it did not need to be written. I am I because my little dog knows me. But was I I when I had no written word inside me. It was very bothersome. I sometimes thought I would try but to try is to die and so I did not really try. I was not doing any writing.

I had always been interested in the good American doctrine you should not prepare anything without having a prospect, that is there should be a buyer for every seller. But then on the other hand there is the inevitable failure. More great Americans were failures than they were successes. They mostly spent their lives in not having a buyer for what they had for sale.

That is of course true anywhere only in America there has not been the habit of recognizing it as there.

Inside and outside and identity is a great bother. And how once that you know that the buyer is there can you go on knowing that the buyer is not there. Of course when he is not there there is no bother.

It was a strange year that year and it is a strange year this year. The blue of the sky looks rather black to the eye.

The Autobiography of Alice B. Toklas after its Atlantic Monthly success was printed and we were to get some advance copies, they had not come yet. Fall was coming and the vintage and Bernard Faÿ was to come which he did later and as yet it was warm yet not hot but warm as it is here in August and September.

We had the telephone.

One evening just at supper we live as people do in the country we eat our dinner at noon and in the evening an early and light supper. Actually country people here eat a very late supper and go to bed immediately after. Well anyway it was just evening and somebody began to say something. He said he was Seabrook, I said yes I knew all about him where was he, in Belley he said, he said he had come because he had just read the Autobiography and it had done something to him and so he had left the midi and here he was in Belley, I said we are just eating supper come over immediately after.

It was a little surprising, he looked like a south European sailor and he looked American. She looked American, she looked like a college woman and together they looked different from anything that we saw around here.

He talked quietly with his eyes fixed in front of him. He said he wanted to see if I was as interesting as my book was. I said I was. He said yes and he went on slowly talking.

And then they said they would go back to the hotel and the next day they would spend all day here.

That day was interesting. There are quite a few paintings of Francis Rose, some of them I had bought from him when I was down here and some he had painted when he was here. Seabrook began to look at them. Do you know what they are he said looking at them. Yes they are very good painting. Yes but he said do you know what they are. Well what are they I asked him. Well he said they have a fascination. Yes sure I said good painting is always fascinating at least it is to me. Yes said he but I cannot make up my mind whether there is any fascination in the painting or just fascination he said. You know what I mean he said, well I said, yes of course he said, yes I know it is your subject I said but I never take it on, well he said it is that, he said, you mean black magic I said and I said how do you tell, well he said you don't tell. Oh well I said, well anyway tell me about him. He is a good man he said and he has religion and it's good painting but there is no doubt about anything, it is black magic in it that is fascinating. Well anyway I said I think it is pretty good painting. We talked all day and he told me that something had to happen and he asked me what I thought and I told him I thought he had better quit the midi. He told me that his father was a preacher on the eastern shore near Baltimore. All my people come from Baltimore and I knew all about the eastern shore. After all preachers' sons will when they begin will drink a lot and it wears them out. There was McAlmon and here was Seabrook.

It is funny about drinking.

66

In the first place it is not true that wine drinkers do not get drunk. Wine natural wine is about twelve percent alcohol and if you drink six or seven litres of that a day and that is what they naturally do when they work all day well by the end of the day there is nothing to say but that they are sodden with drink.

People when they are drunk are not interesting unless they are people who when they are sober are a little queer, and even then well even then it is only in the beginning that they are amusing. Drinkers think each other are amusing but that is only because they are both drunk. It is funny the two things most men are proudest of is the thing that any man can do and doing does in the same way, that is being drunk and being the father of their son.

These are the two things they do exactly as every other man does and they are the two things which make them most proud. If anybody thinks about that they will see how interesting it is that it is that.

I have seen so many people drunk. I do not like to drink, I have no feeling about it but my stomach does not like it and I never do like to do what my stomach does not like to do. But I have seen so many people drunk.

I was very amused with Carl Van Vechten one day. He never drinks now and one day we were together with a friend who was drunk. Carl did not like to see him and I talked to him and Carl said how can you and I said well I have had to be with so many who were drunk that I have the habit of treating them as if they were sober. Oh that's it said Carl. Well I can't, and I said Oh Carl and he said yes I know but I can't.

Well anyway I am very fond of a number of people who are always more or less drunk. There is nothing to do about it if they are always more or less drunk.

As a matter of fact when I was in America I was surprised to see so comparatively few people drunk. It was only in New England where they seemed to be really drunk.

And Seabrook told me about the white magic of Lourdes and how he was going there and be a stretcher bearer and I could understand that they would trust him to be there, and then we all drove over to Aix-les-Bains to have dinner. We picked up Bradley on the way and we went over to have dinner. Seabrook would have to stay there because he could not drive when it was too late to see because to him lighted lights were alive and he could not see to drive.

However we all went over to Aix to dinner. He and I sat next to one another and gradually I told him all about myself and my brother.

They talk a great deal these days about only working a half hour a day and so the work of the world will be done. Well I have never been able to write much more than a half hour a day. If you write a half hour a day it makes a lot of writing year by year. To be sure all day and every day you are waiting around to write that half hour a day. I suppose that will be the way every one will pay their half hour a day.

Well that is another matter but still it has something to do with the story of myself and my brother as I told it that night to Seabrook, I could understand how it happened that it was to Seabrook that I did tell the story of myself and my brother.

It is funny this knowing being a genius, everything is funny.

And identity is funny being yourself is funny as you are never yourself to yourself except as you remember yourself and then of course you do not believe yourself. That is really the trouble with an autobiography you do not of course you do not really believe yourself why should you, you know so well so very well that it is not yourself, it could not be yourself because you cannot remember right and if you do remember right it does not sound right and of course it does not sound right because it is not right. You are of course never yourself. Well anyway I did tell all about myself, -

telling about my brother was telling about myself being a genius and it was a natural thing to tell it all to Seabrook.

It is funny about novels and the way novels now cannot be written. They cannot be written because actually all the things that are being said about any one is what is remembered about that one or decided about that one. And since there is so much publicity so many characters are being created every minute of every day that nobody is really interested in personality enough to dream about personalities. In the old days when they wrote novels they made up the personality of the things they had seen in people and the things that were the people as if they were a dream. But now well now how can you dream about a personality when it is always being created for you by a publicity, how can you believe what you make up when publicity makes them up to be so much realer than you can dream. And so autobiography is written which is in a way a way to say that publicity is right, they are as the public sees them. Well yes.

In The Making of Americans I wrote about our family. I made it like a novel and I took a piece of one person and mixed it with a piece of another one and then I found that it was not interesting and instead I described everything. I had the idea of describing every one, every one who could or would or had been living, but in the beginning I did give a real description of how our family lived in East Oakland, and how everything looked as I had seen it then.

It was funny when we went back one day when I was in America to see how East Oakland, that is Thirteenth Avenue and Twenty-fifth Street as it was then looked. The little houses on Thirteenth Avenue looked very much the same, a good many of them quite as neglected as I remembered them and the hill quite the same but the old Stratton house as they called it where we had lived was of course gone and had been built over with little houses, they looked as if they were the only new houses in all that region. When they used to ask me in America whether I had not found America changed I said no of course it had not changed what could it change to. The only thing that makes identity possible is no change but nevertheless there is no identity nobody really thinks they are the same as they remember. However I did tell Seabrook all about my brother, and myself and my brother.

My brother and myself had always been together. One should always be the youngest member of the family. It saves you a lot of bother everybody takes care of you.

I was the youngest member of my family and there were five of us and this my brother was only two years older. Naturally everybody always took care of me and naturally he always took care of me and I had a great deal of care taken of me and that left me with a great deal of time altogether. Well I suppose you have to do that if you are going to.

The Spanish revolution bothers me so much there is so much to remember. My brother and I went to Spain just after the Spanish American War and we travelled with Jesuits on the train and my brother and they began to discuss things in Spanish and they began to be a little violent and then one of them turned to me and said we Spaniards talk too much but we are very gentle people well they are not but any way it was nice of him to reassure me.

However as I say my brother and I were always together.

It takes a lot of time to be a genius, you have to sit around so much doing nothing, really doing nothing. If a bird or birds fly into the room is it good luck or bad luck we will say it is good luck.

It is better if you are the youngest girl in a family to have a brother two years older, because that makes everything a pleasure to you, you go everywhere and do everything while he does it all for and with you which is a pleasant way to have everything happen to you, sometimes accidents happen to you but after all it is very easy not to have them hurt you and anyway it altogether is a

70

pleasant excitement for you. Anyway as I say my brother and I were always together. He learned to read first and I learned to read after, but reading was something we never did together. Reading is something you have to do alone, and it was something I always did completely alone. So life went on and it was certain enough that life was a pleasant matter. In The Making of Americans I tell about it all and it was all like that, East Oakland is Gossols and the place we lived on Thirteenth Avenue and Twenty-fifth Street was like that.

It is a funny thing about addresses where you live. When you live there you know it so well that it is like identity a thing that is so much a thing that it could not ever be any other thing and then you live somewhere else and years later, the address that was so much an address that it was a name like your name and you said it as if it was not an address but something that was living and then years after you do not know what the address was and when you say it it is not a name any more but something you cannot remember. That is what makes your identity not a thing that exists but something you do or do not remember. It is hard for me to really remember now about my brother but any way that is the way we lived together.

I can remember the first time we were ever separated a long time from one another. He had taken a trip around the world with a rich cousin who had to be taken away to travel and we had not seen each other for over a year and I went over to Antwerp and there we were to be together. I remember being very worried as the boat came nearer the shore lest I should not know him when I saw him. After all one never can remember at least I never can remember how anybody anybody really knows looks like and so perhaps when you see them you wont know them. Dogs worry about things like that, Basket does and sometimes it does happen he does not know us when he sees us, of course it does and can.

71

Well when I saw my brother it was a surprise to me but I knew quite certainly that it was my brother.

After that we were still pretty much always together.

He found a good many books that I would not have found and I read a great many books that did not interest him but I did read a great many of the books that he found that I would not have found. We both liked talking that is we always had argued about anything. That was natural most people do. It always reminds me of the time I heard the two sons of Jo Davidson arguing, they argued in French and it seemed mostly to consist of, You are certain, you are sure and certain, yes I am certain I am sure and I am certain and that could go on without an ending or a beginning. And then once Alice Toklas said that my brother and I had argued for hours about information concerning something and all either of us knew of it was the same article that we had been arguing. Well any way, he continued to believe in what he was saying when he was arguing and I began not to find it interesting.

We did both love to talk a great deal although I do believe that I listened more or at least if I did not listen more I was silent more. I remember we were once arguing my brother and I which one of us talked more and we finally asked our little uncle Ephraim Keyser which one of us did talk and argue more and he looked very carefully first at one and then at the other one and he said well I think you do certainly do both do your share.

As I say we were almost always together.

And then there was Stieglitz. Stieglitz tells a strange story of the early days when we were living in Paris and I had begun writing and my brother was painting and we had begun everything. According to Stieglitz, and I very well remember his being there he was there for several hours and my brother was talking and according to Stieglitz I was not saying anything and he went away with the greatest admiration and said he had never known any woman well perhaps anybody to sit still so long without talking.

He still when I went to see him in New York he still told me this thing. Well perhaps I did. At any rate by that time I was writing and arguing was no longer to me really interesting. Nothing needed defending and if it did it was no use defending it. Anyway that was the beginning of my writing and by that time my brother had gotten to be very hard of hearing.

When we were young together I used to tease my brother. I was very fond of reading Clarissa Harlowe and I used to quote to him, what Clarissa's uncle wrote to her about her brother, remember he is your brother two years older and a man. My brother was two years older and a man and we were always together. We had travelled a great deal together and he was always a very sweet a little older brother when we travelled together, when we had been in Europe and in Spain and in Morocco together, we always had been together, when we were very little children we went many miles on dusty roads in California together, all alone together and he would shoot a jack rabbit and then I would try to shoot after he had shot it and that was in the days when in California you could go miles and miles and be alone together. It was all as it could have been.

I do not think I told all this to Seabrook that evening but that was what I was telling him.

Then we were less together and then when I decided not to pass my last examination and not to do anything with medicine he who had given up biology and history decided to begin painting and I went to Paris to join him.

Just why he began to paint I cannot remember. Of course there is always a reason or at least a combination that makes anybody do anything. But I do not remember why my brother began painting anyway he was going to a regular atelier and he was painting by the time I joined him.

It is funny about anything, we do not remember how Picasso happened to begin to paint my portrait and I do not remember how my brother happened to begin painting, he must have told me if he knew only perhaps by that time well yes he must have told me and he must have known by that time. Well anyway he was painting, he had taken the pavillion and atelier on the rue de Fleurus although he was not painting there, he was painting at the school and drawing from the model at the afternoon drawing class as a matter of fact he never did paint at the rue de Fleurus atelier. I joined him and I sat down in there and pretty soon I was writing, and then he took a studio elsewhere and we lived together there until nineteen fourteen.

The war had nothing to do with that of course not. Wars never do, they only make anybody know what has already happened it has happened already the war only makes it public makes those who like illustrations of anything see that it has been happening.

That is why periods after the war are really so dull and do not really make sense. The French have a word for that the fin de serie when they advertise a sale, the end of a series, and that is what everything after a war is.

Everything has been done before the war and then the war makes everybody know it and then everybody acts as if they were doing something but really they are only carried on by momentum, everybody has finally to get quiet again and begin again, think of the civil war think of any war and anybody will know that thing.

Well anyway now really this is to what Seabrook was listening what I am now telling, I have told it so often, often with a great deal of feeling often with a great deal less feeling often with no feeling often well not really forgetting but now I have forgotten but still I can tell it again even if it is nothing.

We were settled in Paris together and we were always together and I was writing. Everybody began to come in and my brother was talking, and this is what is interesting, what makes one of the things that used to make me say something. I did not care for any

74

one being intelligent because if they are intelligent they talk as if they were preparing to change something.

It is like it was during the war the most actively war-like nation the Germans always could convince the pacifists to become pro-German. That is because pacifists were such intelligent beings that they could follow what any one is saying.

If you can follow what any one is saying then if you are a pacifist you are pro-German. That follows if any one understands what any one is saying. Therefore understanding is a very dull occupation.

I always remember Maurice Grosser. He was a friend of Virgil Thomson and he had a way of knowing how it was possible to play the plays that I have written.

He used to be at the house a good deal and one day we were talking about liberals that is intellectuals, the kind of people that believe in progress and understanding and he said yes I have known a lot of them and they always have had something they always feel that they have had an unhappy childhood. Lots of them have told me a lot about that thing about the unhappy childhood they had had as children.

Well Blum the present French premier he is such a one, certainly he had had a childhood that was like the kind that kind had, that is to say not a happy one, the kind that naturally were not happy when they were children are the kind that believe in intelligence and progress and understanding. Well well.

Anyway my brother needed to be talking and he was painting but he needed to talk about painting in order to be painting, he needed to understand painting in order to be painting.

So we went on.

Gradually I was writing.

About an unhappy childhood well I never had an unhappy anything. What is the use of having an unhappy anything.

My brother and I had had everything. Gradually he was remembering that his childhood had not been a happy one. My eldest brother and I had not had that impression, certainly not however my brother led in everything. He had always been my brother two years older and a brother. I had always been following.

As I say I was writing and well why not I was writing the way I was writing and it came to be the writing of The Making of Americans.

I was writing in the way I was writing. I did not show what I was doing to my brother, he looked at it and he did not say anything. Why not. Well there was nothing to say about it and really I had nothing to say about it. Gradually he had something to say about it. I did not hear him say it. Slowly we were not saying anything about it that is we never had said anything about it.

That was about the time when Stieglitz said I sat for hours and I said nothing, well there was nothing to say because just then saying anything was nothing. How could I say anything when there was nothing to say and how could there be anything to say when I was doing what I was doing which was the writing of the Making of Americans. We were together as much as ever.

Then slowly he began explaining not what I was doing but he was explaining, and explaining well explaining might have been an explanation. Now and then I was not listening. This had never happened to me before up to that time I had always been listening sometimes arguing very often just being interested and being interesting and very often it was just that we had always been together as we always were.

This is what happened then.

Slowly and in a way it was not astonishing but slowly I was knowing that I was a genius and it was happening and I did not say anything but I was almost ready to begin to say something. My brother began saying something and this is what he said.

He said it was not it it was I. If I was not there to be there with what I did then what I did would not be what it was. In other

76

words if no one knew me actually then the things I did would not be what they were.

He did not say it to me but he said it so that it would be true for me. And it did not trouble me and as it did not trouble me I knew it was not true and a little as it did not trouble me he knew it was not true.

But it destroyed him for me and it destroyed me for him.

Because there was this thing it should have been in him, he knew it best so it should have been in him.

It is funny this thing of being a genius, there is no reason for it, there is no reason that it should be you and should not have been him, no reason at all that it should have been you, no no reason at all.

That is the way he felt about it and it was a natural thing, because he understood everything and if you understand everything and besides that are leading and besides that do do what you do there is no reason why it should not be creating, and that is he was that and had always been and I had not been that but I had been it enough to be following, now why should it come to be that it should be something else now just why should it. Well well just why should it. The only thing about it was that it was I who was the genius, there was no reason for it but I was, and he was not there was a reason for it but he was not and that was the beginning of the ending and we always had been together and now we were never at all together. Little by little we never met again.

This was the story I told Seabrook by the side of the lake at Aix-les-Bains.

And then the Seabrooks went away and so did we and we have never met again. It was very nice of him to come.

We are here again and now it is raining but it was not raining at least it was not raining all the time then. Of course water has to go up to come down and when it is raining all the time as it has been doing how can it go up to come down. However it does.

We went on spending the summer here as we have been doing. I never used to think that being in the country could be so pleasing.

Anyway we went on knowing everybody in the country and everybody in the country knows you at least they say how do you do.

Later when we went to America and everybody everywhere said how do you do, people would ask particularly Bernard Faÿ asked me if it did not make me self-conscious to have everybody in America know me and say how do you do, it does seem extraordinary but they all did know me and they all said how do you do, I of course never imagined that they would all know me and that they would say how do you do any one anywhere but when they did it it was afterwards as it is here in Bilignin, everybody here and in Belley knows me and as I go about any one anywhere says how do you do and America is a little larger of course it is a little larger there are a great many more people there but after all if they all do know you and do say how do you do to you once it happens it really does not make it different that America is larger and that there are so many more people over there than here since they all do know you and they all do say how do you do to you.

When it rains as much as this it does not make a flood we talk as if it would but it does not make a flood not here any way.

During that summer after the Seabrooks had been as I say it did not rain not very much and we went on doing what we are always doing.

We changed servants again I just do not remember what happened but we changed servants again, well anyway that had nothing to do with the tragedy that for days excited all of us.

In a French country there are some women who are more interested in hunting and fishing in wine and in food than in anything. There are a great many who are interested in crocheting and hunting and in food and in wine, there are some who are more interested in gardening and in food and in wine and in sleeping and there are some who are interested in chickens and ducks and in food and in wine and in dogs and in nothing more. Madame Caesar was like that.

After all everybody is being now thrown back upon the earth which is all covered over with people and how interesting that can be until somehow there is something to see.

The French peasant used to keep his money or her money in their woolen stocking and as naturally as not that makes avarice come to be and until everybody again can be a miser there will be nothing to see at least perhaps not. However that had nothing to do with Madame Caesar who was not one although perhaps her friend Madame Steiner was one anyway she was always worried about Madame Caesar spending too much money. Madame Caesar was rich and did not have to worry about her two sons they would inherit from their aunt and father, their aunt was feeble minded but not a spender and their father might be poor when he died you can never tell about a man in the leather business, well anyway Madame Caesar did spend her money and later the garage man Monsieur Charles told me that the Englishwoman had paid out all her money for Madame Caesar, that made me at that time not want to see Madame Caesar again, I am not very careful about money, but I do get frightened about it again and again.

Madame Caesar was a big good-looking woman who had had tuberculosis, when she had she had met the Englishwoman who had not had it. She Madame Caesar said she caught tuberculosis when she had been out fishing with Madame Steiner who likes fishing and Madame Caesar had gone into the water to disentangle her fishing hook for her.

Anyway she had been at a sanatorium in the mountains and had met the Englishwoman. After Madame Caesar's father died she bought the place her father had from her sister and went to live there with Madame Steiner. Her father had bought it because he was a water engineer and it had a stream of running water and waterfalls that came down a rocky hillside not far from the side of the house where there were a great many trees. The water was very cold and they raised trout in the water and they would then go fishing in the pools but trout raised like that is not really very good so Madame Caesar said.

After fish came ducks and chickens.

Madame Caesar and Madame Steiner lived there together and Madame Steiner worried about her. Madame Caesar was a tall big woman and had pleasant ways and wore trousers a sort of carpenter's costume and so anybody would worry about her. Mrs. Steiner managed to worry about her and little by little the Englishwoman came to stay there and she worried about her too not exactly worried about her but she did manage to have them be very busy because she began raising chickens in electric incubators.

Madame Caesar liked electric things, she installed electric stoves and electric heaters and electric refrigerators, that in America is nothing, but in that part or any part of France it was not usual it is beginning to be so now but five years ago it was not so.

They raised an extraordinarily large number of chickens and ducks and began to build a very pretty little village in which these little animals were to live, Madame Caesar was pleased that the Englishwoman should have this pleasure.

We knew them very well but nobody else did that is nobody else that we knew knew them very well.

It was this same summer Bernard Faÿ was there that summer. There is a great deal to tell about him.

Well Madame Caesar had not really known very intimately a man who was very important to everybody and who was a sort of agent and gardener for everybody. He now says he had always known her father. That probably is not so, that her father had been a great influence in his life that too is probably not so. Anyway this is a man about whom everybody is always talking. That is something to know just what it is a man is, more often a man than a woman, and when there is silence somebody is talking anybody is talking and they are talking about him.

They are never very successful the man about whom whenever there is a silence and everybody is talking they are talking about him as often men as women are talking about him. I suppose really they do not know why he is not more important or more successful than he is perhaps it is that well anyway this man is such a one and even now, well even now everybody talks about him whenever they do not happen to be talking about something else.

Well anyway the Englishwoman was going to England for a month's vacation and Madame Steiner was going to stay with Madame Caesar and be worried about her.

They were together and Madame Steiner was worried about her and between them and the wife of the gardener they kept the ducks and the chickens going and we had seen them and they were both fairly cheerful but Madame Steiner was worried about Madame Caesar not very much but still worried about her. And then Madame Steiner went away and the Englishwoman was to come back. Bernard Faÿ was staying in the house with us then and George Lyon, George Lyon came from Chicago and wanted to be a diplomat and he was a catholic and now he is in the office of a cannery but that does not make any difference because everybody was interested in him just as everybody is interested in everybody. The man everybody talks about if they are not talking about something else called me up on the telephone and said the English-woman was dead, well I said, yes he said, what happened I said, she is dead he said but she has just come I said yes I know he said but she is dead. Oh yes I said well I am very sorry I said yes he said, well I said, how did she die, well he said well you come and see Madame Caesar, certainly I said but how did she die, well he said they found her dead in the ravine, who did I said, well he said, they did find her dead. Oh well I said what did happen if she is dead well he said the police came why I said did somebody kill her, well he said I think you had better come he said, I said are you there no he said I am not there, and is the dead woman there, no he said she is not there, well I said are the dogs there did they find her, no they did not he said, but anyway he said it would be pleasanter if you went there. So Bernard Faÿ and I went there.

I weep I cry I glorify but all that has nothing to do with that. He weeps he cries he glorifies.

Everybody who has been there has beautiful eyes so Bernard Faÿ said and he was not mistaken Madame Caesar and Madame Steiner had. There was an American woman there too who knew all about Benjamin Franklin. Bernard Faÿ knew all about Benjamin Franklin too, and outside there were two the man who puts in electric heaters and his wife and inside there was a very large woman who was not moving and she was all in black as if it might be evening. She was the mother of the wife of the electrical installer and later she stayed there altogether.

And the Englishwoman was dead. Madame Caesar said that she had come home and they had talked and planned together and the next morning nobody had seen her and then they found her and I said but if she intended to kill herself she should have done it on the boat coming over and not waited until when she did do it it was most inconsiderate of her. Yes said Madame Caesar and she always had been so considerate of me. Then we all said this a great many times oftener. The police from one place had come and taken her but they should not have done so.

Well anyway there was nothing further.

There were two bullets in her head, her Basque cap she often wore one had been put carefully down on a rock beside her.

Doctors said no one ever shoots themselves twice, everybody who had been at the front during the war said that sometimes when a man wanted to kill himself he did shoot himself twice.

82

Anyway it was only once that we saw Madame Caesar, she came to see us and those who wanted to see her were there and in a little while any one was frightened of her and about her and then in a little while although she was always there nobody was there with her that is to say Mrs. Steiner never was there any more and the wife of the electric installer was.

It never bothered us any more but every time I want to write I want to write about what happened to her. Anyway there is no use in not forgetting what you know and we do not know what happened to her.

And then that summer was over.

CHAPTER III

Preparations for going to America

Since the Autobiography I had not done any writing, I began writing something, I called it Blood on the Dining-room Floor but somehow if my writing was worth money then it was not what it had been, if it had always been worth money then it would have been used to being that thing but if anything changes then there is no identity and if it completely changes then there is no sense in its being what it has been. Anyway that was the way it was.

In Lucy Church Amiably I quoted Picasso who had once said that the family of a genius treated him with consideration as a genius until he was successful and then if he was successful then he was like anybody else who was successful, and so they no longer treated him with consideration like a genius.

What is a genius. Picasso and I used to talk about that a lot. Really inside you if you are a genius there is nothing inside you that makes you really different to yourself inside you than those are to themselves inside them who are not a genius. That is so.

And so what is it that makes you a genius. Well yes what is it.

It is funny that no matter what happens, how many more or how many less can read and write can talk and listen can move around in every kind of way the number that is the lack of geniuses always remains about the same, there are very few of them. No matter what happens there are very few of them generally speaking only one and sometimes and very often not even one.

It is puzzling.

What is a genius. If you are one how do you know you are one.

84

It is not a conviction lots of people are convinced they are one sometime in the course of their living but they are not one and what is the difference between being not one and being one. There is of course a difference but what is it.

And if you stop writing if you are a genius and you have stopped writing are you still one if you have stopped writing. I do wonder about that thing.

And what are revolutions, have they anything to do with genius. I suppose a revolution as I have said is so much less orderly than a war. And is being a genius more orderly than other things. No it is not more orderly or more disorderly.

I always remember Pavlick Tchelitcheff writing to us the first time he was ever on shipboard and saying how bored he was with the ocean because it was just like the Russian revolution it just kept going up and down and being unpleasant and annoying and upsetting but it never went forward and back it just went up and down.

No matter how many thoughts are thought and how many characters are described that does not make a genius no matter how wonderfully well everything that is done is done and how like it really is it is described. What is a genius then.

We went back to Paris later. I had done no writing that summer, except for a piece on the war it was the only time since I had begun writing that I had not written.

I tried to write the story of Blood on the Dining-room Floor, and although I did it, I did not really do it and everybody was writing to me and I did not do any writing.

It was then I began to think about am I I because my little dog knows me. Basket left me last night, that is to say he did not stay with me and once a dog has gotten older he does know you but it is not the same thing, of course he does know you, but it does not worry him.

I suppose that really is what it is, it does not worry you. And so being a genius is not a worrisome thing, because it is so occupying, and when it is successful it is not a worrisome thing because it is successful, but a successful thing does not occupy you as an unsuccessful thing does, certainly not, and anyway a genius need not think, because if he does think he has to be wrong or right he has to argue or decide, and after all he might just as well not do that, nor need he be himself inside him. And when a dog gets older there is less of it and it does not worry him. When a genius gets older is there less of it and does it then not worry him.

Not always. Some have stopped, the few there are, others have gone on then.

I used to be fond of saying that America, which was supposed to be a land of success, was a land of failure. Most of the great men in America had a long life of early failure and a long life of later failure.

I am also fond of saying that a war or fighting is like a dance because it is all going forward and back, and that is what everybody likes they like that forward and back movement, that is the reason that revolutions and Utopias are discouraging they are up and down and not forward and back. Look right and not left look up and not down look forward and not back and lend a hand. That used to be called a Lend a Hand Society when I went to school and all the children had to write once a week when the society inside the school met, how they had lent a hand, most of them had an easy time, they could mind the baby or watch the cow or cut the wood or help their mother. Nobody wanted us to do these things and I and my brother who spent our time at home mostly eating fruit and reading books, never could remember how we had lent a hand. I wonder. I can still see the school room and hear the things read out and how that neither I nor my brother had lent a hand.

I never really did care very much about hearing any one lecture. My eyes always have told me more than my ears. Anything you hear gets to be a noise, but a thing you see, well of course it has some sound but not the sound of a noise.

A hoot owl is about the best sound. We hear it here a great deal.

But speaking voices always go at a different tempo than when you listen to them and that bothers me, things seen might too, but then you do not have to look at them, but things said have to be heard, and they always go on at the wrong tempo. I suppose really that is the trouble with politics and school teaching, everybody hears too much with their ears and it never makes anything come together, something is always ahead of another or behind, it does not even make any bother but it does nothing either but make a noise and a noise is always a confusion, and if you are confused well if you look at anything you are really not confused but if you hear anything then you really are confused.

Well Alice B. Toklas would say that depends on who you are. Perhaps, anyway there is no beginning and no end.

I had not heard any lectures since I had left learning for ex-aminations and the winter before I had gone. Bernard Faÿ had been appointed lecturer to the College de France which by the way had its four hundredth birthday just then, not that that mat-tered, not to him or to us, but anyway we were very close friends then and we had talked about how you came to be appointed professor and he was and so we went to hear him. We went to every lecture, it was a pleasure, it was interesting, I did not know then that I was going to lecture and it was polite always to be there at every lecture.

It is best not to talk about hearing anything.

Sound can be a worry to any one particularly when it is the sound of the human voice.

It is quite natural that some hear more pleasantly with the eyes than with the ears. This is true of me. I do.

When we went to school my brother and I although he was two

years older for a little while were in a class together. This was the second year in high school.

He never did recite very well because he had not that kind of a memory, I did not have that kind of a memory either but I could hold it a little longer. I never liked hearing any one recite or any one ask questions that needed an answer. And when he began it was a difficult matter not to believe that hearing did not matter. Anybody at school with a brother or sister knows how that can come to matter. And then there were recitations of poetry or prose, that happened every Friday and that was even much worse because then you had to stand on the platform alone and it was no longer your brother but some one who certainly could not remember and anyway what he had to say was so far away and more and more what you heard had no reality. What you say yes that was a picture but what you heard really did not matter.

It has always bothered me a good deal that and as in America hearing plays such a large part in everything it is a thing that makes any one really creating worry about everything. It does not worry me but it might if I could listen, that is if I could hear, but hearing tires me very quickly. Lots of voices make too much sound, any one voice sounds too much like that voice, and soon I do not worry, hearing human voices is not real enough to be a worry. When you have been digging in the garden or been anywhere when you close your eyes you see what you have been seeing, but it is a peaceful thing that and is not a worry to one. On the other hand as I write the movement of the words spoken by some one whom lately I have been hearing sound like my writing feels to me as I am writing. That is what led me to portrait writing. However lecturing is another matter.

All the time that I am writing the Spanish revolution obtrudes itself. Not because it is a revolution, but because I know it all so well all the places they are mentioning and the things there they are destroying.

When we were in England when the nineteen fourteen war began after all we never did think that we would have to speak of it by its date, we did think it would be the only war anybody can remember just as they always do with any war. When I was very young it was the civil war and when they said long before the war they meant that war. And then there was the Spanish war. One always does mean the war they had and I suppose sooner or later everybody has had a war.

Well anyway the Spanish revolution obtrudes itself because I know Spaniards so well and all the things they are destroying. When we were in England before the nineteen fourteen war and just at its beginning the Whiteheads worried me they were so much more interested in the destruction of libraries and buildings in Belgium than they were in the war and why not, now I understand why not that is just the way I do feel about Spain and yet why not. Everybody in the opera Four Saints in Three Acts thought it was funny when they asked Saint Therese what would she do if by touching a button she could kill three thousand Chinamen and the chorus said Saint Therese not interested.

But of course Saint Therese was not interested she was building convents in Spain why should she be interested in Chinamen.

When I was about seventeen I remember with excitement having decided that all knowledge was not my province. After all, you have to be able to imagine a thing to know it is there and how could Saint Therese imagine the three thousand Chinamen when she was building convents in Spain.

Actually that came to me rather differently. Years ago when I knew Hutchins Hapgood, he was a philosopher then and liked to think of the number of angels on the point of a needle and the things scholastic philosophy was interested in and he always complained of me that I had too good a time for anybody who was so virtuous. My virtue consisted in my not drinking or liking too much excitement or doing anything that he considered was normally a vicious thing to be doing. And so one day he gave me a test question. Would I if I could by pushing a button would I kill five thousand Chinamen if I could save my brother from anything. Well I was very fond of my brother and I could completely imagine his suffering and I replied that five thousand Chinamen were something I could not imagine and so it was not interesting.

One has to remember that about imagination, that is when the world gets dull when everybody does not know what they can or what they cannot really imagine.

And so it was about the works of art they are destroying. I would worry about them if I did not remember that they are always that they always have been destroying works of art. I remember being awfully upset in reading very long ago about the destruction of all the things they destroyed in Greece and Rome and then suddenly remembering that probably I would not have seen them anyway and there were lots more works of art than I would ever want to look at anyway left after everything had been destroyed as they are destroying them.

Picasso and I used to dream of the pleasure if a burglar came to steal something he would steal his painting or my writing in place of silver and money. They might now they certainly would not have then and after all if a work of art has existed then somehow every one can feel that it has been and so that makes the few geniuses there are a continuous line even if what they did is not there any more. Of course one always does want one's own to be left perhaps not so much now as in the beginning and so perhaps after all they are right the Americans in being more interested in you than in the work you have done although they would not be interested in you if you had not done the work you had done.

Anyway we did come back to Paris and I had not yet begun to write.

The life we were leading was not the same we had been leading, to be sure when anybody predicts what is going to happen to you they tell you that everything changes completely for you about every four years. That is more or less so. The war lasted four years pieces of peace have a way of lasting about four years.

I said in the Autobiography that when one is young a great deal happens in a year I do not think more happened in a year then than now. An awful lot happens in a year now, not so much happens in twenty years it is hard to believe that it is twenty years since nineteen sixteen but every year is full of things that make everything change completely.

After the Autobiography was printed different people were interested to see me and I found different ones of them interesting. Of course once you have written everything about anything it is out of your system and you do not have to see them again.

Everybody invited me to meet somebody, and I went. I always will go anywhere once and I rather liked doing what I had never done before, going everywhere. It was pleasant being a lion, and meeting the people who make it pleasant to you to be a lion. Bradley my agent was most encouraging, he was going to America to arrange about everything. And then I said but remember I want printed all the things that have not been printed yes yes he said, and the Making of Americans I said. Yes yes he said, and I had just before I wrote the Autobiography written Four In America which was very difficult reading so they said, and I wanted that printed. Yes he said and he went away.

So we went on accepting invitations and going out to see the people, Daisy Fellowes and others like that and we had engagements a week ahead for every day and sometimes twice a day always before that they used to come as they came but now it was all arranged to come. We did not yet use a tiny engagement book and look at it in a nearsighted way the way all the young men used to do as soon as they were successful but we might have. Being successful is all the same and we liked it. I did not do any writing but we liked it.

I have wondered a great deal about everything since then. Over in England I have just given a lecture which I have written about what is a genius and why are there so few of them.

After all a genius has to be made in a country which is forming itself to be what it is but is not yet that is what it is is not yet common property.

The minute you or anybody else knows what you are you are not it, you are what you or anybody else knows you are and as everything in living is made up of finding out what you are it is extraordinarily difficult really not to know what you are and yet to be that thing. Very difficult indeed because not alone you but the whole country in which you have your being has to be like that and that is the reason there are so few of them so few geniuses come to be existing.

Well anyway in spite of all this not writing I was always wandering around Paris a good many hours with Basket in the evening.

Dogs have not changed they have been dogs for a long time but now they never howl or bark at the moon because no matter how small any village or how far away they have electric light to light it and if they do not then automobiles pass and make more light than any moon and the dogs see it so often they know light when they see it and so now they never see the moon. I doubt if they would see it as light if they looked at it but now they never look at the moon.

I wandered every evening I always do but I wandered a long distance every evening with Basket I like to go up one street and down another and even if all the streets are wider and the houses are not any of them very old certainly not very much older, it does feel like any Paris used to and I never get used to it and I like to wander with Basket all about it.

Everybody thinks that this civilization has lasted a very long time but it really does take very few grandfather's granddaughters to take us back to the dark ages. Here in the country most everybody does not remember but the twelfth century is where in a way they can remember and it does not worry them to remember. Anybody can do it.

Any country man can do it. So I like to wander around Paris with Basket. I like the climate of Paris most people do not, Alice Toklas does not she says she was raised in a temperate climate and she never can forget it. I think Paris has a temperate climate, any way that is the way I feel about it. Janet Scudder used to feel that way about it. Now she is in New York and feels that way about it there.

I was amused at the easy way Roosevelt wanted to take the farmers away from where they lived. It is like the American soldiers who used to argue about the land with the French farmers and try to persuade them it was no good that it never had been any good. It is nice to leave a place when you want to but it is not nice to be taken away from it even if there is nothing left of it, anyway there always is something left of it.

In the evenings several evenings that winter a very tall thin young fellow used to watch Basket just before we went in, and gradually one evening we took to talking, and then gradually we took to walking, his name was Jones and he was an American and he called hinself a child of the depression.

He was the first child of the depression I had met and it was interesting.

I had known the generation made by the war and the generation made by the peace I used to call them the children of the armistice, I told a good deal about one named Celestine in the first part of the book called As a Wife Has a Cow a Love Story.

Celestine came to us from the cows, Janet Scudder had her sister, it was not long after the peace. Celestine had never seen an electric light or a bed, she had slept in a bunk as they do in Brittany. The first night she came some one came in, she was told to let him in so she let him in and then when he stayed she came in and she said where is he going to sleep, what do you mean asked Alice Toklas, will I have to give him my bed she said, no we said later on he is going home oh later on he is going home she said.

She looked liked a Modigliani Brenner said and then in half a year longer she was a Rubens. She bought picture postal cards and made herself over, not the lower half but the upper not by anything but the feeling inside her. She was a child of the armistice and it was not possible that it would not change her. Inside of a year she had been put out of a cinema by being with some one she should not have been with and then we lost her. A year later she came to see the concierge she was upper servant in a house and was a good Bretonne and later was a rich one and a prosperous one. Before the war it could happen but it would have taken so much longer, the time was reduced to two years from ten.

Jones was the first child of the depression that I had ever seen and as I always want to know what they do and what their fathers and their mothers do I asked him. His father had been a salesman, a salesman who normally should have earned at most a couple of thousand dollars if he did well but with the after war boom he had been earning twenty and twenty-five thousand. So they were all living like that and when the depression came he was too old to begin again or to do anything not that he was old but he was too old to do anything, the mother also was not old but she was too old to do anything so they lived on the dole and they lived in an apartment for which they did not pay anything, no one did just then and there were younger brothers and sisters. Jones had a talent for drawing and he was seventeen and he went East and somebody gave him a job doing book covers and then he did illustrating and he had enough money to take a vacation and he came to Paris and he had a way with him, everybody has a way with them and I was interested in him and I asked him what was going to happen to his father and his mother and the younger children and he said all I can do is not to think about them and I never do. You never hear from them. Oh no he said I have to go on. Well I do not suppose he will ever amount to anything. Anyway I know nothing more about him.

Paris was changing, it had commenced to change by everybody beginning again talking. Talking is natural to Frenchmen, and the activity of post war life the constant moving around interfered with conversation. Slowly it was commencing again, they were beginning to play checkers and indulge in conversation, it almost seemed as if it might be that they would naturally begin again but it is very complicated to begin again. It mostly does not happen until there has been a good deal more.

Basket is a white poodle. When I first came to Paris everybody every concierge had a poodle as they later had a fox terrier, then Alsatian police dogs came and then wire-haired terriers, and then we had a white poodle and we named him Basket. The French children and the French men and women would all stop and look at him, they said each one as if it was a new idea one would think he was a lamb. And Basket always liked it naturally it is always more pleasant to be flattered than anything and admiration is the most pleasing flattery.

One day, Basket had just been washed, a little boy came along and said, one would call it marriage he is so white, and then when the little black dog came and he was beside him then one day a little girl said mamma look and see the two dogs one alongside of the other.

So Basket was accustomed to that and so was I.

And then just as conversation had begun again and checkers and economizing and there were quite a few poodles to be seen and it looked as if everything was going to begin again it did not begin. Instead there began to be on all the walls political posters and everybody instead of commencing began to stop and silently read them. When French people read political posters they do not comment about it or about anything. They have been through so many things and they know that it makes trouble for them that naturally when they read them they just silently read them. It is like the women in Bilignin the farmer's wives the first thing they asked me when we came down this summer it was well before the Spanish revolution they asked me is there going to be a civil war oh dear is there going to be civil war, that is one of the curious things about a European democracy they do not feel that they have any more to do or to say about what is going to happen than when it was a kingdom that is the reason to our surprise the return of the empire or the kingdom is not at all a surprising thing, after all they do not know who decides these things all they know is that there is a decision.

So I took Basket and I stood and read everything. The only thing that was amusing in among the attacks on Free Masonry and declarations by the pretendent the Duc de Guise and the communists and the socialists and the center and the conservative republicans and the old soldiers was one day a serious long one printed on yellow paper saying that if they were going to begin they should really begin and go back to the original king, Louis Merovingian and that there was a direct descendant of those ancient kings in Algeria named Alexander Merovingian and they should have him as king.

The notice was all regular with an office and a place to subscribe and a place to meet just as all the others had. Everybody read it just as seriously as they read the others and they were renewed three or four times and if it was a joke it was a fairly expensive one or if it was something to make such fun of the present pretendent that everybody would laugh at him, nothing was mentioned about it anywhere and we all went on reading everything.

Gradually more people were getting together and every evening at the corner of the boulevard Raspail and the boulevard Saint Germain they were gathering and every evening more and more were gathering.

Every evening when I was walking I was watching them gathering and one evening a woman next to me said we do not see anything, no not much I said and she said but if we climbed up on something, in a French street there is always something to climb on and I said yes we might then see something yes she said but if anything was happening and we were on something it might be more dangerous than if we did not climb up on something yes I said and she said we had better stay where we are and I agreed with this thing. Basket is always a dog that everybody looks at and says why one might think he was a sheep and they say you do not see many of them and they say what race is he and I say a caniche a French poodle and they say I have not seen one before and is he sweet and I say yes very sweet and they say and he must have cost a lot of money and I say he was given to me and they say but what a care to take care of him he must be bathed every day oh no only twice a season and in betwen just brushing oh yes they say and this is always the conversation and to everybody it is pleasing. Once up at Montmartre he was in the car and another dog came up to him and the window was closed between them and a woman said to her dog my poor dog you had wanted to play with a rich dog but it was not to be no my poor dog.

Anyway one evening we were walking and a man came along and he said in a song as he was walking, Piss you dog piss against the side of a house in passing, if it was my house I would take a gun and shoot you, piss dog piss against the side of the house in passing, Piss he said piss against the lamp-post in passing, a poor street cleaner has to clean the lamp-post that you have pissed against in passing, Piss dog piss against the lamp-post in passing.

Every evening then there were people who were gathering and then the sixth of February men with women who would not leave them and some of them had bandages over their head and then in our street it is a quiet street but there were two men and their hands were bandaged and one of them the head, and then they told me that they had been at the Place de la Concorde and everybody had been fired upon and that was the beginning.

It was not the beginning nothing more was happening.

There was no connection between anything happening this winter.

I was not interested in anybody painting. Except Picabia.

I do not care about anybody's painting if I know what the next painting they are painting looks like. I am like any dog out walking, I want it to be the same and I want it to be completely unalike.

The painting anybody was painting just then was not the same and it was completely alike. Except Picabia.

I took some interest in a new man, he was a Pole named Balthus. I found him the day I was leaving for the summer but when I came back at the end of the summer I did not bother.

But all that winter everything was happening. The Autobiography of Alice B. Toklas became a best seller and I was not doing anything. Then came the opera, Four Saints the opera was to be given. That was most important but it was to be given in February. It is just as well to have been born in February because February is a month when things are apt to happen. It is a funny feeling but it is always surprising to know anybody who has been born the day of the month you were born even though it be another year, as a matter of fact I have never known any one who was born the third of February, the fourth yes but not the third.

However.

The opera Four Saints in Three Acts was to be given. I did not really believe it, I rarely believe anything, because at the time of believing I am not really there to believe. This is a natural enough thing. Anyway the opera Four Saints in Three Acts was going to be given.

Before that, there had been a decision about printing a popular edition of the Making of Americans. That would please me more than anything.

And then before that Bennett Cerf cabled for the rights of Three Lives for the Modern Library and that was the beginning of a good deal because Bennett Cerf was to come to do everything.

Alice Toklas, when she decided to print the Plain Edition, had written to him asking him to distribute this edition and he had said at the price she was paying for printing and the price they could ask for it it was not interesting. He did not hesitate about his decision. Now he wanted Three Lives in the Modern Library, and that was pleasing, and then three days after signing a contract with Harcourt Brace for an abridged edition of the Making of Americans he cabled asking to do it complete in his giant edition of the Modern Library. I am still regretting that it was too late but perhaps now again it will happen. The Making of Americans is a very important thing and everybody ought to be reading at it or it, and now I am trying to do it again to say everything about everything, only then I was wanting to write a history of every individual person who ever is or was or shall be living and I was convinced it could be done as I still am but now individual anything as related to every other individual is to me no longer interesting. At that time I did not realize that the earth is completely covered over with every one. In a way it was not then because every one was in a group and a group was separated from every other one, and so the character of every one was interesting because they were in relation but now since the earth is all covered over with every one there is really no relation between any one and so if this Everybody's Autobiography is to be the Autobiography of every one it is not to be of any connection between any one and any one because now there is none. That is what makes detective stories such good reading, the man being dead he is not really in connection with any one. If he is it is another kind of a story and not a detective story.

Harcourt Brace did not really want to print the Making of Americans, they made him, but Bennett Cerf did. It is important yes I think so that it should be looked at by every one.

There is no doubt about it, in the twentieth century if you are to come to be writing really writing you cannot make a living at it no not by writing. It was done in the nineteenth century but not in the eighteenth or in the twentieth no not possibly. And that is very curious, not so curious really but still very curious. In the eighteenth century not enough read to make any one earn their living and in the twentieth century too many read for any one to make their living by creating, the nineteenth century was just right it was in between.

Too few is as many as too many.

The end of the nineteenth century already they could not make a living writing.

Some did make a lot of money in the eighteenth century, Pope did but then he could wait until he did. Well I suppose really in a way anybody can if they can wait until they do. In the twentieth century you have to wait longer and that is because there are so many who can read and write and if everybody can read and write then what is the use of reading. I always remember the daughters of the major from whom we rented our house in Palma de Mallorca, they explained that not being able to read and write did not mean that they had not been taught. Of course in ·the convent they had been taught but as in their life they had no need of it they had forgotten how to do it. It is not like swimming that cannot be forgotten but like bicycle riding which can be forgotten. That is what writing and reading is.

Some one has just suggested that I make a lot of money writing cigarette advertisements. So naturally I begin to write them, how can I not naturally begin to write them that is what reading and writing is, naturally the ones advertising will not want them and just as naturally I will not send them and just as naturally I do write them.

Now although I never do think anything is going to happen things were happening, Roosevelt was being elected, the opera was going to be given, the Autobiography was selling, everybody wanted to meet me, and I began lecturing. All this happened that winter the winter before the summer that I went to America.

There is one thing that is very funny, one is happy reasonably happy on the whole life is reasonably amusing and mostly everybody likes living but if you keep a diary when you are young when you are not so young when you are middle aged or when you are older it sounds as if your life had not been a happy one. It sounds like that in writing and that is very important because it is that that makes them ask all the time about proletarian literature. If you write about proletarians it sounds as if they were very bitter, if you write about yourself or anybody if sounds as if you were very unhappy and very bitter but generally speaking everybody living has a fairly cheerful time in living, if not why not, but naturally they do.

Any life you look at seems unhappy but any life lived is fairly cheerful, and whatever happens it goes on being so.

I remember being so surprised when I was a little girl reading what I had written as my thoughts, they were very awful thoughts but naturally I had a good time then as I have had a good time since.

So this winter it was a very different winter, Picasso used to be fond of saying that when everybody knew about you and admired your work there were just about the same two or three who were really interested as when nobody knew about you, but does it make any difference. In writing the Making of Americans I said I write for myself and strangers and then later now I know these strangers, are they still strangers, well anyway that too does not really bother me, the only thing that really bothers me is that the earth now is all covered over with people and that hearing anybody is not of any particular importance because anybody can know anybody.

That is really why the only novels possible these days are detective stories, where the only person of any importance is dead.

Lloyd Lewis said his mother told him when he told her that I said the novel as a form of writing is dead, I think she is right, characters in books do not count in the life of the reader the way they used to do and if they do not the novel as a form is dead.

I tell all the young ones now to write essays, after all since characters are of no importance why not just write meditations, meditations are always interesting, neither character nor identity are necessary to him who meditates.

The world is completely covered with people and these people would like to be completely organized to live.

But anybody can get tired of anything, except living, and perhaps they will get tired of organizing. I used to have a friend who said if perfection is good more perfection is better and that is certainly true of organization.

Well anyway that winter Roosevelt was elected and Bernard Faÿ I said Bernard Faÿ was the one we were seeing more at that time than we were seeing any other one.

Bernard Faÿ was a Frenchman he is a royalist, he says his family has been royalist for centuries but any French family has been indeed it is astonishing how many of them still would like it better if there was a king not because they really want a king but their habits and their language and the things they would like to have be the country does not really suit a republic, and besides that Frenchmen do not really think they have anything to do with anything that governs, they live their own life and they fight for that country and besides that they have no responsibility. Their life is secret that is it belongs to themselves and up till now that is what has made French elegance and French style, it is a funny story.

It was just that winter that the French newspaper the Intransigeant asked me to write and tell them why I like to live in France. Well the reason is very simple their life belongs to them so your life can belong to you and I tell this story to illustrate this thing.

In the days when Helene our servant for many years was with us we talked about anything and one day I think something was happening. I did not take any interest in French politics, but something was happening so I said Helene what political party does your husband belong to, she looked at me firmly but she said nothing, well I said, and she said nothing, is it a secret I said, no she said no it is not a secret but one does not tell it. Well I said supposing women had a vote would you have a political party, I have one now she said, is it the same as your husband's, I said, she knew me too well to be suspicious of me but she did not like what I was asking and finally she said as she had already said, no it is not a secret but one does not tell it, one does not tell the political party one belongs to.

I then was interested and I asked all kinds of people and they all had the same expression the expression of it not being a secret but of their not telling it, and so I wrote for the Intransigeant, with any people but the French you would imagine that this well not secrecy but not telling would have something a little unpleasant about it but with the French it is a serious comedy that makes them just more attractive. Their lives are their own it is not a secret but one does not tell it.

Bernard Faÿ was a French college professor only like so many Frenchmen the contact with Americans during the war made the romance for them. French people living so completely the life of Frenchmen have always needed something exotic to make a relief for them, and to the Frenchmen of the war generation it was the American.

. The French felt themselves such an old worn out people and here was something so different from them. They did not care for any one to be blond if they were English or German or Scandinavian but they did like it to be American.

The Americans pleased and puzzled them, they were like a strange flower to them and each one of them had at least one who was completely a romance to them. They were also a puzzle to them. I remember just after the war I was in a garage having my car fixed, I like garages, I like a great many things but I almost like garages best, and the man fixing my car a young Breton said to me, you are an American, I said yes he said I would like to ask you something that has always been a puzzle to me. I was with my regiment at Nazaire when the American troops came to France, it was just the time of the Spanish grippe, and we Bretons had gotten discouraged with France we said after the war if we had not been killed we would emigrate to America and take a chance and then the American soldiers came and they had the Spanish grippe and they took all precautions, so many more than we took, they had masks and they were isolated and nevertheless they died like flies, those great big chaps who looked so clean and strong as if they could stand anything we Frenchmen died too but not like that not so quickly nor so many and as we watched them we little Frenchmen got frightened we said that if men coming from that big country and looking so big and strong could die so quickly what chance would there be for us little Frenchmen to live over there and so after the war all of us who were alive we did not go over. Now he said Mademoiselle you are American please explain to me why they died so many and so quickly.

So America was like that to any Frenchman a romance but puzzling and Bernard Faÿ was another one and he liked everything American and he was a Frenchman and the way of living and feeling was not the way of a Frenchman but he almost felt that he was an American.

He had been a boy in bed for nine years and his mother had read to him, he always likes rainy weather best because ducks quack and his brothers would be in the room with him. A great many French people like rain best, why not you can go out better in rain than in snow, in rain than in sun. Alice Toklas says not, but nevertheless it does rain. I like it but Pépé the little Mexican dog does not.

Bernard Faÿ was read to for nine years by his mother ten hours a day as he could not sit up at all during the day and French mothers are that way, they are as untiring as the French army, one day Alice Toklas said to a French general who talked some English at what age does a French general retire, Madame said the general the French army is never tired.

And so Bernard Faÿ became a historian and the war came and he was just ready to begin and he met the American army as it came. Naturally as he was lame he could not fight but he could do what he did which was to help every one and naturally helping the American army was fascinating.

Perhaps America since the depression will never be so young again. I suppose it has to happen it does to any dog that he can never be so young again. But then after they get old they do get young again and so this can happen. It is almost happening in Europe but then America is not old enough yet to get young again. They believed the depression was a depression, before that booms had busted a busted boom is not a depression. I know I was so surprised when a banker cousin of mine said he could not believe really believe that the depression was a depression although he did believe it and that worried him. When a boom busted everybody knew it, they used to say who is holding the dollar this week, but now for the first time they were taking the dollar seriously. Well.

I used to worry about that just before the war. I began to worry that employees in America were getting to feel themselves employed and not potential employers, I used to worry because Americans no longer were feeling themselves potentially rich they were still talking that way but they were not feeling that way and yet it was not a settled thing as it is here in France. As a matter of fact now that I know the French country it is astonishing how often somebody without any money makes a fortune. Here in Belley the rich are always getting poor and the poor getting rich.

Then there is the other thing about the Frenchmen that they

know from the time they are born what is to happen to all those who go into government service and into the professions and a very large part of the population do.

Bernard Faÿ was certain to go on to be an Academician he is not yet but he will be and so on, and in America after all sooner or later the earth is always all covered over, and so very well where else is there to go from. Not that it is not a pleasure, to do so, a pleasure to go on.

Well anyway to go back again. I was beginning writing and I began to write the Four In America. I was bothered about it. I have always been bothered but mostly I am bothered because after all I do as simply as it can as commonplacely as it can say what everybody can and does do I never do know what they can do, I really do not know what they are, I do not think that any one can think because if they do then who is who. And anyway except in daily life nobody is anybody.

So in the Four In America, I took four Americans, Washington, Henry James, Wilbur Wright and General Grant, and I wanted them to be what their names would be. Hiram Ulysses Grant, Ulysses Simpson Grant, supposing he had been a religious leader, and Washington supposing he had been a novel writer, he might have been, and Wilbur Wright he might have been a painter, and Henry James he might have been a general, a real general with the career of a general and I wanted to find out why war was and camp-meetings. I remember so well when I was young going to camp-meetings in the woods in California.

Moving forward and back the two things that made me know that, the camp-meetings in the woods and the minuet as we were taught to dance the waltz a little but the minuet made me feel that.

In the camp-meetings there was always a plank walk and some one to walk up and down on it and everything followed that, as some one went forward and back moving it did something to every one watching.

That is what war is and dancing it is forward and back, when one is out walking one wants not to go back the way they came but in dancing and in war it is forward and back.

That is what I tried to say in Four In America.

And now the last evening that Thornton Wilder was in Paris last winter we wandered about together and I told him that what worried me was narration, no one in our time had really been able to tell anything without anything but just telling that thing and that I was going to try once more to try to simply tell something.

I am telling it now so simply that perhaps it is not anything. Perhaps not, and if not there is no why not it just is not.

So I had been writing the Four In America and I was beginning to quarrel with my literary agent because he wanted me to sign something. I am always ready to sign anything a bank tells me to sign but anything else fills me with suspicion. I wanted the Four In America printed and he wanted me to sign a contract for another autobiography. Anyway why sign anything, unless you really need it if they give you the money ahead they do not give it to you afterward and that is then a very great deception so why sign up ahead. That is what I told him. Besides I said I wanted them to go ahead and print everything, it has always been my hope that some day some one would print everything, it does not bother me so much now, well partly because it does not and partly because if it is not printed some one will discover it later and that will be so much more exciting or they will not and that will be so much more disturbing.

And then I quarreled with my literary agent about going to America to lecture. So far I have not quarreled with Bernard Faÿ but then with a Frenchman quarreling is another matter. Combat is so natural to them that quarreling is not really anything. I suppose that is the reason Frenchmen so rarely mean quarreling. I know Georges Hugnet was so upset when we never met again why he said he took it for granted that the quarreling had been a literary quarreling.

I always enjoyed watching a little American girl all in brown in the Luxembourg Gardens who used to say she would now play her father. And that consisted in saying with a gesture I am going I am through. Any American is through but not any Frenchman.

So I quarreled with my literary adviser all that spring, he not being a Frenchman we finally never met again.

In the meantime they had played Four Saints in America and that was exciting.

And now I should write Spain a play and it would begin, Act I First Spaniard. There is no second Spaniard. Second Spaniard. There is no first Spaniard.

I used always to say that the only thing about which Alice Toklas was not impartial was Spain. Anything can bias me but the only thing that could bias her was the charm of Spain. And it does do something. I can always remember when we were the first time in Granada my brother and I and there was an American there and his daughter and there was a fearful sound and she said what is it and he said it is the last sigh of the Moor. It was a bray of a donkey of course and if one has never heard it it is a fearful thing.

America can almost bias Alice Toklas as much as Spain did, perhaps not quite as much but there is something of the same thing, after all there can only be religion and the charm of religion where there is a desert country. That is natural enough. Deserts do not make painters but they make charm and religion, because where there is nothing to do and nothing to see anybody can not know that the time is passing and so naturally there is religion but there is no painting because there is no pleasure in looking. There can be architecture and religion there cannot be painting and looking of course there can be writing anywhere even when writing is talking or singing.

And so America and Spain have something in common and each

one can bias Alice Toklas so that she cannot be impartial. They can always accomplish that.

And so it was natural that when I wanted saints that they should be Spanish saints. There are saints anywhere. There have been saints in Italy and in France and even in Germany and I suppose in Austria, I do not know anything about them, but the important saints have been Spanish and Italian and that is natural enough, there must be really weather in which to wander in order to be a saint.

A saint a real saint never does anything, a martyr does something but a really good saint does nothing, and so I wanted to have Four Saints who did nothing and I wrote the Four Saints In Three Acts and they did nothing and that was everything.

Generally speaking anybody is more interesting doing nothing than doing something.

And after all Americans like Spaniards do spend so much time doing nothing. They like to move around so quickly because naturally they mostly are standing or sitting and doing nothing. Frenchmen and Englishmen are always doing something they are either conversing or eating or sleeping or alive inside them but Americans and Spaniards so much of the time are doing nothing.

I remember years and years ago Sayen was a painter in Paris and I used to say to Sayen of course all this was long before there was a war and Americans in Europe in any army and I used to ask Sayen when Americans stand or sit at the Café de la Paix not doing anything and then they go away what are they doing what are they thinking what are they saying. He always said nothing. But said I being accustomed to Europeans that is not possible. Yes it is he said well then I said why do they not stay on forever. Oh he said because one of them says I am going, and I said why did he say it then, for no reason said Sayen.

Well there is something in it Europeans have something to do but Americans have not and so in a way do not Spaniards and

Saints do not have anything to do they are very busy but they do not have anything to do.

So I wrote Four Saints In Three Acts and when it was played it was a success.

Another thing that is like Spain that is like America is that they make them alive and they make them dead.

Anything dead is dead and that too has to do with a desert and with religion.

I said in England when I was talking to the Cambridge students that although it was the same language anybody could tell right away whether it was an American writer or an English writer who had written and that has a great deal to do with their making them alive and their making them dead, in England the dead are not dead because they are connected with the others living, in America the dead are dead there is no connection with those left living. That has a great deal to do with deserts and religion.

I think I felt this first definitely when I was very young and read Huckleberry Finn by Mark Twain.

And then having the Four Saints that is the two saints Saint Theresa and Saint Ignatius anything could be a saint.

Anybody can like saints. I was pleased when somebody wrote to me and told me that they had never known what saints were before.

I was surprised the day the Four Saints was played when I had cables and a quantity of them, I knew Carl would but I expected nothing from any others of them.

What is it that makes anybody certain that nothing is really going to happen. It is all that about time and identity not existing undoubtedly it is.

And so they cabled and it was surprising, people that I did not know were in America and some I had not known about for a long time. It was astonishing. I had become accustomed to fan letters but this was once more astonishing.

And then came a letter from the Kiddie. In the war there was the Kiddie so we called him, this was after he left and he did not know about it because like all the American soldiers he never wrote to us.

Mildred Aldrich had a charming story about that. When the American soldiers who had been in a French hospital left of course they never wrote to any one afterwards. The sisters naturally thought they were dead as they had not written and Mildred Aldrich could not explain that they might be alive and had not written there was no such explanation.

So the Kiddie who had been with us in Nîmes and had supplied us there with cigarettes called Darling and had visited beauty spots with us and had written to us as long as he was a soldier had never written after. And now he wrote a long letter. We had thought he was to be a business man with his father I suppose because he used to tell us about driving to dances in a car and that his father was in business, well anyway he had become a school teacher had been married and divorced and become a writer for a newspaper and he lived in Springfield and he had gone over to Hartford and seen the opera and this for some reason had made writing to us proper. Anyway we were delighted to hear from him and he was to come over that summer and come to Bilignin.

All this time America was coming nearer. Not that it had ever really been far away but it was certainly just now coming nearer that is to say it was getting more actual as a place where we might be.

Ford Maddox Ford for many years had been saying that I should go over. Come with me he would say, they feel hurt that you do not come, and you would not like to hurt their feelings, come with me come this January he used to say persuasively.

As I say I am a person of no initiative, I usually stay where I am. Why not as long as there are plenty of people about and there are pretty much always plenty of people about why not. So it used to be Paris and Spain and then it was Paris and Bilignin and what was I to do in America when I got there. After all I am American all right. Being there does not make me more there.

And besides we had had the whole American army over here and it had been natural to be with them and they were not changed from the America I knew in fact what could they change to. But Ford always said you had better go over. Do come along. Well I did not go not then.

But now it was getting a little exciting. Carl Van Vechten sent me photos with my name in electric lights on Broadway and that was very exciting.

Mildred Aldrich had once gone to America and when she came back we all crowded around to ask her what she had felt. She said what she found was the trouble over there was that there was no place to sit down, you walked along a while and then there was no place to sit. Well now in Paris you cannot sit as much as one used to sit, Mildred would now not really find Paris very different from New York.

And my literary agent who was in America cabled me that he was making arrangements for me to lecture, and through the people who had sent the man who said interesting if true. This naturally made me very angry and I said not at all, I would not lecture. Anything can make one get angry and say not at all and this certainly did so.

I often wonder about getting angry. Somebody objects to your letting your dog do something and you know very likely he will and anyway it is all right anyway and yet often as it can happen you suddenly get really angry.

It is like Monsieur Pernollet of the Hotel Pernollet. All Belley is very excited, yesterday morning was market day and suddenly everybody knew that the Hotel Pernollet had closed its doors. The Hotel Pernollet was the glory of Belley after Brillat-Savarin. It was the famous place where everybody ate and it was a number of generations and today it suddenly had shut its doors and Monsieur Pernollet said it was not to open, his employees had decided to follow the fashion and strike and he said the hotel was not doing very well and they could all get out and he would shut the door and he gave all the food that was left to everybody out of the window and that was the end of that. He was suddenly angry and that was the end of that.

I remember in my youth in America there used to be things called spite fences. I remember there was one in East Oakland, a fence I do not know why but they did build a fence that was high higher than the house.

I have though as it happened lectured twice that winter but that was an accident that is the first was an accident.

Bernard Faÿ was to lecture at the American Woman's Club and he asked us to come. We had never belonged to any club and we had never been there. When I am not out walking I am at home, it is extraordinary in Paris how little visiting one does. In Latin countries you do not visit, families live together but that is another matter but visiting is very little done. One Austrian servant named Betty once bitterly complained of us that we lived French, from the French standpoint not from the Austrian American standpoint yes. Well anyway Bernard Faÿ was to lecture about France and America.

Bernard Faÿ was away he was in Sweden and he had an American secretary whose name is Hub and Hub was to meet him in the car and bring him back. Hub had been to dinner with us before leaving and I went out walking in the evening and we walked together down the Boulevard Raspail. And so you are to be back Saturday evening I said as Bernard is to lecture. Are we said Hub. Well of course they did not get back Bernard Faÿ had remembered to forget but I was there and they asked me would I do it for him.

But that is not what did matter I did but the thing that I remember is that Hub Murphy said are we.

I began to think then and later more and more that Americans can and do express everything oh yes everything in words of one syllable made up of two letters or three and at most four.

And in some fashion the letters chosen that make up the words of one syllable although they are so few are like letters which would make up a longer word. Are we for example.

I have wanted to write a whole book about words of one syllable. In a play I have just written called Listen To Me I keep thinking of words of one syllable. It is natural to write poems of words of one syllable and some live with words of three letters and some live with words of four letters. In the play Madame Recamier I did it and it makes a very good poem. Are we. And then after all I can remember that I am one of the masters of English prose and that there are not many of them and when I get low in my mind that revives me and Carl Van Vechten says so.

So I said that if they would ask questions I would answer them and I did and it was very amusing and so once more I began to think of lecturing.

After all I do talk so much to anybody who will listen so why not call it lecturing. And yet why not. It is not the same thing.

When Janet Scudder wrote her autobiography Modeling My Life and made a great deal of money, Mrs. Harden the mother of Emily and Elmer Harden said to them and when I think how often you tell the history of your lives for nothing.

When I was about eight I was surprised to know that in the Old Testament there was nothing about a future life or eternity. I read it to see and there was nothing there. There was a God of course and he spoke but there was nothing about eternity.

This could not happen again.

We had a book about the excavations of Nineveh and the civilizations that were over were very interesting. They were just as real as anything finding those enormous heads, anything one finds is very interesting, just now I am hunting hazel nuts and each one I find is exciting just as much so as any other hunting. I spend long hours at it, it is very interesting. Basket goes away but he always comes back when I call him, Pépé being little is a little afraid to go away and so he mostly does stay.

It was frightening when the first comet I saw made it real that the stars were worlds and the earth only one of them, it is like the Old Testament, there is God but there is no eternity. And now that is what everything is there is a God but there is no eternity.

The French have a funny phrase. All these vast sums that everybody votes nowadays to do anything they call astronomical.

Then there was the fear of dying, anything living knows about that, and when that happens anybody can think if I had died before there was anything but there is no thinking that one was never born until you hear accidentally that there were to be five children and if two little ones had not died there would be no Gertrude Stein, of course not.

Just today nobody knew just what skin the peau de chagrin was made of and looking it up it was made of anything mule calf or horse and I said how did it happen to be called peau de chagrin and Madame Giraud said and how did you happen to be called Gertrude Stein.

Well how did I.

Steins were called Steins in the time of Napoleon before that any name was a name but in the time of Napoleon in any country he went through the name of any one had to be written and so they took the name they gave them and Stein was an easy one. Then when any of us were named we were named after some one who is already dead, after all if they are living the name belongs to them so any one can be named after a dead one, so there was a grandmother she was dead and her name not an easy one began with G so my mother preferred it should be an easy one so they named me Gertrude Stein. All right that is my name.

Identity always worries me and memory and eternity.

I read a poem of George Eliot when I was very young I can not often remember poetry but I can remember that. May I join the choir invisible of those immortal dead who live again. Well I was not at all intending it but like anybody I knew about that.

In the bath this morning I was drumming on the side of the bathtub, I like moving around in the water in a bathtub, and I found myself drumming the Chopin funeral march and I might have stopped doing it but I went on because they used to play it on Golden Gate Avenue in San Francisco and I was worrying then about identity and memory and eternity, and I am not worrying now but there it is if the stars are suns and the earth is the earth and there are men only upon this earth and anything can put an end to anything and any dog does everything like anybody does it what is the difference between eternity and anything. As I say there was a God but there was no mention of everlasting. Anything is a superstition and anybody rightly believes in superstition. Because it is certain that superstition means that what has been is going on. I always rightfully believe and believed in every superstition.

It did not really help much when I was young it helps more now. Now superstition is really realer than it was then. There is one thing though that has never changed and that is if you start putting on anything inside out you must continue, otherwise it would change everything. I can know that that does happen because of absentmindedness by reason of something troubling and all the same the fact remains one should not change. I do not mind the dark now. But high places well that has to be talked about later.

Seeing superstition has nothing to do with believing anything except what anybody is seeing. Just the other day I was talking to a Princeton professor and I was talking about the way it is not at all interesting to take working men so seriously if by working men one means only those who work in a factory. There is really nothing so very moving that there are so many of them, there are so many of them because there was so much virgin soil that could produce so much food and so factories were produced in such quantity because as they could be so easily fed why should they not be in a factory. But now when the virgin soil is used up and there is no more because all of it is known all the earth is known so then just at this time the factory working man is being self-conscious completely conscious of his own existence just when inevitably virgin soil being used up he will have to go back to dirt farming, and in dirt farming it is not easy to regulate anything because things do happen, in factories anything can be regulated because really nothing does really happen. I remember when I first came to Paris waiting to get a pair of shoes that I was having soled and the owner of the shop was having a row with a workman. They got madder and madder until finally the boss said and what are you you are just as stupid as anybody who works in any factory and the workman could not answer, how could he answer. Well I was talking like this to the Princeton professor and he said well if these are the facts there is no hope and I said well what is hope hope is just contact with the facts. Alice Toklas always says I do not look facts in the face well anyway what are facts, one thing is sure that everybody has a knowledge of gods even if they have no knowledge of eternity.

When I was just beginning high school I knew a girl whose name was Cora Moore. There were two things about her she could make turban hats decorated with pansies or nasturtiums as a flower and her mother believed in spiritualism, so perhaps did my father anyway they both believed in prophecy but anybody does that and why not since prophesying is prophesying. The mattress maker in Belley says he does not believe in the predictions of the almanac because when they say there is going to be good weather as the country is large enough somewhere in France there is good weather and so the almanac is never wrong. In California everybody was interested in prophecy. That is natural enough as gold was still something somebody could remember. Cora Moore said why should her mother go to another spiritualist when she could be one and so she and I used to go together while she was one.

One can do anything all over.

She said that she knew just what they did, they had spirits come all over and then they told what they had told her. And so Cora decided to do it too. She was the only Cora I ever knew.

She did do it but it did not then really interest me because after all the difference between whether she believed it or whether she did not was nothing. To me it really had nothing to do with anything that was interesting. I never did take on spirits either then or later they had nothing to do with the problem of everlasting not for me, because anybody can know that the earth is covered all over with people and if the air is too what is the difference to any one there are an awful lot of them anyway and in a way I really am only interested in what a genius can say the rest is just there anyway. In a kind of a way even then I felt like that, I could not see why there being so many of them made it any more interesting.

I had just been writing that after all the only difference between man and animals is that men can count. No animals count. And of course the thing they count when they count is money, no animal can count money only men can do that and in a queer way just now when eternity is not all troubling any one because every one knows that here on this earth are the only men and everybody knows all there is on this earth and everybody knows that there is all there is to it just now counting is a more absorbing occupation than it ever has been, people thinking in millions, they love the sound of numbers, it is the religion of every one just now counting is all there is of religion for them.

But in those days in California I was interested in everlasting and I wondered so much about everything that I was almost alone and if you are almost alone well all that there is is almost alone.

So the winter after I wrote the Autobiography was almost over and I had almost thought I would go to America to lecture.

This time it was Bernard Faÿ who thought I should go and still if you have not been anywhere for thirty years why not go.

Sometimes in Paris people used to turn up that I had not seen for many years. I remember one year two or three that I had not seen for eighteen years turned up. Certainly there is no use in seeing anybody you have not seen for eighteen years, and I hoped it would not happen again. Alice Toklas always liked a poem that used to go, Give me new faces new faces new faces I have seen the old ones and just then well there did not seem any reason why one should see the old ones any more.

Having written all about them they ceased to exist. That is very funny if you write all about any one they do not exist any more, for you, and so why see them again. Anyway that is the way I am.

Picasso used to say during the war will it not be awful when Braque and Derain and all the rest of them put their wooden legs up on the chair and tell about their fighting, but it never did enter his head that this generation would completely not think about those happenings and that if they did he would not be there to listen as they were certainly not to see each other often.

After war for this generation has turned out to be more oppressive than war even now when a good many of them are the age of grandfathers when it would be natural to be reminiscing.

Nobody even remembers first going to Russia when everybody was interested in Soviets, now they all look upon Sovietism as being out of fashion. Oh yes they say the communists do not know that they are very conservative, the only thing that is never out of fashion are the anarchists but really there never can be very many of them because they are not out of fashion.

In those early days of Russia just after the war I happened to come back from the garage where I kept my car, lots of young men had come to see us just then and they were full of Sovietism. I laughed, I said one of the chauffeurs over in the garage has just come back from Russia where he has been with the French general for whom he was driving, I said and how is Russia he said, Russia they put down far too much tar far too much tar they cover the roads with tar. Well I said but how is life under communism, not as expensive as I thought he answered it cost me about as much as it does at Deauville.

In a French village they understand all about that, they say the men in politics are like the women in dressing, sometimes the skirts are long and sometimes the skirts are short, well perhaps it was I who said that well anyway they said they agreed with that.

After all it is troublesome.

There is no difference between men and animals except that they can count and never has there been so much counting as is going on at present. Everybody is counting, counting is everybody's occupation. And that is because everybody is certain that there is the difference that is what makes men men and as everybody wants to be sure that men are men just now wants to have it as an affirmation everybody is counting. I always liked counting but I liked counting one two three four five six seven, or one little Indian two little Indians three little Indian boys counting more than ten is not interesting at least not to me because the numbers higher than ten unless they are fifty-five or something like that do not look interesting and certainly when one goes higher than a hundred there is not much difference, of course there is but yet again there is not.

The queen was in her parlor eating bread and honey the king was in his counting room counting out his money.

Counting is the religion of this generation it is its hope and its salvation.

It is troublesome, not counting, anybody can count, even if like the Spanish women and Chinamen they count with pebbles what is troublesome is religion and when counting gets to be religion it gets to be troublesome.

Lightning never strikes twice in the same place but that is only because there is not enough of it, nuts always fall in the same place which makes one say brother brother go find your brother. When you drop one nut there is another just there which you had not seen before there was a pair.

Well that may have nothing to do with it but they have just asked me to write an article as to why any one who writes as I do which is not understandable can be so popular which means can be so understood. Has that anything to do with lightning not striking twice in the same place because there is not enough of it or nuts falling in the same place because there are so many of them. I wonder.

Every time I go out I meet some one and we talk together of revolutions and the weather.

Revolutions do and many of them can never do better than come. The Spanish civil war has frightened the French.

Every time we talk about revolutions we know that there is going to be another. After all and that does make me know that when I was frightened when I first knew that civilizations came to an end and cities were buried that it was nothing to frighten because after all the earth is round and do what you like it can only be round and so a civilization must end a mechanical civilization as well as any other. After all two hundred years is not a great deal of bother. And two hundred years is as much as anybody can remember.

And so I do know what a genius is, a genius is some one who does not have to remember the two hundred years that everybody else has to remember.

But really believe it or not it is strange to see that a mechanical civilization can end just like any other.

I just met a French woman Madame Chabout the wife of the doctor and I was telling her that now they talked in America about something they called dirt farming. What is that, she said. I said that is touching the earth with your hands. Indeed and she said why not and I said because for a hundred years they almost did not. And we she said we are just learning not to. Yes I said the farmers in Bilignin tell me that if they had to thresh grain the way they used to they would none of them raise any. Well she said as the French are logical they may stop before they begin. That is what makes them all now think of a king.

That is what I suppose does take the longest to realize that a republic in Europe is never a natural thing. In America we really have not known anything else, but in Europe they like to count them. I am always pleased the careful way that the present republic in France is always spoken of as the third republic.

The more I think of everything the more I realize that what worries every one is that the earth is round. That is what I liked in being in an airplane the earth does not look round as it does on the ocean. It looks flat, but is it, everything seems to tell everybody that it is not. It is round.

I detach myself from the earth being round and mechanical civilizations being over and organization being dull although nobody knows it yet but they will and go on with what happened the summer before we went to America.

They ask me to tell why an author like myself can become popular. It is very easy everybody keeps saying and writing what anybody feels that they are understanding and so they get tired of that, anybody can get tired of anything everybody can get tired of something and so they do not know it but they get tired of feeling they are understanding and so they take pleasure in having something that they feel they are not understanding. I understand you undertake to overthrow my undertaking.

I always did like that you did it like this:

stand take   to   taking

I   you throw   my

That was almost as exciting as a spelling match.

That is all understanding is you know it is all in the feeling.

My writing is clear as mud, but mud settles and clear streams run on and disappear, perhaps that is the reason but really there is no reason except that the earth is round and that no one knows the limits of the universe that is the whole thing about men and women that is interesting. All the rest is human nature and I have written Alice Toklas says and she is always right so much so that I often ask does it not tire her that I have written altogether too much about what is human nature.

So we did go to the country as usual before going to America although we did not really know as yet that we were going to America.

You have to go on telling something although these days there is always less and less of it, that is what it is, the earth is round and even airplanes have to come back to it. And so naturally there is less of a beginning and a middle and an end than there used to be and novels are therefore not very good these days unless they are detective stories where the hero is the dead man and so there can be no beginning and middle and end because he is dead. It worries me in detective stories that they do not tell you what happened to the money in English detective stories there is always money. More and more I am certain that the only difference between man and animals is that men can count and animals cannot and if they count they mostly do count money, and one of the things I really liked about Napoleon is that he used to make out the daily spending of any character in any story he was reading. That always interested me a lot in English novels, nowadays well money in detail has a little lost its meaning, anyway you have to have some even if the detail of it is not fascinating as it used to be in the old novels and that really is why novels really now are not very well written really it is. Anyway we did go to the country as usual that summer and I was quarreling with my agent about my editor and about my becoming a lecturer. He wanted me to be managed by somebody. I always am managed by somebody because naturally there is nothing to manage, but to be managed to go anywhere without my knowing where and doing there what anybody would want me to do there whether afterwards I wanted to or not naturally I did say not, I was very angry. One always is very angry and I was very angry and we wrote it in letters and said it over the telephone and that was the end of that matter. I said I would not go to America. However I did go to America but that was an entirely different matter.

This year it is the end of September and there is snow everywhere and this has never happened before not ever before the end of November. And in these days when they are all so troubled and so certain that everything is going so badly nobody not even the most simple minded of them think that the strange weather has anything to do with the matter. Things are not that way any more and nobody feels that way just the same way as dogs no longer bark at the moon because there are always even in the most far away places lights that are so much brighter. Trac told us something about that. Trac comes with this because it was he who saw us off to America and it was he who was there to meet us when we came back after.

We like to eat well and live simply.

And now the French were not doing it not in France, during the war the fathers complained that their sons were becoming Americanized they said Frenchmen should be French and now everybody is saying that French people should be French and that is the reason they all say they want a king because they say the French were frenchest when they had kings, but the factory people, do not want to be French and it is commencing to be a tug of war, we used to like to play tug of war. A whole lot would get on the one end of a rope and a whole lot would get on the other end of the rope and then they pull and for a long time neither side moves they all pull hard and they all stay still and then slowly one begins to yield and then in a minute the other side can run at full speed away with the rope. Well that is the way it is. Bennett Cerf asks what are we going to do this winter. I would not mind doing something else but very likely we will be watching the revolution if there is going to be one and hoping all the time that we can just go on looking. It might be nice to go to America again where they are not likely to have one at least not just now, yet. But now in this book we are not in America yet not yet so of course we cannot yet talk of going again.

After all the struggle with French couples we decided to have an Indo-Chinaman. They are French but not so absorbing not as yet being Frenchmen, that is coming. So we had a lot come and we chose Trac. Trac has only been with us a couple of months at a time but we love him and he loves us. When he is with us it is very pleasant for every one and in between he leans between the kitchen and the dining room against the door and goes on talking. He told us about when he was a little boy, he is little now that is he is a little man but then he was little he was a little boy. He lived just outside of a village and it was not a big one and a little farther away was a bigger one and there from time to time a circus used to come, they do have them in Indo-China and they only perform in the evening, so Trac used to go to join others to see them, and he had to go quite a little way alone and as he went and came home he said he used to see phantoms rise up and rise and rise and rise and it was a fearful thing they used to come out of nothing and rise and rise before him and it was awful and now a friend had just come from Indo-China and he was talking to him and he said to him it is nice to be in France where there are never any phantoms, oh said the friend in Indo-China there are no phantoms anywhere, since the war everything has changed and now there are none.

Before we had Trac we almost had an American not almost because naturally we could not but all the same we did go to see him.

It is funny about being afraid. There are so many things more dangerous than they used to be but there are so many more doing them all the time that in a way there is no more fear than there used to be in a way there is less.

We went out to see the American he had advertised that he wanted to do everything so we went to see him. He let us in, he was living so he said with a Russian but the Russian was not there she was a woman and she was not there but he and his wife were there we did not see his wife she was a Bretonne. We asked him and so he told us everything that had happened to him since the war. He had lived with a Frenchman, that is to say the French-man was rich and had a big property in Normandy and the Ameri-can had given him all the money he had which was considerable. They had a nice house and garden and the American did all the gardening, he began to grow the largest vegetables that were grown in the region, they were the admiration of every one, he wrote to Vilmorin the big horticulturalists who told him exactly what to do with everything and he did it and the results were marvelous. Often people came to see them, the Frenchman had brothers and often when they came the American helped to serve them, and anyway nothing meant anything. And then something happened to the Frenchman he was put away somewhere for something and his brothers he then had two of them came to take everything and the American had put in lots of money twenty thousand but he had no way of making any brother know that so he went to law about it and so lost everything. He then married a Bretonne, he had gone somewhere else and there he was doing something mechanical and there he met the Bretonne. The Bretonne was an excellent cook but she did not like doing cooking, she had done enough perhaps however she would be pleased to come and cook for us he did not think so but you never can tell with a Bretonne. Then they had a child and they were very happy as they both loved children, she did not care about animals but she liked chil-dren. And then the child who was a baby was not well and they went to a hotel and they called in a doctor who was not used to children and he said the child was very ill they had better take it to a hospital for children and there the doctor said why had not they brought it before anyway they took it away again and it was hardly living and it died then.

Then he went to work for this Russian his wife was often there but she did not like cooking and as for himself he thought of leaving. When he went to see them at the American Legation they said of him that he was a very nice man and why did he not advertise for a position. So he did and we went to see him. He said do you see that woman she can see us by mirrors she is a Scandinavian. Yes I could see her, she is always watching watching by arranging mirrors, I am afraid he said, why, we said, because she is always watching, and your wife, oh she may be going to have another baby he said we do not want one but maybe she will have one. She is a fine woman he said and then we left him. We thought an American man would not do in the kitchen and I guess we were right.

I am always interested in American men marrying foreign women you do not expect it of them and yet they do very often. Once I wrote a history about a number of them I had known who did. Just now an American painter Ferren is one but with him it is natural enough. Ferren ought to be a man who is interesting, he is the only American painter foreign painters in Paris consider as a painter and whose painting interests them. He is young yet and might only perhaps nobody can do that thing called abstract painting. I often tell him there is no such thing. The minute painting gets abstract it gets pornographic. That is a fact. However he is married to a foreigner and I know them.

The Kiddie the one we knew in Nîmes who was in the ambulance and was the first American uniform we had with us in our automobile and who never wrote to us and then did write when Four Saints was given did not marry a foreigner although it was proposed to him by our neighbor the Baronne Pierlot, but he did come to see us and when a tire deflated and so he missed his train and had to come back again to wait with us he decided us to go to America.

Everything that summer was in confusion just as it is this summer, only then the confusion was inside me and not outside me and now it is outside me and not inside me.

I had quarreled with Bradley and said I would not go to America, he said but I wanted to get rich certainly I said I do want to get rich but I never want to do what there is to do to get rich.

Just at present my passion is avarice. To be avaricious I think the greatest value in the world and I say so and I do want to be so. For instance the house we have has always been in the hands of the family the most completely miserly in the country hereabouts. So now we have a home which is really seventeenth century, all the other houses around here were changed as people were married or were buried and in the long history of the country here there has been a very great deal of that and so now every one comes to see ours because nothing has ever been changed in it neither the house nor the garden nothing has ever been done. Even the few new wall papers have always been put one over the other one. Once Francis Rose was staying with us and I went into his room to speak to him and there he was with absorbent cotton and water and he was finding Empire paper and Louis the sixteenth paper under the Directoire paper which was the last that had been put on.

Avarice is a good thing, it would be a wonderful thing to be really avaricious and so occupying. It is true though the Americanization of everything has driven avarice out of every one and I do not like it. I am hoping a good many millions are to be avaricious again and I want to be the first one. Not that there are not a good many in America who are perhaps Jay Laughlin is and

128

that is why I believe in him, but unfortunately Europe does not know about him but now I will tell them.

So Bradley my agent said he had made all the arrangements for me to get rich and now I was upsetting everything.

I was upsetting everything, I definitely did not intend to do any of the things that Bradley wanted me to do. I would not sign a contract for an autobiography the idea of which at that time I did not find interesting and anyway I was certain that I would not sign a contract to do anything, and I had not quarreled with my editor Harcourt because I had never written to him or met him actually when I did although he only wanted autobiographies to print and I wanted everything I did not quarrel with him. Everything is being printed by Bennett Cerf and this autobiography too, even then Harcourt and I did not quarrel and anyway nobody could quarrel with him, Americans do do everything for you so how can you quarrel with them. Bradley and I had become European and so quarreling was a natural thing, anyway there was a complete explosion and I refused everything and we have never seen each other again, I told him that there were somethings I could not do even to become rich as he was saying.

There are some things a girl cannot do. Ronda is a town in Spain. In the summer there is a great deal of dust blowing as it is on a high plateau as almost all of Spain is. It has very small houses that look almost as if an Englishman in the eighteenth century had built them with bay-windows and in the middle of the town in nineteen-twelve or thirteen there had been built one of the two or three up-to-date hotels built at that time. We were staying there just about then. I always liked Ronda and when we were in Spain we used to stay there a while and take walks and sometimes the little rivers were dry and sometimes they were wet and there were stepping stones over them. Once we were crossing them and Alice B. Toklas was frightened by them.

It was a really big hotel and nobody was there not any French or American or Spanish but there was a mother and daughter who were English.

We began talking, the mother said that her husband, he was naturally in England he was never there with them and they were never in England with him, she said that her husband had always said of her that she had the eye but not the hand of an artist. Were we either of us by any chance artists. No I said but I was a writer, oh yes she said that was interesting.

The daughter began to talk about Spanish people, she had known a good many of them and then we were tired and we said we would go to bed and we did.

I never go to sleep when I go to bed I always fool around in the evening and somebody was knocking. Come in I said. The daughter came in she said she wanted to ask my advice about something. She began to tell me about her life with Spaniards and her life in England before she had come to Spain, she went to the door to listen but there was nobody listening. She told me about how any Spaniard wanted to marry any woman who was English, and she told me how nearly she had come to marrying. She told me how often she had nearly come to marrying. She was to marry an Englishman only that had not happened to happen and now again she could begin again and she said I have told you everything, will you tell me what I had better do. Why I said I think you had better marry the Englishman, oh she said, there are some things a girl can't do. Then I said why dont you tell your mother something I will she said when she is on her death-bed, but she is not ill I said, oh no she said but when she is on her death-bed then I will tell her everything, but why upset her last moments I said, oh she said it would not do for her to go to heaven without knowing because when I met her there no it would not do, she said, my brothers understand that, she said, they will do so too, they will tell her on her death-bed, well I said I think you had better get back your Englishman. Ah she said you do not understand that that is something that no girl can do. At last she left and the next morning we left and what happened to them we never knew.

So I too having refused everything and being left with nothing, we went to Bilignin that summer.

And now this is Bilignin and now this is the Spanish revolution. I do not have to talk to myself about the destruction of the El Greco paintings, Picabia has just been here with us and he had seen Picasso in Cannes, he said he said to him well how about their making you director of the Prado and Picasso did not answer him, Picasso woke him up at six o'clock in the morning to talk about Spain. It seems said Picabia that he has given the Madrid government two airplanes and that is the reason he was given the directorship of the Prado. Yes I said and when the king was sent out Pablo and Ortiz came Ortiz from just having gone to see the king come to Paris and Pablo was furious at Spain becoming republican. Oh it is just surrealism said Picabia and I said no I think it is Sarbates he knows Pablo would never go to Madrid and he could represent him, and Pablo hoping that his youth was coming back thought it would be rigolo to do this thing. Well said Picabia angrily what difference does it make to any of us what any of them do and it is true and what difference does it make to any of us what any of them do. El Greco meant a great deal to me once and now I would not go anywhere to look at them. And so I do not have to talk to myself about them but I do. It is like nutting. You go over the same ground ten or a dozen times and each time you see nuts that you had not taken. The pleasure is in the eye seeing them but if you did not take them there would be no pleasure in the eye seeing them and that is why avarice is so occupying, anybody who is not avaricious can get angry suddenly without any reason. Just now everybody is angry there is no more reason to be angry now than there is always but just now everybody has an angry feeling. Perhaps the time comes when there are no nuts left when you go to look for them but then you do not go to look for them when there are no nuts left, of course then you do not go to look for them.

I have just found another pocket-full of them and that is a pleasure.

So we did just before going to America come to Bilignin and we brought Trac the Indo-Chinese along and we had made up our mind not to do anything. It is always best to resist doing anything, if you stay where you are long enough you have to leave it but if you do not stay where you are long enough you do not have to leave it.

Louis Bromfield explained that he had taken the lease of his house for seven years, yes we said but why not for longer, well he said I have no idea where I will be in seven years but I certainly will not be here. I am wondering though if he has not noticed that after all he did stay there.

Airplanes are nice and automobiles are nice and yet you do have to stay somewhere, the earth keeps turning around but you have to sit somewhere. Since the war we had not gone anywhere, except the one lecturing in England we had not left France, we had just gone from Belley to Paris and from Paris to Belley and so we decided not to go to America.

Then the Kiddie came and then Carl came and with him came Mark Lutz and then Bernard Faÿ came and with him came Laughlin and then we did go to America.

But first we came to Bilignin and Trac came.

Thornton Wilder writes to us these days and says he is shamelessly happy, and now he has no father. That has of course nothing to do with Trac although Thornton Wilder's childhood was passed in China. Trac had more or less not a father at least not for very much longer and he himself had nothing in him that would make him want to be a father. Fathers are depressing and China was more a land of mothers than it was a land of fathers.

Mothers may not be cheering but they are not as depressing as fathers.

Bennett Cerf has a father but he is more than a father and Bennett himself is more a brother and a nephew or a great nephew than a father, that is the reason we like him and like him as a publisher.

But to come back to Thornton Wilder. We never met him until we went to Chicago, we might have met him earlier because he had been in Paris at the same time as all those of his generation, but Thornton always likes to think of himself as older which so nicely makes him younger now than any of his generation. He then had a father now he has not a father.

There is too much fathering going on just now and there is no doubt about it fathers are depressing. Everybody nowadays is a father, there is father Mussolini and father Hitler and father Roosevelt and father Stalin and father Lewis and father Blum and father Franco is just commencing now and there are ever so many more ready to be one. Fathers are depressing. England is the only country now that has not got one and so they are more cheerful there than anywhere. It is a long time now that they have not had any fathering and so their cheerfulness is increasing.

I have been much interested in watching several families here in Belley that have lost their father and it is interesting to me because I was not grown when we lost our father. As I say fathers are depressing any father who is a father or any one who is a father and there are far too many fathers now existing. The periods of the world's history that have always been most dismal ones are the ones where fathers were looming and filling up everything. I had a father, I have told lots about him in The Making of Americans but I did not tell about the difference before and after having him. I am always interested in the families here in Belley who have lost their father or who have lost their mother when the family is more or less a large one. We were five children and our mother was dead and we were living all together with our father. My brother Michael was our oldest brother we called him Mike or Mickey, and so there were three brothers and two sisters that made us five.

It is funny how in a large family they all are alike or each one is extremely different, I suppose there are in betweens but I do not notice them. Here in Belley is a family where there are four brothers and four sisters and a mother, I think I have mentioned them, they are horticulturists and the mother wears a wig and bows in a peculiar way her eldest son does exactly the same not wear a wig but bows in the same way and all his brothers and his sisters, I used to call him aîné or the first because I always imagined there was no father they all came through him and his mother this was easy to imagine but not easy to have been as his sister was only three years younger and then they came each one not too long after the other one. However.

Mostly in a large family there is a family resemblance and each one is extremely different from every other one. It was so in our family of three brothers and two sisters they were called Mike and Simon and Bertha and Leo and then I came, two died in baby-hood or else I would not have come nor my brother just two years older and we never talked about this after we had heard of it that they never intended to have more than five children it made us feel funny.

Alice Toklas when she met my oldest brother in San Francisco many years later after the rest of us had left thought he was an only child. She has a tendency to think that any one is an only child because she was one, that is to say she had a brother but he came so much later that she was an only child. That is right enough because after all by the time any one meets any one they are only children, the family has died away from them so that it has never been. If not why not. As I say fathers are depressing but our family had one.

134

We had a mother and a father and I tell all about that in The Making of Americans which is a history of our family, but I can tell it all again, why not if it is interesting.

So then there were five children and they were not at all alike. Mike I suppose sometimes was younger than about sixteen, he surely had been because there are photographs of him but for me he was always about sixteen in his beginning. Simon was two years younger but for me he began even a little later. I remember him when I was about eleven so he must have been about seventeen, there is no reason why I should not have remembered him earlier, but I suppose just about that time he began to be funny to me and before that I had been living my life with my younger brother who was two years older than I was. My sister four years older simply existed for me because I had to sleep in the same room with her. It is natural not to care about a sister certainly not when she is four years older and grinds her teeth at night. My sister Bertha did. She was a little simple minded so was my brother Simon that is to say they would have been natural enough if no one had worried about it but Simon was very funny. He was always very funny. He never could learn anything not that it mattered except to my father. He naturally did not like it. My sister Bertha could not learn anything and that annoyed him even more. I suppose when there are a number of children there are sure to be some like that. I always liked the way the Spanish women explained that if they wished to have four children they must bear twelve because two thirds of them would certainly naturally die before they could grow up. After all it is all right for them to be like that, they are just as likely as not to have interesting children why not. Whenever I read Edgar Wallace I am always pleased the way the detective hero is always ready to marry the girl no matter what happened to have been her mother and her brothers and her fathers.

So Simon was funny. When I first began to think about him he was very large and heavy he was good-looking he had straight black hair and a very good nose and forehead but not silly eyes, and he loved eating, he could eat a whole rice pudding and he liked going into any kind of business. There always was an attempt to educate him and there was a time when I undertook to teach him that Columbus discovered America in fourteen ninety-two. I used to ask him every morning and every evening, that he could not really remember that it was Columbus was not surprising but that he could not remember fourteen ninety-two was not really a bother to any one neither to him nor to me. This must have been when I was about eleven. And then a little later he began to go into partnerships. Everybody in East Oakland was delighted when he went into partnership with a house painter, the house painter disappeared and everybody went to see Simon carry out the order, they had an order and then I must have been about twelve then I had to help him write out an advertisement to be put into the Oakland paper announcing that he was not responsible for the debts of his partner. I do not know who told him about this but we both liked doing it. He was very funny he did not like my brother Leo so he would take Leo's violin out into the barn and get it to smell of horses, he used to be worried because he thought that from time to time he paid a five dollar piece for a five cent piece, that could happen in East Oakland because five dollars was in gold then and five cents in nickel and he always had things in his pocket, candy he did not care very much for candy he preferred more solid eating and cigars he never smoked cigars but that was to please Mickey and make anybody else happy. He had his own ideas of what was funny. Anybody does have but his were very funny.

Everybody has their ideas of being funny. Spaniards have. It is a difficult thing to like anybody's else ideas of being funny.

A French officer of the navy was just telling me today, he was visiting in the country and he told about a French admiral who has

136

just recently been in Barcelona. The French admiral landed to have a conversation with the French consul general. He did not let his sailors or any officer land because he did not want to be the cause of any trouble so he decided to go himself on foot to the office of the French consul. Just after he left his boat they saw him come to a corner and fall they followed to see what was the matter, and on the corner was an automobile and in place of the two front lanterns there were two heads of somebody and the admiral's eyes had rolled and then he had fallen.

Simon of course had no such idea of being funny his were simple and satisfying ideas, and in a way he was funny very funny. Later on he decided that he would do something, my father was vice-president of a street railroad then and Mike was a manager of one of the lines. Simon thought he wanted to be a gripman, and he became one and that really suited him, he liked every one, that is almost every one, and he liked giving the children candy and the men cigars and he did not have to think about five cents and five dollars looking alike and almost to the end of his life he was a gripman, to be sure most of the time only on Sunday or when they were very busy and finally he was too heavy to stand so long, and then he stopped.

That was Simon and then there was Bertha. Bertha too could not really learn anything and Simon and Bertha were not very pleasing to each other which is natural enough. Simon I liked but I did not like Bertha.

Some one has just sent me a book they have written called A Miner My Brother and I have been wondering why they do so much like to say brother. Once some years ago I met a man an American I had known him casually and he said to me and how is your brother. Oh I said I have not seen him for a very long time in fact I never see him any more, Oh yes, he said, I know, consanguinity.

So Bertha was not a pleasant person, she naturally did not like anything and later very much later she married a man who well they married and after all one of the sons is very interesting, he is the one about whom I wrote Dan Raffel a nephew, he is a Johns Hopkins man and a biologist in Russia.

Daniel was my father's name, it is a good sounding name and yet not a very real name to me and I never have found out whether it is a name that I like or not, anyway it was my father's name.

My mother had been dead a long time, there is a great deal about her in The Making of Americans and the family she came from, except herself, they are all a long-lived family they are very small in stature and they do go on living pleasantly for ever.

Here in Belley it interests me very much when the father dies or the mother and it is a large family and the children are all old enough to like it better. Whatever happens they do like it better.

When my mother died she had been ill a long time and had not been able to move around and so when she died we had all already had the habit of doing without her. I have told all about her in The Making of Americans but that is a story and after all what is the use of its being a story. If it is real enough what is the use of it being a story, and anyway The Making of Americans is not really a story it is a description of how every one who ever lived eats and drinks and loves and sleeps and talks and walks and wakes and forgets and quarrels and likes and dislikes and works and sits, and naturally a longer description of some than of others and a very long description of my mother and my father. This is not a description of them at all, what is the use of remembering anything. There is none. And now really really remembering is very little done.

That is what makes today today that there is very little remembering done.

After my mother died we went on doing what we had done but naturally our father was more a bother than he had been, that is natural enough. Hitherto we had naturally not had to remember him most of the time and now remembering him had begun.

138

Mike had come back from the East, so we were all together, except that Leo had had typhoid fever and they thought he ought to become a vineyardist naturally that was not very interesting, and they thought that Simon should become a rancher but it was not very amusing to any of them and he came back to be a gripman, and Mike came back to manage a street railroad of which my father was vice-president and I stopped going to school Mike thought I ought to be a musician, not that I was ever interested in music naturally not, and Bertha was to do the housekeeping.

Naturally my father was not satisfied with anything, that was natural enough.

And after that we did all do that.

Naturally our father was very often irritated.

He told Mike that he had to make up his mind to take out his sister, that was Bertha, he would have to do it sooner or later. Mike muttered that he would take his later.

Later Mike when my father was very irritated said that after all if a man could not manage to have what he wanted he should not come home and be irritable as after all it was for him to decide what he wanted. Mike was always reasonable that is to say he always was until he had a son of his own. He said fathers should not be irritable because they could not manage outside matters.

Many years later not so very long ago when Mike was impatient with his son I said but Mike you always understood so well that every one wants what they want and you always let Leo and myself have it, Mike had been our guardian after our father died, and now you have a son and you are irritable and you see no sense in what he wants. Oh said Mike you do not understand it is different, a son irritates you differently from any other irritation and when a son irritates you you are irritated.

Well feudal days were the days of fathers and now once more these days are the days of fathers.

Well anyway we all went on. And I like to have been it, because

139

everything that was inside could be inside where anything is, and so we all went on. And then it was the spring or summer.

Before this Mike had come to be in San Francisco and we had come to know a lot about everything. That is what happened when things were being done.

Much later on I first was interested in Fitzgerald because in This Side Of Paradise he described what happened when there was no longer any money in street railroads. He only stated it but it made me like it.

Street railroads were interesting. Now the last tram has just been taken off the streets of Paris but street railroads were only interesting to us when they were in San Francisco.

The only other that ever interested me were the trolleys without tracks they had in an Italian hill town and in Chambery, not that it had anything to do with me I never went on it but it was interesting.

And so we began to know what every one did who did anything. I often have said that it is a puzzle to me that a boy just out of school goes into his father's office and they give him a lot of papers and nobody gave him papers before and he seems to know what to do with them.

We asked Mike what he did because he was supposed to be managing a branch line and they were to do some new work on it. Where do you get your men we asked him. Oh you lean on the wall and first one and then more come, he said. That is the way they did then. We then used to be puzzled because he said he was very good at making up time-tables and we knew he never could do arithmetic, we always used to have to do percentage for him and division and addition and subtraction but he was very good at making up very complicated time-tables so everybody said. And then sometimes he came home and he was pretty sick. He said that was because they wanted to have a new franchise and he had to meet the men who could give it to them. No one in the family ever liked drinking. They smoked very good cigars very good cigars and they knew a lot about tobacco as was the habit in California but they never did care for drinking. And so we were interested in what they did, but all we knew was that Mike would be pretty sick and did not care much about anything then. But what we liked most Leo and I was to go and call for him at his office. We had by that time been given an allowance for spending, but naturally we bought books with it, we always bought books with it, I bought a Shelley in green and Morocco binding and we bought an illustrated set of Thackeray and we had a simple book plate made and when we went to call for Mike in the evening when we had gone to the city as everybody in Oakland going over to San Francisco called San Francisco we never had any more money, Mike would always sigh but he liked to have us with him and so he would take us out to dinner but before that we would sit and watch him disciplining.

Any gripman or conductor who had done anything he should not do would be sent in to see him. Mike who never knew what to say unless he was really angry and then would say if this kind of thing goes on I will throw up the whole damn business, used to stand with his head down, the man would go on and Mike his face very solemn would stand with his head down and then would mutter something. And we in the background knowing what Mike was feeling were thoroughly enjoying the situation. The men dreaded being sent in to Mike because he never said anything and only looked solemn.

Then he would take us out to dinner, and San Francisco was a nice place in those days to be taken out to dinner by a brother.

And it all went on until one spring or summer.

Then one morning we could not wake up our father. Leo climbed in by the window and called out to us that he was dead in his bed and he was.

Then we stayed where we were a little longer and then we

141

moved to San Francisco. Mike was our guardian as Leo and I were minors and I remember going to a court for the only time I was ever in one, to say that we would have him.

It was a funny place it all seemed to have so much raw wood in it the floors and the walls and all sorts of things in it, and we were in and we were out and that was all there was to it.

Then our life without a father began a very pleasant one.

I have been thinking a lot about fathers any kind of fathers.

After all civilization has only lasted about five thousand years and five thousand is an awfully small number to see anywhere now. This is the epoch of big figures and five thousand is not much of a one.

And fathers come up and fathers go down. That is natural enough when nobody has had fathers they begin to long for them and then when everybody has had fathers they begin to long to do without them. Sometimes barons and dukes are fathers and then kings come to be fathers and churchmen come to be fathers and then comes a period like the eighteenth century a nice period when everybody has had enough of anybody being a father to them and then gradually capitalists and trade unionists become fathers and which goes on to communists and dictators, just now everybody has a father, perhaps the twenty-first century like the eighteenth century will be a nice time when everybody forgets to be a father or to have been one. The Jews and they come into this because they are very much given to having a father and to being one and they are very much given not to want a father and not to have one, and they are an epitome of all this that is happening the concentration of fathering to the perhaps there not being one.

Well anyway, we had a time with only a brother not a father, and a father as Mike later so well explained to me is different after all he is a father.

Soon we left East Oakland and went to live in San Francisco. We went to live on Turk Street, of course at that time everybody lived in a house alone, they still do pretty much in America, and it was a pleasure to see all those wooden houses a wonderful pleasure but all that will come later.

We did move in all of us together and once we all were tired of unpacking and Mike had been left alone in the cellar and we all had commenced eating and Mike came up in the dining room and he was furious with every one and he said if this sort of thing was going to go on he would throw up the whole damn business. Whenever he said that we all surrounded him to placate him. Anything but that he should throw up the whole damn business. He used to make nice little jokes too that pleased us and Leo and I always liked giving him a book to read, he never read any book except one that we gave him and that he always read from the beginning to the ending. He always had these pleasant little ways he still has them.

One night there was a big fire one of those nice American fires that have so many horses and firemen to attend them and Mike very frightened came up to see that we were all safe and none of us were awake and he was furious with us because none of us had heard anything and he was the only one awake. And then one night the night-watchman woke us up because some one had left the front parlor window wide open, and he had to go down and close it to please the watchman not that it made any difference to any of us but Mike said we had to please the watchman. We lived like this for a year or more. I know I was most awfully shocked when Mike brought home my father's business books and Leo and I went through them with him. There were so many debts it was frightening, and then I found out that profit and loss is always loss, that did not worry us as much as there being estate debts, but Mike explained that this always happened in a business and it was all right, because we always had a habit in the family never to owe anybody any money.

I have been writing a series of articles in the Saturday Evening

Post about money and what is money. And it is awfully funny about money. I am sure that there is no difference between men and animals except the power to count and if you count you do count money. Just now nobody counts in any small numbers such as thousands and millions they have to go very much higher, but then any counting was counting and large sums were just beginning. They really did begin first with England in the Napoleonic wars and later with us and the Civil war and now they are not overwhelming because the imagination has gotten used to them which is natural enough. After all there is one one one and there are the stars' light traveling and anything else there can be. Do not forget that everything is as it is even if it is. All right we lived in San Francisco more than a year. During that time we sometimes had visitors from the East, that is relatives and cousins. Naturally we had not known them but they came to see us. The first one that came was another Simon Stein quite another one. He was a gentle Simon Stein and a quiet one and he said nothing that is to say he did not say much of anything and that evening when he left my brother Simon went with him to the train and when Simon came back he said that Simon Stein had said to him thank you for seeing me to the train when you come to Baltimore I will be sure to do that for you. And we all laughed and we all laughed louder and Simon said he thought all the way home that there was something funny about Simon Stein when he said good-bye to him.

Later another one this time not a Simon but a Hattie came and she had just been married and her husband was a big man. They talked more than Simon Stein had and nobody went with them to the train.

These were all on my father's side of the family those on my mother's side naturally never came.

Anybody can think a lot about money. It is funny about money, there are such different ways of counting money, but everybody anybody is counting and is counting money. The Keysers my mother's people and the Steins my father's people had very different ways of counting money. So have we all.

When I was at Radcliffe I was to pass my entrance examinations after I had been there some years. I had left the high school young and I had never learned French and German having had it and forgotten it and I knew a lot but still there were some examinations that knowing a lot did not help advanced Latin was one and so Margaret Lewis a graduate student was to teach me enough to get through. We worked together and I was to pay her at the end of the month. I had paid her and then one month I had spent all my month's money in going to the opera and so I said to her do you mind if I do not pay you as I have not got any money. She said no reflectively and then she said what do you mean when you say you have no money, Oh I said I mean I have spent my month's money and I haven't any. Well she said reflectively your father and mother are dead you have your own money haven't you. Yes I said. Well then she said you have the money to pay me now I do not need it but you have it so you must not say you haven't got it. Yes I said but you see I cannot use that because that is what I have not got I only have a month's money, yes she said but you see those who earn money have not got it but then when they have not got it they have not got it. I was much surprised and I never forgot it. Now I am not so much surprised because after all an income is an income whether you earn it or whether you have it and I was right and she was right about it. Sometimes everybody wonders whether there is going to be one kind of income or another kind. Jessie Whitehead used to say during the war, after the war there is not going to be any more cream to put on strawberries and when I am an old lady I will tell my grandchildren there used when you ate strawberries to be something called cream and I will describe it to them and they will marvel at it. Anyway there does seem to be a great deal of cream all the same, more cream than ever one might say, and so Jessie Whitehead cannot tell her grandchildren about the wonderful thing called cream which they have never seen just as Picasso cannot listen to his old friends sitting around with their wooden legs telling about their war campaigns. Jo Davidson says that what he wants is everybody to have an income then nobody will worry about anything, well anyway an income if it does not go away is very comforting and does not need so much counting as other kinds of counting. Afterwards while I was still at college I did realize that my uncles and cousins they were richer than we were and they knew less about everything they did not realize that anybody needed to be paid right away, they always paid of course but they did not realize that waiting was complicating. But now what happens, well now nothing happens, there are a great many more who have an income, but even so counting is really pleasant when there is something to count.

Naturally Leo and I spent all the money we had on books, I still like that only now I buy only the cheapest detective and adventure stories and then I bought the most expensive history and poetry and literature. As I say incomes are incomes and counting is counting and reading is reading. Why not.

And so our life in California came to an end and we left that is Leo and I left and my sister left. Mike and Simon stayed on.

Years before Leo and I were to go East with my mother. I was about nine then and he eleven. We bought as many books as we could to take along. We bought Jules Verne lots of them and then we did not go my mother went but we did not go but we had already bought the books to read in traveling. There was the Cryptogram and Twenty Thousand Leagues Under the Sea and The Children of Captain Grant we had already had that in German, we seemed to have Jules Verne in everything except in French of course I only read him in English and the English at the North Pole and The Mysterious Island we had bought all these for traveling and Around the World in Eighty Days. You can read a book over and over again until you remember everything and even then you can read it over again if you begin at the beginning. That is very important about reading a book over again you must really begin at the beginning. In that way you can read it over and over again.

I do not know why we did not go East with my mother, I suppose there was something instead we went to Marysville and stayed with the relations of a governess we had then. In The Making of Americans I have told about all the governesses we had and this was the one who finally married a baker. I have written a very good description of her. Marysville was hot and there were mosquitoes and the beds were made of feathers and there were lots of animals. Anyway we came home in the autumn, and when my mother came back she was never well again. Mike was at that time in Baltimore at Johns Hopkins University and he wanted to marry some one there and my mother wanted this to happen she liked anything to happen, but it did not happen and it was then that Mike wrote the poem that Leo and I found and it said that he always had looked at a plot of grass and it had been a plot of grass to him and then he met the one he loved and then when he looked at the plot of grass there were birds and butterflies on the plot of grass and before that there never had been. That was what love was. Then we also found letters he had written or she had and they consisted of a great deal of Latin and hopes of Latin. We enjoyed finding them. This was after Mike came back from the East and he had come out with the G. A. R. celebration, you had cheap tickets if you belonged to that organization. Naturally Mike was much too young for that but he grew a beard to make him look like one. Perhaps he had the right as the son of one, or his uncles may have been of them although as a matter of fact the one who went all through the war fought on the Southern side. My mother used to tell us stories of Baltimore and the Northern

147

soldiers being stoned as they passed from one station to the other you always had to change in Baltimore. The Civil war seems far away now but then it seemed quite near. If your grandfather was an oldish man when your mother was born and you are the youngest of a number of children it is extraordinary how few generations can cover the history of civilization. Everything is as exciting as it can be but not that.

Any time is the time to make a poem. The snow and sun below.

When they came to see us the relations, from New York and Baltimore and they said they loved to read we were always surprised that they had not read anything. It did not worry us but it surprised us. Nothing about them worried us and that was all about them that surprised us. Really nothing was very surprising or worrying just then. We had no parents and each one of us was where each one was. That was what we were doing.

We all stayed in San Francisco for a year and then we all went somewhere. Bertha and I went to Baltimore and Leo went to Harvard. Mike stayed in San Francisco and so did Simon. Mike said Simon could be a gripman on any car except one of the lines that belonged to their system and Simon was one for years on the California street line, he finally only drove on Sundays and he was even so big he could hardly stand in between where he had to stand and his pockets were always full of candy for any one and cigars for any one and he went on until the fire and after that he gave it up and went fishing, but Mike had also left San Francisco by then he was in Europe then and so Simon was the only one left in California.

When we left San Francisco for Baltimore we left Mike all alone Simon did not count and Mike was alone, later he married but at that time he was alone and he had to save everything for all of us and he did it but he never knew quite how he did it.

Street railroads do not exist any more they have taken the last one off of Paris but then they did exist and we all used them, there was no other way to go up and down except to walk and in San Francisco and everywhere distances were too long to always walk and horses were slow and street railways were quicker. To be sure street railways once were drawn by horses but except in Baltimore and many other places that was almost over. Anyway in San Francisco there always had been street railways. Then there was the dummy, the dummy had four seats in front almost like a cow catcher and Alice Toklas likes the story of when she and three others were together they were sitting on the front of the dummy, the dummy gave a jerk, it often did, and Ada said I almost fell off the dummy, who almost fell off the dummy said the other three, I almost fell off the dummy said Ada. Alice Toklas still says and who almost fell off the dummy.

Well anyway, when my father came to California he had the money that he had made with his brother in Pittsburgh, Pennsylvania, that is how we all happened to be born there, and then when the sisters-in-law were no longer able to get along together, one brother went to New York and we all went to Europe. My father was interested in everything and when we all came back from Europe we all went out to California. There my father waited a considerable while before he was interested in anything and then he became interested in street railroading. There were at that time several systems which sometimes transferred to another one but each one was by itself and one was called the Union, that was the one that my father came finally to become the vice-president and of course we all heard all about everything the way anybody does without listening, the word franchise was a common word.

Then my father was dead and Mike was doing something, we used to go to see him do it and we knew George Leroy was to help him. George Leroy was the French brother who was not a wicked Frenchman like his brother Eugene. At any rate he was a large and quiet Frenchman and he used to come and sit and neither he nor Mike said anything. That was much later after everything was done that I saw them sitting that was after Mike was married and everything had been done and I came from the East to California to visit them.

After we went away Mike's troubles really began.

My father had been one of the early ones to believe in consolidation and he had worked out a complete system for the street railroads of San Francisco. But he was a man who frightened any one because he was too impatient to finish what was not yet begun. And so he was vice-president of a small part of the system of San Francisco street railroads. When he was dead naturally what was small was still smaller and everything else was getting bigger. Mike who like his mother's family dislikes responsibility and dislikes business it makes him nervous when anything has to be done knew that it had to be done. Anybody wants to do what Mike wants them to do and so everybody did but what could they do. How it was done nobody ever knew. Mike's own statement was that he knew if it was not done he had us all on his hands because none of us could earn anything not even Simon enough to live on and something had to be done and so although the Southern Pacific street railroads could have had the Mission line for nothing they took it on on an equal footing. Mike persuaded them. Then afterwards when they realized what had been done they were so impressed by him that they made him manager of the whole system and that was frightful for him because it does make him nervous to decide anything besides he likes to be very busy just arranging any little thing, but he was manager for two years and then he decided to either go to Paris or to the country and by that time he did come. When it was all done he said now at last it was satisfactory, we had enough to live on if we lived very quietly and we all did live very quietly until the war began, other things have happened since but we did live very very quietly until the war began.

And so we all left San Francisco, Simon died there still fat and

150

fishing, and Mike has gone back there again now to bring up a little grandson and Leo is in Florence and I am in Bilignin.

It was in Bilignin that I finally decided to go to America again after years of not having been.

So we were in Bilignin and I was quarreling with Mr. Bradley about lecturing. We were here and we had as a servant an Indo-Chinaman.

One thing I can always remember going back again to East Oakland is wearing gloves and books. Bertha was being put at another school and I went with her and while they were talking to her I was left in the superintendent's room and there was a bookcase there. I was wearing gloves I was just beginning to wear them and I saw a book and I began reading, it was Jane Eyre and I had not read it and I held it tightly and I read it and then suddenly I saw that my thumb had made a black mark on the page I was holding.

I can never touch a book with a glove on and I get very troubled when any one touches a book and they have a glove on. Dirty hands do not dirty a book as much as a glove can.

Knowing so many people is curious and yet everybody knows them. Again and again I have known practically nobody and again and again I have known a great many. Just now here in Bilignin we know a great many a great many more than we know in Paris. This happens again and again.

In East Oakland sometimes we knew a great many and sometimes we did not know any.

It does change very much who you know and when you know them.

In East Oakland we knew the people who lived in the houses near us, the people my father knew knew us but we did not know them their children knew us too but not enough to matter to us or to them. And then we knew others as we had come to know them. You never know just how you will come to know them.

We were in a hotel at Belley and we only knew the people of the hotel and the people from whom we had bought anything. And then one day, we had noticed her several times a very good-looking woman who sat at a table behind us and then being a French-woman one evening she could stand it no longer and she said to us, do you really eat the same fish every evening. Yes we said we did. And I said but you always read a new magazine every evening. Ah yes she said I do. Well we came to know her. Somebody had predicted that we would come to know somebody that summer that had blue eyes and had a garden. And she did she had blue eyes and she had a garden. But a little later and in a simpler man-ner because we were taken there by some one who had sold us flowers, we met another Frenchwoman and she too had blue eyes and had a garden, so how can you tell what is going to happen.

When we went to live in San Francisco we did not know any one. Naturally everybody we had known in Oakland we did not know any more because we were not in Oakland and in San Fran-cisco we did not know those who knew our father and mother be-cause there was no reason why we should know them even if they wanted to know us and so we did not know any one. Naturally we began to know somebody each one of us naturally would but not very many or very much.

Then we went to Baltimore and there everybody knew us and it did not make any difference about our knowing them since they all knew us.

I have just had a postal card from one of them, I had not seen or heard of him for so many years that there was no use in there having been any years in between. All I knew about him was that he once loaned me five cents because I asked him to pay my car fare and I forgot to pay him back and he never said anything about it but he never forgave me for having forgotten. How did I know that, I do not know but probably somebody told me.

So Baltimore was full of everything which was natural enough and soon it was natural enough that there were so many and we knew them. Not now but then.

If anything begins then it has begun and if it is begun then it is like that. That is the way it was living in Baltimore and everybody knowing us. Of course they did know us, had not my mother's father and mother well anyway it was a hundred years and my father's people fifty years and so naturally anybody could know us. It was not unnatural and it was not natural, and pretty soon and that is the reason changes in anything are not really exciting pretty soon it was only unnatural if it was natural. I wrote a little story about that when I was at Radcliffe and being still under the influence of George Eliot I called it the Red Deeps.

I was very fond of my aunts and uncles on my mother's side particularly the one named Fanny, Fanny is a nice name, I do not quite know why but it is a nice name.

I was interested in the way she counted, she said the only way that you could save with dignity and then use the money that had accumulated was by counting one one one. You should never say three or even two, you should keep strictly on a basis of one. If you kept counting by ones and had purses in which you kept the separate ones you could always keep everybody well fed and prettily dressed and the furniture renewed whenever the covers grew shabby. And she did. Her husband David Bacharach, was the ugliest man in Baltimore but a pleasant one, he was one of the very early followers of Henry George. I was much pleased on receiving a letter from some one just yesterday about my writing in the Saturday Evening Post about money and they said it would be different if I knew about Henry George. I knew about Henry George. David Bacharach knew all about Henry George every day and any day. I do not think I really am very interested in any of it although I can and do get excited about it. Government is really not interesting, because the reason for it is that it has to go on and if it has to go on then there is no reason for it.

After all it is very simple, we are on the earth and we have to live on it and there is beyond all there is and there is no extending it because after all there it is and here we are, and we are always here and we are always there and any little while is a pleasure, and a pleasure is a pleasure or yes it is a pleasure is a treasure. Any way my aunt Fanny did always count by one and one and she still does and she still can manage to have everything come out the way it should by the simple process of counting one and one. I saw her when I was in Baltimore and she had again won by counting one one one.

So then there was the Keyser counting money and the Stein counting money and they all like to spend money, unless you can really have the pleasure of being a miser there is no pleasure like the spending of money, and it is hard to be a miser, a real miser they are as rare as geniuses it takes the same kind of thing to make one, that is time must not exist for them. There must be a reality that has nothing to do with the passage of time and it is very hard for any one to have that in them, not hard almost impossible, but there is no way of having it unless you have it, I have it and so had Hetty Green, oh yes.

There was no opposition in knowing all the family and the families in Baltimore none at all. How could there be any opposition after all the opposition had been. Leo went to Harvard and I went to visit him. And then I went to Radcliffe. They are foolish in Radcliffe at least it seems so when they send me their printed anything. When I was at Radcliffe it was not Radcliffe it was the Harvard Annex and living in a boarding house was interesting and knowing a whole new lot whom I had never seen before, it is a thing that is so natural and yet is it natural, that you know a whole lot of them that you never knew before. The landlord at the boarding house was funny, he sat at the end of the table and he did not like low lights, he said if they had another light like that he would be in total darkness. He did not say funny things. His wife was a very good boarding-house keeper, I think he kept an employment agency, we did not know it then but still we must have or perhaps not. Everybody was New England there. I was there for four years.

Well anyway when I wrote The Autobiography of Alice B. Toklas for the first time I received really a quantity of fan letters and also for the Four Saints. I was always reading something and I never wrote any fan letter to any one why should I have been so pleased when they wrote to me but I was.

It is natural to believe in superstitions and hand-reading and predictions. I like hand-reading better than predictions, predictions are a little more frightening. Well anyway there was the summer before we went to America and we were not at all certain we were going. There was every reason for not being certain.

Well anyway I am reading and rereading the book I wrote after being in America, The Relation Of Human Nature To The Human Mind and I would not have written it if I had not gone to America and that would have been a pity anybody can know that. So we did go to America but first we spent the summer in Bilignin and it began badly, there was Trac.

Trac was our first Indo-Chinaman and he loved us and we loved him. I imagine that often happens with anything although Nyen who came later was better to be sure he drank, but you cannot have everything.

Francis Rose is now in Indo-China and he has just sent me all the drawings and water colors he has made there and he has made drawings of Indo-China boys he had as servants and he says on the back of them a Chinese boy probably from the island of Hanau went away first day.

Annamite boy sent by the Cochin China government house. He had worked many years with the governor and had been personally sent by the governor's wife. He went as far as Phnen Pararge with me and then I had to send him back knew nothing about clothes. Placed all empty bottles and cigarette tins in cardboard boxes old empty tubes of tooth paste. He was aged forty and when I returned to Saigon he brought me flowers and asked to be taken back.

Annamite boy stayed a day or two was not bad but knew nothing about being a valet was formerly engineer but smoked opium which makes it impossible to keep them.

Anig boy Mother Tonkinoise traces of Lo Lo in facial construction. Silent and willing but quite untrained could not leave Saigon and could not speak French.

Beri Annamite boy pleasant but lazy from Hui lasted two days. So Trac was our first Indo-Chinaman since then we have had so many that we can not remember all of them but Trac was the first one. He went to the country with us and we all enjoyed eating the Chinese patty he made which is delicious for a picnic, and a Chinaman even an Indo-Chinaman is always pleasant to have with one and so we had Trac. Carl Van Vechten photographed him and so did the Kiddie but they came early to see us before Trac had left us. It was pleasant beginning the summer in Bilignin.

The other evening Francis Picabia was here with his son Poncho almost twenty-three. Poncho complained that his half and illegitimate brother Lorenzo was going off to be a sailor on a sailing boat, how can he said Poncho confine himself to a boat. After all said Francis Picabia you are confined to the earth and possibly the air how can you like being confined to it. Well anyway more and more we like Bilignin we are not confined to it but we do like it. So Trac began the summer with us but really we knew he would not like it. How could he since there could be phantoms in Bilignin when there was none any more in Indo-China since the war. Anyway coming down and settling in was everything and then Carl came, just for twenty-four hours and he made ninety photographs but he did come and we met him. Trac has never forgotten him naturally we never have but neither has Trac.

Trac was with us in Bilignin the summer before we went to

156

America, you have to think it over in detail to know whether it is two years ago or a year ago or longer, it might just as well be.

I have time to meditate longer but that does not matter because once again now I am sitting to a portrait painter, I sit and he sits and we do not talk together, I look out over the roofs and sit not very comfortably and he draws to get acquainted with my portrait, it is not that he says it. It is interesting me to do it again. Yes again.

I come back again from America and then a year or so later I am sitting again to a painter.

Trac anybody can remember what Trac is, nobody has seen him lately but that does not matter. Trac is always faithful to his memory, and his memory is being present ever after.

And so Trac went with us to Bilignin and was there with us when Carl Van Vechten came with Mark Lutz or rather when William Rogers came first. William Rogers was the Kiddie who was with us in Nîmes when the war was. We had not seen him again and now we saw him, it was nice seeing him. Later much later when we saw him and his wife in New England and she had set fire to the gas oven in the kitchen he said let it be a lesson to you but this was only what his grandfather would have said when it happened and the Kiddie did really say it. However. We were glad to see him very glad to see him. We always at least I always and then Alice Toklas always well anyway we always tell everything. Anybody can only some do not. We did and we do and so we told the Kiddie everything about going to America and how we could not go. It really was getting very exciting that we could not go, it excited us and it was an exciting thing to tell.

The Kiddie had been with us in Nîmes he had come to Nîmes not because he knew about us, they naturally did not know about us then but he came there because he wanted to see the Pont du Gard that the Romans had built over the river Gardon.

We saw him then every day and he went with us and then he

went away, he wrote to us and we wrote to him until the war was over and then he never wrote again.

Then so many years after when Four Saints the opera was played in Hartford he wrote all about it and all about himself and we were pleased and we told him so and he said he was coming to France and could he come to see us and we said it would give us a great deal of pleasure and it did give us a great deal of pleasure and he came to see us in Paris.

I did not remember what he looked like I never do remember but he did look as he had looked only he looked older. We talked all that evening and we liked him, you never can tell but we did like him naturally he liked us and we talked about everything not anything as it happened but we talked about what we said was everything. We were leaving for Bilignin the next day and he said he would come down. It is always very difficult to know whether you should say up or down, going anywhere, everybody has their own feeling about that. Some Americans who live in Russia were here last night and when they talk about Russia they say he is coming out or going in, they are not going to or from but in or out. Well everything means something even if it is only a habit. My father always used to complain of my brother Leo that a great many things he did were only a habit. Well.

The Kiddie came to Bilignin.

Carl Van Vechten and Mark Lutz had already been. When they were there Carl was mostly photographing but we did tell about going to America and quarreling. Carl did not say anything he never does if you tell him about quarreling, he says if you behave correctly well if you behave correctly not that there is no quarreling but quarreling is not existing, and indeed nobody knows anything about that once it is all over but if you do quarrel then once it is all over only it does go on. Well anyway we had a good time and Mark Lutz was nice to Basket and Pépé, and after Basket had his photograph taken nobody paid any attention but Pépé and then Pépé had his taken. Basket just now and for the first time is loving a dog and her name is Sugar, perhaps that is why he loves her, he is a poodle and she is an elk hound, and will it be a next time or not, an elk hound is about the same size as a poodle but otherwise there is no resemblance. After January we will know.

So after Carl and Mark were there America was not any nearer or any farther.

And then the Kiddie came otherwise known as William Rogers. I suppose there is something in a name there was Billy the kid, and we had William the Kiddie. All right he came.

After he was there while he was there we took him everywhere. We always had taken him everywhere.

That is when he had been with us in Nîmes during the war, the nineteen fourteen war which was pretty well now forgotten and anyway it was pleasant to have him.

He stayed two days and then he had to take a train. On taking him to the train the tire broke down and it was just outside of Bilignin and so we came back again.

When we were waiting for the next one we told him everything we had not told to him before but now we told him we told him how we were not going, not going to America, and how we had quarreled with Mr. Bradley and he said he could see that it could be arranged and arranged as I wanted it, not as they wanted it. We always believe every one as we listen to them. We believed him. It was pleasant believing him and then he caught the next train.

Trac had been very pleasant all this time Trac the Indo-China-man and each one had photographed him as well as us and everything. And now we were alone in the country and nobody was photographing.

Trac did not go out in the evening, that is to say he did not like to go out in the evening because if he did it might be frightening and he began to talk about everything. He naturally always had talked about everything Chinamen always do, but he talked about just that just then that after all he did not go out in the evening.

To be sure in Belley there was a family the mother was an Indo-Chinese the father a Frenchman, and there were a lot of children. Belley is small but we had never known about them but Trac found them. Even so they were not really a comfort to him so he said and he did not go out in the evening.

And then he began to talk about having a comrade with him. Yes we said. But will he come, well no said Trac he will not not when I tell him how it is about not going out, yes but when there are two of you you can go out we said well anyway said Trac it is very distracting and I do not work well when I am distracted, yes we said but you said you would, yes he said well I will write to my comrade again.

Three days after he announced the comrade was coming. That is fine we said tell him to telegraph the train by which he is leaving and we will go and call for him we said. Yes said Trac here is the letter. Yes we said but this is written by a Frenchwoman she is writing for him, no said Trac that is the comrade, what said we, yes said Trac that is the comrade. Oh no we said not at all, and I said, if I want a Frenchwoman I will choose her, not for me said Trac, no I said no you have to telegraph her off I said, it is too late said Trac she has her ticket, well telegraph it off we said, I have no address says Trac besides she has started. Well I said come on we will meet her and Trac and I went to meet her. We met her. She was the largest fattest Bretonne I have ever seen and dear me. Well there we were. And little by little Trac began to go out of an evening and leave her. He could go out in the evening if he left her behind him. And then he said he thought he would go away altogether and leave her and then he would come back again, not at all, we said if you want to go you will go together. And they did go together but Trac always comes back again and he loves us and we love him.

And so we were without anybody and we have to have somebody.

Two came.

It was funny.

When we had taken Trac another Indo-Chinaman wanted to come. I liked him he looked like a Chinaman and he was sad. Alice Toklas went to telephone for his references. We had already decided about Trac but then when they come you talk to them and think some time you will have them.

The reference was some one whose mother an Englishwoman had had him in the South. He was the best Indo-Chinaman she had ever had and she had had many of them but he left and after he left others of his compatriots said that he was a communist. Well perhaps that might make a difference and perhaps it might not. Well anyway we had taken Trac. I like to keep things so we had kept his address. And now that Trac left we wrote to him that is Alice Toklas did.

We had his handwriting and he wrote back in that handwriting that he would like to come. Alice Toklas wrote back saying when he should come. He wrote back in another handwriting saying that he would like to bring his brother with him and would we send tickets for them to come. Alice Toklas wired them the money for the two tickets. They wired back that the name was another one and so they could not get the money. So she wired it again changing the name. They wired back the train they would come on and we went to meet them. There they were but neither of them was the other one. I said you see we know Chinamen. Chinamen do not look alike to us and neither of you are that one. Oh yes they said they were and they remembered all about coming. Well anyway they were there and that was something one said he could cook and he could, what a cook Nyen was, and the other one said he could do anything which he could not and soon the two of them were quarreling in high Chinese voices and it was a pleasure to hear them but it was not a pleasure for them.

Nyen one day talked to me in the garden, he said get rid of him,

I can do everything and you are not brothers I said, no he said I never saw him before I started on the train with him. But I said he is not the other one either. Oh no he said he is nothing. All right we said and we got rid of him. Not so easily but we did he had a high thin Chinese voice but we did. He had been in the ministry so he said he had the papers he had been a government clerk and he had never had done any work and the other one that was Nyen was drunk so he said and we would regret everything. It was true Nyen was drunk but he could and he would work and we still like him. Nobody can keep him but we still like him, and he stayed with us until we left, the thing is that Latin races are not drunk but in a village they are as much so as any other race is. And Nyen was. He was not Latin but he drank with the Frenchmen. Well anyway that was Nyen and I have just written a story about him called Butter Will Melt and the Atlantic Monthly thinks it is delectable and if it is it is because it was like his cooking.

We quieted down and I began working and naturally I began writing lectures to be given, as if we were going to go to America.

I began writing them and I had written several of them, and when I began writing then I gave up thinking about anything. What is the use of thinking about anything and then our ordinary way went on.

A little later Bernard Faÿ and Jay Laughlin came. We had been writing a great deal about everything and we knew nothing about Jay Laughlin but he came. Charles Henri Ford was there already but that was not interesting. One does like to know young men even though as soon as that they are not any longer young. As soon as one really knows them they are not any longer young.

We now have here in the kitchen a Polish-American girl. She says, Mrs. Simpson, I do like that name. She also says that Paris is an earthly paradise because you might say there are no black people there. There are black people all over Ohio she says, and you can be afraid of them.

Well anyhow Bernard Faÿ and Jay Laughlin came and stayed ten days with us and before it was over we knew that we were going to America and I was going to lecture.

I read the lectures to them. Bernard Faÿ lectures and he listened to them. Jay Laughlin listened to them too. In France everybody reads everything aloud. In America they talk over the radio but they do not read aloud.

In France they never think of giving it to you to read by yourself they read it to you out loud. I never could get either to hear or to read. I do not like it. I like to read with my eyes and not with my ears. I like to read inside and not outside. However if you are going to lecture and to write the lecture beforehand you have to read it out loud. And it is not possible not to write it beforehand because in that case it is not written and what is spoken is never written and as spoken it is not really interesting.

Bernard Faÿ was ready to help us about everything and we were going. We had no one to do anything and he would find that one and he did. He was found.

Jay Laughlin was to make a synopsis of the lectures and he wandered around. It was all a little worrying but it all was decided then.

The last thing was the war and now it was going to America, otherwise I had always been doing what I had been doing that is going and coming in a regular way. I like diversion but a diversion that is not a change. The war was a change and now we were really going going to America. As Tom Peters once wrote spring has come and nothing can stop it now, and we were going nothing could stop it now, and nothing did. We went. But first we had to prepare. After all it was thirty years since I had been and thirty years are not so much but after all they are thirty years.

We decided to have all our clothes made in Belley and we did. That is one of the nice things in France if you are anywhere near Lyon you can get very good clothes made. Near Paris is not so good, Paris is a capital and anywhere near it is suburban, but once you are away and anywhere near Lyon, there is good cooking and good dress-making. So we had all our clothes made in Belley. I went on writing my lectures, and everything was getting ready, I was not worried any more, worrying is an occupation part of the time but it can not be an occupation all the time.

Bernard Faÿ told me what would happen to us in America, we were not sure that he knew. After all you never do know what is going to happen anywhere. Carl Van Vechten knew we knew that after it happened because he had told Bennett Cerf before but then as I never know what is going to happen at any time, I never try to know what is going to happen at any time. Jay Laughlin could not make the synopsis but that was not discouraging. I had been having a pleasant correspondence with the Choate School for some time, they write very well there and Jay came from the Choate School and I was to go there. I was also to go to the Harvard Signet Club. Well anyway we were to make our expenses and there was a pleasant man from Columbia who also wrote and arranged, and from Amherst the president Mr. Stanley King wrote and it was getting pleasantly exciting, but it all was far away.

After all if you never have done it before.

The earth is covered all over with people but geniuses are very few. Interesting if true and it is true.

So we had everything made and we stayed at Bilignin until we left for Paris. And in Paris we only stayed a few weeks and Trac came back and Alice Toklas bought an umbrella, this was later left at a restaurant in Central California and after she wrote for it sent to San Francisco and by that time we had left America and it was sent to Carl Van Vechten in New York and just this week Eddie Wassermann has brought it over to her. She is sorry about it because she says if it had stayed over there it would have been something to go back to get. And in between she had bought another one just like it at any rate we both thought it was just like it but now the other one has come back we see that the handle is different. Also today we met just this afternoon New Year's Day the Indo-Chinaman who came when he said he was a brother and had a high voice, and he said he had not been a brother but now he would like to come back again. Perhaps he will come back again. And Trac has started an Indo-Chinese restaurant.

So we left for America.

CHAPTER IV

America

We were going to America. We had a special case made for the lectures, they make very good leather things in Belley, and this fitted exactly and we packed everything we could find to pack and Trac was more and more excited, Trac loves to travel and he always wants to go with any one who is going away. Finally we went and Trac took us down to the train. Of course I had many new shoes, I am very fond of new shoes, I do not care a great deal for new clothes, I have to let them hang a long time before I can wear them but I do like new shoes and at Chambery they made me a great many of them. I was wearing one of them and as I stepped up on the train the button snapped off. Oh Trac, I said. He said wait a minute and off he went and he came back with a button and a needle and a thread and he sewed the button on and there we were once more ready to go away. Three came to see us off, Trac and Georges Maratier and Jay. Jay that is Jay Laughlin is six foot and something very considerably something, next to him was Georges Maratier a stout middle-sized Frenchman and Trac a tiny Indo-Chinaman and there they stood one two three of them as we went away.

We were on the boat and it was different than it had been. Boat travel had changed but later I found that train traveling had not, they said over there it had but it had not. You were much more comfortable on a boat than you had been, you were not really more comfortable on trains than you had been. They use words like air-conditioned but it smells just about the same.

But first we were on the boat and we liked it. It was the beginning of traveling being a celebrity and all the privileges attached to that thing. Everybody had always been all right to us but this was being a different thing.

The French have a nice way of respecting anything that has to do with creating anything. Writers and painters and students and academicians are always nicely treated by every one.

Once I came back from the country and there was no place in the garage. A number of cars could not get in. But I must come in I said. Ah yes, said the man at the gate, let me see yes there is just one place, and that of course is yours, it is in a corner and there is no other car there except that of the academician. It was quite all right, the academician and the writer should of course be accommodated when the others were not. Any one could know that.

It is very pleasant that. They are not interested in you as they would be in America but they respect you and you and you have that as your right.

I have just been writing a long letter to the Kiddie explaining about class distinction and this is this.

That is what is nice about the French they are not foolish, they know that as there are occupations and habits and character and intelligence and personality and force and dullness that all that always does make a class, anything you do every day makes a class that will stay, and so they admit the class as a class but that has nothing to do with the being as a being they are only now finding it a little confusing but not really, they know really that a class is a class and why not. Every class has its charm and that can do no harm as long as every class has its charm, and anybody is occupied with their own being. Of course the French do believe in metier that is in knowing your occupation and so do I.

And so we were on the Champlain. Being a celebrity we paid less than the full price of a small room and we had a very luxurious one. That was a very pleasant thing. People always had been nice to me because I am pleasing but now this was going to be a different thing. We were on the Champlain and we were coming.

I used to say that was long ago in between I never had thought of going, I used to say that I would not go to America until I was a real lion a real celebrity at that time of course I did not really think I was going to be one. But now we were coming and I was going to be one.

In America everybody is but some are more than others. I was more than others.

Thirty years before being on a boat was being on a boat there were bunks and benches you slept in a bunk and you sat on a bench in the dining room or on a chair that was screwed down and now you slept in a bed and you sat in a chair at a small table just like any hotel. The trains have not changed, they make up the berths exactly as they did all the gestures were familiar but on a boat there is nothing unless you go and look for it that can remind you of the water. We liked it. That is to say we did like it.

Everybody talked to us and we talked to everybody but there were not many then one day a family talked to us a father and mother and little boy, we had noticed everybody and we had noticed them they were pleasing. They looked very prosperous, not very rich but rich and prosperous.

If you are used to living in France you are used to people not looking poor there are very few poor people in France but they do not look rich and prosperous, simply rich and prosperous, in America a great many do, this family did. He was a doctor in Newark and we talked a great deal together and how he had it I do not know but he had The Autobiography of Alice B. Toklas and we signed it for him. He was a throat specialist and I was beginning to have qualms, I had never bothered about my throat, in France when you say anything you say it very loudly and it is like standing, they can stand and stand but while they are standing they talk. In America they stand but as they stand they do not talk that is not much and never very loudly, but in France standing is always accompanied by violent conversation, and so I had never thought about my throat but now that I was going to lecture I at once was certain that my voice was failing me and meeting Doctor Wood was perfect because I could tell him all my symptoms and he could console me. He did but even so I knew it would happen and it did, and when I was to give my first lecture I had a cold and my throat was troubling me, he had said I might and we telephoned to him, hearing his voice was already soothing but having him come and feel my pulse was everything and he was there at the first lecture and so was my voice and we have never seen him again but we do not forget him. New York was coming nearer and we were nervous but not really nervous enough. You never are when a thing is really happening. If things happen all the time you are never nervous it is when they are not happening that you are nervous. I have just found a nice sentence in a detective novel. It says, when you have no job you get into the way of spending as much time anywhere as you can.

So the Statue of Liberty began and Staten Island. I did not remember Staten Island, it did look awfully pretty it was so white and green, and then there was the silhouette of New York. I did not care as much for that as I had for Staten Island, it was just as I remembered or as the photographs of it remembered it, it did not look very high. I was disappointed. And just then we saw the boat coming, and there was the Kiddie and that was comforting, there he was and there were a great many with him.

It was coming to be nearer but the Kiddie had been with us in France and so perhaps it was not yet America and after all America is where we had been born and had always been even though for thirty years we had not really touched it with our feet and hands and so it was as if we had come often but really it was not just the same. The Kiddie called and we called back and we were all waving and then he was on the boat and he said come. We always go when anybody says come. How can anybody say no. You either have to say no all the time or yes all the time. It is very rare to know when to say yes or no. So yes all the time or no all the time is easier. Anyway when the Kiddie or Carl say come we come and we came. Anyway they were all reporters and we sat down all of us together.

Everybody who has ever done anything has seen reporters. After all there always are newspapers and one has always read them. They are not interesting like books or detective stories but one does read them. You usually read the same one, you read it every day but it is the same one. Well anyway there we all were and it was very lively and I liked it, I always like talking and I like asking questions and I like to know who everybody is and where they come from. This first lot asked me questions later on I was able to ask them.

Then I went somewhere else on the boat, they were photographing me and then I was taken by the arm by some one else and they said I was broadcasting, and then some one else came later it turned out to be Jo Alsop, he has not yet read what I said about him in the Geographical History of America but that did come later anyway he said he really wanted to write something and could he come to the hotel, I said yes of course of course I said yes, and then we were landing. There we were it was all easy, Carl and Bennett Cerf were there and everything was easy and nothing was really happening and then we went out of the station into the street and then at last I knew something was happening something that I had not really known would happen we were here or we were there, anyway it was where we were and it was all right, we knew where we were it was all right but it was strange really strange.

After a while we were moving, we were in Bennett Cerf's car that was all the same just as any car had been but not those we saw, the taxis looked different and the trucks completely different. It was like the camouflage in the war. They all meant it to be the same but as it was done by different nations it was not the same.

During the war I was interested that the camouflage made by each nation was entirely different from the camouflage made by another nation but I had not expected the cabs and the trucks to look different in America from those in France after all there are lots of American cars in France but they did. The little lights on top made them look different and the shapes of the trucks were completely different and then the roadway seemed so different, that is what makes anything foreign, it looks just as you expect it to look but it does not look real. For a moment America that is the New York streets did not look real.

And then we were in the hotel. That was exciting because by that time we were excited and we knew that it was all exciting which it was. Everybody arranged everything. We had four rooms, we had only thought that we were going to have one, and there was no noise or anything but everybody was coming and there were a great many of them there. We did what they did. That is we did what they said we were to do. There were so many of them and it was no bother, they were friends and there were flowers and they were photographing and they were sitting down with us and then two of the reporters came in to talk some more. That was pleasant it always is pleasant to talk some more. Jo Alsop was one of them, he turned out to be a cousin of the Roosevelts but before that we had talked a great deal together. I told him everything and he said that I talked so clearly why did I not write clearly. I do write clearly. That is not the answer that is a fact. I think I write so clearly that I worry about it. Not really, but a fact. However I began to explain to him then and at intervals all that winter I explained it to him and then at last I wrote him letters about it explaining to him how explanations are clear but since no one to whom a thing is explained can connect the explanations with what is really clear, therefore clear explanations are not clear. Now this is a simple thing that anybody who has ever argued or quarreled knows perfectly well is a simple thing, only when they read it they do not understand it because they do not see that understanding and believing are not the same thing. Well anyway. I never did not like reporters, later on I almost preferred press photographers but all that will come later.

Then more came and more and more and then it was decided that I would be cinemaed and read to them, and we rehearsed that. I always do what they tell me to do and I did and our things were everywhere and perhaps some things disappeared and there was a great deal of apparatus, and finally we had dinner. We were not at all tired yet.

We had our first dinner in an American hotel and it did excite us because one of the things that had seemed most foreign to us although we did remember everything about it had been the hotel and restaurant menus the Kiddie had sent us to Bilignin after we had made up our mind to come. In France you talk about food but then you talk about food in any country. When the doughboys came to France they called it the eats and they did not like it. Nobody ever does.

Eating is a subject and a habit and the country in which one lives needs the kind of eating everybody eats in it. All of our French friends who had been in America had always said that the eating was inedible. Jeanne Cook had said that in all America there were no lettuces and no salads. Now of course there is nothing but, but that after all that is what America needs it needs to do all of it as long as it does it.

The country where we live in the summer is a French country where Brillat-Savarin was born and it is a country where they talk about eating. Every country talks about eating but in that country they talk about about talking about eating. Lamartine came from that country and Brillat-Savarin and Madame Recamier. They might all have liked eating, and perhaps the most charming book about eating that has been written is one written by Tendret, an extraordinarily charming one. Well anyway. They eat and they talk about eating while they eat and while they are talking about eating they eat. Madame Recamier had a niece and the niece married Monsieur Lenormant. Monsieur Lenormant had a son and his son had another one and then there was Henri Lenormant who several years before we went to America was a young medical student. His father was a famous surgeon, Henri is pleasant and talks a lot and likes to walk and he has begun to meet Americans in Paris, American girls who are studying there. His father had a patient who was still ill, an American and when he unexpectedly had to return to America before he was quite well, it was suggested that Henri as an embryo doctor should accompany him and stay in America just a week and then come back. He did, he flew to California he went to Cincinnati and to a number of other towns where the girls he had met had come from and he came back and we all asked him everything and he was interesting about it all and then we all said and the eating. Ah he said that is interesting. I liked the food over there but I know why Frenchmen do not like it. The food is moist. And so you cannot drink wine. Besides it is moist well it was too moist for me, I liked it but it was too moist for me. We all wanted to know more. Well he said in France a thing is cooked dry and there is a sauce made, it is cooked in butter and the butter cooks and the thing cooked by the butter is dry and then a sauce is made with cream or butter and that sauce is not very moist. No French sauce is really moist, it is not like American gravy which is moist.

So now here we were and he was right the food was moist. The oysters are moist well of course tomato juice and all that is but even American bread certainly hot breads are more moist than French bread.

We liked that moist food. I suppose since American climate and certainly American heated houses are dry food has to be moist. On the contrary in France where there is always lots of humidity food has to be dry. That is natural enough. But anything is if it is.

So then we began and we liked it. It was foreign but also it was

173

a memory and it was exciting. I then began to eat honeydew melon, most of the time I was in America I ate honeydew melon every morning and every evening and I ate oysters and I ate hot bread that is corn muffins, they were moist and I ate green apple pie and butterscotch pie, pumpkin pie not so good but twice superlative lemon pies, once at Katharine Cornell's and another time at the Hockaday School. Then they make much better cream mushroom soups in America than in Europe the best was at the Choate School, I will of course always tell everything we ate, but that first night it was exciting, and then as enough had happened we then went out walking.

We went out on the street and then we went up the avenues and then down them, and it was wonderful. Strangeness always goes off very quickly, that is one of the troubles with traveling but then the pleasure of looking if you like to look is always a pleasure. Alice Toklas began to complain she said why do they call Paris la ville lumière, she always prefers that anything should be American, I said because when they did there were more lights there than anywhere, you cannot blame them that they still think so although there are more lights here than anywhere. And there were. And more beautifully strung as lights than anywhere except in Spain, and we were walking along and talking and all of a sudden I noticed that Alice Toklas was looking queer and I said what is it and she said my knees are shaking and I said what is it and she said I just happened to see it, the side of the building. She just had happened to see it, and if you do just happen to see one of those buildings well her knees had not shaken not since the first bomb in 1915 had fallen in Paris so the sky-scrapers are something.

So then we went on and people said how do you do nicely and we said how do you do to them and we thought how pleasantly New York was like Bilignin where in the country everybody says how do you in passing the way they do in any country place in the country and then we saw a fruit store and we went in. How do you do Miss Stein, said the man, how do you do, I said, and how do you like it, he said, very much, I said, he said it must be pleasant coming back after thirty years, and I said it certainly was. He was so natural about knowing my name that it was not surprising and yet we had not expected anything like that to happen. If anything is natural enough it is not surprising and then we went out again on an avenue and the elevated railroad looked just like it had ever so long ago and then we saw an electric sign moving around a building and it said Gertrude Stein has come and that was upsetting. Anybody saying how do you do to you and knowing your name may be upsetting but on the whole it is natural enough but to suddenly see your name is always upsetting. Of course it has happened to me pretty often and I like it to happen just as often but always it does give me a little shock of recognition and non-recognition. It is one of the things most worrying in the subject of identity.

Well anyway we went home to the hotel as the English say the Americans say and so we did always come to say and we went to bed and so after the thirty years we went to sleep in beds in a hotel in America. It was pleasing.

The next day was a different thing everything was happening and nothing was as strange as it had been, we could see it and we were looking but it would never be again what yesterday had been.

Lecturing was to begin. Carl Van Vechten had arranged that I was to give one a little privately so as to get used to everything. Thank him.

And then Potter of the university extension of Columbia came to see me and he was a nice man. I used to be so pleased with the author of the Girl Of The Limberlost, Gene Stratton Porter, because she spoke of the men everybody met in her books and said, Mike O'Halloran said they are such nice men. That is really the difference between America and Europe, all the men in America are such nice men, they always do everything, they do. Everybody in Europe knows that about Americans. In England they say American men are so attentive, well anyway Potter came. He had been the first person to ask me to lecture, and this was the university extension of Columbia. We had had a pleasant correspondence and there were to be four lectures and he had described the audience as being a few hundred and after the private lecture this was to be my first one.

He was a nice man. We liked him.

He said he was pleased that everybody now that everybody had been so excited at my coming everybody was coming to hear me lecture and that there would be many over a thousand in the audience. I lost everything, I was excited and I said but in that case I would not come. What do you mean, he said, well, I said, I have written these lectures they are hard lectures to read and it will be hard to listen to them, anybody not used to lecturing cannot hold the attention of more than a roomful of that I was certain and I certainly was not going to read a difficult lecture to more than a thousand of them, you said that there would be no more than five hundred and if there are more than that I will not come. But what can I do, said Potter. I do not know anything about that, I said, but if there are more than five hundred there I will not come. Does she mean it, said he perplexedly to Alice Toklas, If she says so, said Alice Toklas, she probably will not come. What can I do, said Potter, I do not know, I said, but I am definitely not going to read a difficult lecture to more than five hundred people, it cannot be done, I said. Well, he said and he was a nice man and he left. Of course I was awfully upset I was to speak the next evening before two hundred and that was bad enough. Carl Van Vechten had arranged all that but here was all this trouble and then I was not accustomed to heated apartments, we heat very sparingly in Paris and besides Paris is moist, the food is dry and the air is moist and in New York the food was moist and the air was dry, so gradually I was certain that there was something the matter with my throat and I would not be able to speak anywhere. New York was nice but I was not accustomed to decisions if you lead a quiet life you talk about decisions but you do not really make them and here we were, and everything was moving. We were high up not as high as we might have been, we were much higher later and nothing was strange any more but it was very exciting, letters and telephones and everything. Anyway before we went to bed Potter telegraphed, everything arranged I have done the impossible sleep peacefully. And that was over. Nothing is immediately over with me but that was over.

Carl Van Vechten said that they had asked him to introduce me for the first lecture and he did not think I would care to be introduced and I said I would not. And I could refuse him because that would be all right and if I refused him then I could never of course accept any one. Besides it was silly everybody knew who I was if not why did they come and why should I sit and get nervous while somebody else was talking. So it was decided from then on that there would be no introduction nobody on the platform a table for me to lean on and five hundred to listen.

But my throat was not any better and so we telephoned to the nice doctor we had met on the Champlain and he came and he said there was nothing the matter, of course there was nothing the matter but it was a pleasure when he said there was nothing the matter and he gave me something and it was a comfort and I was almost ready to begin lecturing. Many people say you go on being afraid when you are alone on the platform but after the first one I never was again. Not at all.

Much later on very much later on when I spoke at the Dutch Treat Club and there I had to be introduced because somebody had to be funny, you always have to be when there are that many men and the introducer has to be so as to be sure that somebody will be funny. During lunch I was sitting next to the introducer and to my astonishment he was eating nothing and was pale and his hands were shaking. What is it. I am nervous, he said. I said, you are making believe being nervous in order to be effective, I said, aren't you. I dont know he said. Are you always like this, I said, always he said and how long have you been doing it, for three years once a month, he said. Dear me, I said.

I still do not know whether he really was nervous or not anyway I never was except the first time. After all once you know an audience is an audience why should it make any difference. I suppose I in that respect was like my aunt Fanny I count by one one one, and since that is what an audience is and I am never afraid of one unless he or she does something unexpected and sudden I am never afraid of them, and that is what an audience never does it never does anything unexpected or sudden so if one has not a sensitiveness to numbers and naturally counts by one one one then there is no trouble in talking to them.

We settled down to be in New York for a month and lecture with a few excursions out. We settled down to be accustomed to it. And we were accustomed to it. It was not as if we had always been there but we were getting accustomed to it. It never became as if we had always been there. Everybody speaking to you everybody knowing you, everybody in a hotel or restaurant noticing you everybody asking you to write your name for them that was not the strangest thing. The strangest things were the streets, they were American streets, they really were, the people were American people but that was not such a difficult thing.

I have always been accustomed to talking to anybody and to have anybody talk to you, it always happened in America when I was there and before I came over here and it has always happened over here and then went on over there, more of them of course but once you admit adding what is the difference to your feeling. None.

Just yesterday I went to the studio of a man whom I had known as a street acquaintance for almost three years his name is Benno.

178

He is an American that is to say yes he is an American, he has been a sailor for twelve years ever since he was fifteen and always under the American flag he was a real sailor and gentle.

He is a painter and he had always asked me to come. I had seen some of his things at the surindependent and I was interested in them and he told me Picasso was interested in him really interested and I went on meeting him from time to time on the street and talking to him. Then one evening just a few days ago there were two of them the other one was a young doctor and he was shy and I said would they come in, Benno came in and the other one was sad but he had to think about having met me and so he could not come in, that is what Benno said after he came in. Then I said again I would go to see him but I did not and then some time again and we met again and I invited him to come in and he came and that time we made an appointment to go to see him and we went, he was living up several flights of stairs and the stairs were open and I never like that so he came down and he said yes that was one of the things that really stopped him from going on being a sailor for many years he knew nothing about that and when he did know about that he began not to be a sailor any more he had once again gone on a scow but that was all now.

He had a little bit of a studio with a great many paintings in it and we looked at all of them it was astonishing, he was the only one who ever understood what Picasso was doing. Sometimes well I am sure when everybody is dead lots of his will be sold as Picassos. Not that he copied them not at all but he realized them and sometimes completed and balanced them and he made them from within.

I was very much interested in this thing. He said that a great many artists were buying his things and I understood that thing, he made it clearer than Picasso could to them this thing this writing which is the painting everybody is now doing. I do not mean the writing of their poetry but the writing in their painting, it is once more the Oriental thing introducing into the Western the later painting of Picasso is writing, just as my middle writing was painting and that is all reasonable enough and anybody looking at Benno's painting can understand this thing. He told me that Picasso had written a recommendation for him for the Guggenheim Prize but he had not got it. I was surprised, I knew that they never gave it to any writer I recommended but I was surprised that they did not give it to a painter Picasso recommended, Alice Toklas says that I am easily surprised but I was surprised. Well anyway Benno is interesting, he had been painting for five years and always before that when he was being a sailor and he is interesting.

And so meeting everybody on the streets of New York that is they all knowing us was not troubling. I often wonder about the world being covered all over with people. A young Benedictine father in Hautecombe has just written a book about a sixteenth-century abbé of Hautecombe. I read the manuscript when I was in Bilignin and he says in it that the first abbey of Hautecombe was built at that time and on a much frequented road. I asked everybody what in the fifteenth century would have been a much frequented road, would it mean that somebody passed at least once a day, they all seemed to think that frequented would mean more often. It is hard to know just what frequented does mean, that made me interested and I was interested in Prokosch's book The Asiatics, he makes his own kind of way of the world being full of people and they are going about very much as they did when a road was frequented in any period. Prokosch has done it and I think it is very interesting.

The way the people moved on those broad side-walks in New York was very different from the way they move in Paris and I liked to go with them, sometimes some one would stop me to speak and tell me something, I always like that, and always they said everybody said there is Gertrude Stein and Alice Toklas always heard it, I do not always hear it so well and we liked it. When Carl Van Vechten was with us in Bilignin before we left for America one day Alice asked him Carl will there be any one over there who will say there goes Gertrude Stein I have heard of their doing that and I would love it to happen. Oh yes, said Carl looking at Mark Lutz, I think it will happen. You mean, Alice asked him, you will hire some small boys to do it so as to give me the pleasure of it. Perhaps, said Carl, we will not have to hire them. Later on he teased Alice Toklas about this thing.

So then there we were and we were liking it lecturing and everything. Almost always liking it very very much. I was always eating honeydew melons and oysters and an egg and green apple pie before lecturing, and I was enjoying everything. We went to Princeton that was the first time we went away from New York and the first experience with a college audience. I liked it and I liked meeting them afterwards. The head of the English department had arranged everything. When we got there he was laughing. I said, what is it. Well, he said, I think it is a great joke. You will not allow more than five hundred in the audience. No, I said, and I began to explain to him why not. Yes yes he said but the joke is that usually in university lecturing I have to get an audience for the lecturer so that he will not mind there not being many present when he is lecturing. I go around and I persuade the students after all they hear enough of lecturing and I persuade them to come and at last I get sometimes as many as two hundred to come and you say you will not have more than five hundred and to keep it down to five hundred I have had an awful time, I think it is a great joke he said. And it was but all the same I was very solemn about this thing.

I like college audiences they inevitably are more flattering.

It was in going to Princeton that I found that train traveling was as bad as it had been thirty years before it had not changed, we had to wait and the train was late and coming back it was worse. I said if we had only known, anybody in Princeton would have come in an automobile and they or somebody else would have taken us home again, after that they always did everybody always did, and we never got into a train again, well yes once in a while but not often.

We were in New York a month and during that time went to Philadelphia, Chicago, Cambridge and Vassar. In going to Philadelphia we first saw again the wooden houses the American wooden houses and American graveyards and American country. We went to Philadelphia and Bryn Mawr and we stayed at Bryn Mawr. The male professors were bearded, one of them promised me a photograph of the most interesting wooden house we saw there but he never sent it. In America if they do not do it right away they do not do it at all in France they very often seem not to be going to do it at all but if it has ever really been proposed at all sometimes it really is done. No American ever expects it to be done but really sometimes it is done.

The wooden houses of America excited me as nothing else in America excited me, the skyscrapers and the streets of course and everybody knowing you of course but not like the wooden houses everywhere. I never stopped being excited by the wooden houses everywhere. I liked them all. Almost best I liked those near the railway stations old ones not very old once but still old ones with long flat wooden surfaces, painted sometimes not and many near automobile dumps. I liked them all. I do like a flat surface that is the reason I like pictures and do not like sculpture and I like paint even if it is not painted and wood painted or not painted has the color of paint and it takes paint so much better than plaster. In France and in Spain I like barracks because they have so much flat surface but almost I liked best American wooden houses and there are so many of them an endless number of them and endless varieties in them. It is what in America is very different, each one has something and well taken care of or neglect helps them, helps

182

them to be themselves each one of them. Nobody could get tired of them and then the windows they put in. That is one thing any American can do he can put windows in a building and wherever they are they are interesting. Windows in a building are the most interesting thing in America. It is hard to remember them because they are so interesting. Every wooden house has windows and the windows are put in in a way that is interesting. Of course the skyscrapers it is a wrong name because in America there is no sky there is air but no sky of course that has a lot to do with why there really is no painting in America no real painting but it is not necessary when there are houses and windows and air. Less and less there are curtains and shutters on the windows bye and bye there are not shutters and no curtains at all and that worried me and I asked everybody about that. But the reason is easy enough. Everybody in America is nice and everybody is honest except those who want to break in. If they want to break in shutters will not stop them so why have them and other people looking in, well as everybody is a public something and anybody can know anything about any one and can know any one then why shut the shutters and the curtains and keep any one from seeing, they all know what they are going to see so why look. I gradually began to realize all this.

It is a funny thing when the Americans first had their meeting place on the Raspail and they left it all open that is they never closed the shutters or the windows and everybody looked in and everybody was uncomfortable in looking uncomfortable for themselves and for them but now a funny thing has happened. As I wander around in the evening with Basket I notice that shutters are much less shut in Paris than they were. Lots of apartments never shut their shutters. They would never have done that before. Perhaps it is because there is less money and there are less servants, perhaps they are affected by seeing no shutters and no shutters shut in American movies. Why it is I do not know but I do know that where all Paris always shut its shutters as soon as the daylight failed they now do not that is a great many of them do not shut their shutters. They still have shutters but they do not shut them. Will they like the Americans come not to have them. I am wondering. Nothing changes but just the same Paris shutters are now more open at night than shut and when I began to notice it I found it astonishing.

So we went to Philadelphia and Byrn Mawr and we went on liking everything.

When we were at Bryn Mawr we were given Miss Thomas' old room in the Deanery. And that was surprising not that we were given it but that it was as it was. That and the railroads were still where they were. They even had the photographs of the same works of art that we used to have in our rooms in college in ninety-seven. It was exciting. Clive Bell used to be funny when he objected that Roger Fry and Mrs. Bell always went to see capital works of art. In those days he was amusing. Well in the Dean's room all the photographs of the works of art were of capital works of art and of course capital works of art were what we used to have as photographs then. I wonder if anybody still does in their college rooms. As a matter of fact we did not go into any of them.

While we were in Philadelphia and at Bryn Mawr there was some disturbance, we had too many telegrams and telephones and it all had to do with the only time we did something we should not do.

Carl Van Vechten told us when we first came, you are not likely to make any mistake but if you are ever in doubt ask me before you begin. Which is what we should have done.

We had refused everything except what we were really doing that is lecturing and having a pleasant time.

Some one had asked us to do something that seemed all right it had to do with the opera and singing we were not to sing I was just to tell them about the opera and it was a charity and they wanted to pay us a good sum. It was suggested in such a way that we did not quite say no we said yes and we imagined nothing would happen and anyway no confirmation had come that the date was set and then we went to Philadelphia and Bryn Mawr. It seems that a date had been set that is there had been a description of what I was to do in the paper again and again and of course and that was difficult for any one to really think we did not read the papers not very much any way. I had been used to reading the New York Herald ever since I had been in Paris, I read it in bed and I know where everything is in its pages and there is just enough there so that a war or a revolution or a flood or a crime if it is a very important one a kidnapping if it is very important one or anything local in Paris very exciting or very usual does not escape one but after once or twice looking at all the pages there were that made a New York paper I gave it up and did not look at them. I decided nothing really very exciting would happen before we were back in Paris again and really in those seven months except the Lindbergh trial and that every one told you all the detail nothing did happen that made any difference whether we knew it or not and so all that had been announced we had not seen and naturally nobody in New York would think of that even Carl Van Vechten who knows our ways was a little surprised that we had not known anything and so we were astonished when the Bryn Mawr Deanery was worried lest we should be disturbed or lest they should be disturbed and they were they began to ring up during the night and said that they were sending two secretaries to tell us more about it. There was also a clerk in the telegraph office who said he could quiet everything but would we send him our autograph we said we would send even a letter of thanks if he could quiet everybody. There was even some talk of having a policeman stationed so that no one would be disturbed, anyway we finally said we would do the best we could. We did get there for a few minutes and then we left and we left everything to charity and then we left. I am afraid it was a racket, said Carl Van Vechten. There was only one other time that we did anything that should not have been done. Bennett Cerf was giving us a pleasant party and everything went off nicely and we liked everything and everybody liked everything and then suddenly there was a very drunken young man who began to kneel on the floor and kiss the hem of one's gown, so he said and they all said who is that, who asked him to come. Alice Toklas said she had asked him that Bennett had said ask any one you like and he had come and wanted to see us and we were busy and she had said come to the party and he had come. Carl Van Vechten said reflectively if you are not perfectly certain you had better always ring up and ask me. But the thing that was really extraordinary was that with all the publicity and the talking to every one and going in anybody's automobile and my wandering around the streets in any town we never had anything unpleasant happen and no letters from cranks or crazy people or anything. Everybody was perfectly nice and friendly and nobody was insistent or troublesome not anybody. I happened to speak of this last year in London in talking to Lord Berners and he said an interesting thing. He said cranks and abusive people never bother writers or artists however queer or well-known they are, people who are a little off their head are only attracted by something official. As a musician and writer Gerald Berners is very well known and he has lots of fan letters but nothing abusive or troublesome while as a member not very active of the House of Lords he does get crank letters quite often. He says and I imagine that is true once he has said it that is the nice thing about saying a thing if it is really said it is true, it is true that there has to be something official to bring out the craziness of a crank which is a very interesting thing about officialdom, and if one has never even been a member of any committee or anything and is just known for writing and reading well then a great deal may happen to one but not that kind of thing, as a matter of fact nothing did happen that was unpleasant not one single thing.

We went to Cambridge over night and I spoke in Radcliffe and at the Signet Club at Harvard. It was funny about Cambridge it was the one place where there was nothing that I recognized nothing. Considering that I had spent four years there it was sufficiently astonishing that nothing was there that I remembered nothing at all. New York Washington East Oakland Baltimore San Francisco were just about as they were they were changed of course but I could find my way there anywhere but Cambridge not at all. I did not go back again perhaps I might have begun again but that day Cambridge was so different that it was as if I had never been there there was nothing there that had any relation to any place that had been there. I lost Cambridge then and there. That is funny.

In between everything I wandered around the streets of New York.

The ten cent stores did disappoint me but the nut stores not. In the ten cent stores there was nothing that I wanted and what was there was was not there for ten cents. It was a disappointment, I had looked forward to it looked forward to going in and buying at a ten cent store. Alice Toklas says they were not a disappointment but nothing in America was a disappointment to her but they were really they were. But the nut stores I had first known of their existence accidentally from Carl Van Vechten when he happened to say that he one day met Henry McBride as Henry was coming out and Carl was going into a nut store. What is that we had asked excitedly what is a nut store. Then later when he was back in New York he did not forget to send us an ad of a nut store and now here we were and there they were. I was always looking into them.

I also lectured in Brooklyn and that was interesting it was a nice audience but it was not because of that but because I met Marianne Moore and because an attentive young man accidentally

187

closed the door on my thumb and we had to go into a drug store to have it fixed. It was dirty the drug store, one of the few things really dirty in America are the drug stores but the people in them sitting up and eating and drinking milk and coffee that part of the drug store was clean that fascinated me. After that I was always going in to buy a detective novel just to watch the people sitting on the stools. It was like a piece of provincial life in a real city. The people sitting on the stools and eating in the drug store all looked and acted as if they lived in a small country town. You could not imagine them ever being out in the streets of New York, nor the drug store itself being in New York. I never had enough of going into them.

Then we began to have trouble with Chicago, not with the city but with the arrangements for lecturing. There is always war and peace anywhere and we always have a good deal of both of these things and we proceeded to have them. You have to have peace after war and you have to have war after peace and then there is the tug of war when both sides pull and any side starts then the other side goes, there was a good deal of Chicago I like Chicago. I liked Texas and Chicago. Chicago because we had a good deal of trouble with it and Texas because we had none.

We did have trouble with Chicago.

Muriel Draper has just been here she has been in Spain and we talked about all that and we said she said that and I said that and that was that and then we said yes it is good to look at and New York and Chicago are good to look at and Oklahoma and we said that.

Yes Chicago too was good to look at but at that time we did not know that. We were having trouble.

We had said that I would lecture in a university any university for one hundred dollars and mostly well really gradually I liked that best. And in Chicago nobody in the university had asked me but still I had been asked. It turned out that some students were arranging it and they were to charge a dollar apiece for anybody and of course I did not want that. If I had wanted that everything would have been different and I did not want that. So the trouble began. Everywhere else it had all been easy but here the trouble began. For the first time they were making arrangements that did not please me and I was beginning to say so, and the long distance telephoning that we had heard that everybody did began.

Some one has just sent me a Camel pen from America, you fill it with water and it writes ink. But you have to press hard on it to make it write ink if you fill it with water and as I like to press lightly when I write I began to fill it with ink. Well yes ink is better than water. So we went on struggling. I said I would not go unless they arranged it the way we wanted it and there we were.

I had not seen the opera played naturally not because we were not here and now they were to give ten days of it in Chicago. They telephoned to us would we go but then how could we go. We wanted to go but how could we go it would take too long. We always think that everything takes long. Well it does.

If things do not take long it makes life too short.

They telephoned there is plenty of time if you come by airplane. Of course we could not do that we telephoned back, why not, they said, because we never have we said, we will pay for your trip the two of you forward and back they said, we want to see the opera we said but we are afraid. Carl Van Vechten was there while all this was going on, what is it, we explained, oh nonsense he said of course you will fly, we telephoned back if Carl Van Vechten can go with us we will fly, all right they telephoned back we will pay for the three of you. All right we said and we had to do it. Everybody is afraid but some are more afraid than others. Everything can scare me but most of the things that are frightening are things that I can do without and really mostly unless they happen to come unexpectedly do not frighten me. I was much more easily frightened before the war. Since the war nothing is so really frightening not the dark nor alone in a room or anything on a road or a dog or a moon but two things yes, indigestion and high places they are frightening. One well one always hopes that that will not happen but high places well there is nothing to do about them. I thought after all our airplaning and being on top of high buildings it could not happen again but it does. I told all this to Carl and he said I am coming and so we did not think about it again. We went on doing what we were doing and then one day we were to meet Carl and fly and we did very high. It was nice. I know of nothing more pleasing more soothing more beguiling than the slow hum of the mounting. I had never even seen an airplane near before not near enough to know how one got in and there we were in. That is one of the nice things about never going to the movies there are so many surprises. Of course you remember something, two little terriers that belong to Georges Maratier began fighting their servant had been visiting her uncle who is our concierge and the two of them a wire-haired and a black Scottie both females they should not but they do were holding each other in a terrifying embrace. The girl came and called me, people always think that I can do something, any way as I went out I always go out when I am called I remembered I had never been near a dog fight before I remembered in the books you pour water on them so I called for cold water in a basin and poured it on them and it separated them. The white one was terribly bitten. Reading does not destroy surprise it is all a surprise that it happens as they say it will happen. But about the airplane we had known nothing and it was an extraordinarily natural and pleasant thing much more simple and natural than anything even than walking, perhaps as natural as talking but certainly more natural than doing any other thing. And so we liked it and whenever we could we did it. They are now beginning to suppress the noise and that is a pity, it will be too bad if they can have conversation, it will be a pity.

I was not really surprised that being high was not frightening.

The inside of the plane that is the pilots and the stewardess were more like the efficiency of war than either the American or French army had been. That was interesting. Being ready for war makes you more war-like than being in a war. I liked them in their uniform with their pistols on and coming in and out. They did come in and out and very often. The stewardess came too very often. They were more like the thing we had heard about than anything we had seen. They did come in and out and they looked as if it was necessary to come in and out very often.

It was then in a kind of way that I really began to know what the ground looked like. Quarter sections make a picture and going over America like that made any one know why the post-cubist painting was what it was. The wandering line of Masson was there the mixed line of Picasso coming and coming again and following itself into a beginning was there, the simple solution of Braque was there and I suppose Leger might be there but I did not see it not over there. Particularly the track of a wagon making a perfect circle and then going back to the corner from where they had come and later in the South as finally we went everywhere by air and always wanted the front seat so I could look down and what is the use, the earth does look like that and even if none of them had seen it and they had not very likely had not but since every one was going to see it they had to see it like that.

I was bothered as to why being up so high nothing happened. If you go up into the mountains not very high everything happens, you feel funny even if you are not afraid because being so high makes you feel high but being really high as high as you can be does not make you feel high. And at once I knew and it was true that the air below is solid when you are above it, it is as solid as water. If you are on something solider next to it then it is not solid at all, but if you are directly above it and not looking forward at it then it is solid as solid as water and so there is no fear. And then after all everybody knows that somebody has fallen from any cliff and not been killed so anybody can remember that but anybody falling from the air is killed so no one can remember that. Anyway I was not at all afraid. I thought I would never be afraid again in the hills and going around a curve when there seems to be nothing below but I am, I was again last summer, perhaps not quite so much but enough. But in an airplane never. It was nice going from Paris to London over France and England but not so wonderful as America, no one can be grateful enough that there were quarter sections when they first made the country, it makes a regular division that makes everything clearer. I did want to write a play about the States the way I did about the Saints. I have always wanted to write about how one state differs from another. It is so strange that the lines are ruled lines on paper, I never can stop having pleasure in the way the ruled lines separate one state from another. Ohio from Indiana Kansas from Nebraska Tennessee from Alabama, it always gives me a shock of pleasure the American map and its straight lines and compare it to any other with the way they go all over nothing neat and clean like the maps of America. Well that is the way the earth looked to me as we flew to Chicago. They all came and talked to me the pilots and the stewardesses and then I went into the pilot place and talked to them and I sat down in one of their chairs and made the wheel move a little and it was all a pleasant matter but most of all the looking down and finding it a real America. Straight lines and quarter sections, and the mountain lines in Pennsylvania very straight lines, it made it right that I had always been with cubism and everything that followed after.

Being above the clouds was nice and something but not so interesting as seeing everything below.

And so we came down into Chicago, and after that going up and down was everything, I like waiting in an airplane field the wind is always blowing, it may not blow any where else but it always does blow there.

So we landed in Chicago and there were many there to meet us, and naturally I had to tell them all about it, somebody always took me away and there were always lots of them there, and I always have something to say and I like to say anything I say.

All right anyway Fanny Butcher then drove me away with her and we talked everything over not airplanes or the opera but the arrangements that were being a bother.

I always remember the day that Fanny Butcher and Alice Roullier came to see us in Bilignin, some days rain more than other days, but that day rained the most of any day. I remembered that Fanny Butcher's eyes were brown, perhaps they are not, and I remembered her so well but when I saw her well I never do remember but I liked her even better. It is awfully hard to remember.

And I was beginning to know a little what an American city looked like and Chicago did look like that but it did look larger than that it looked more like an American city that I could remember. Later on when we came back again and then later on when later on we came and lived there for two weeks and I had a car it came to be more the one I can remember.

So we went and rested and then we went to hear the opera. I was less excited about that than I had expected to be. It was my opera but it was so far away.

When I am writing a play I am writing one now I am writing about Daniel Webster, whenever I write a play it is a play because it is a thing I do not see but it is a thing somebody can see that is what makes a play to me. When I see a thing it is not a play to me because the minute I see it it ceases to be a play for me, but when I write something that somebody else can see then it is a play for me. When I write other things not plays it is something that I can see and seeing it is inside of me but when I write a play then it is something that is inside of me but if I could see it then it would not be. And so I do write a lot of plays and they are things for somebody to see and somebody does see them, sometimes there will be lots more of them given. They are doing one in London Lord Berners has put music to it and Pépé the little Mexican dog is going to be on the stage not in person of course but a little girl to play him but even the littlest little girl is going to be a very large little Mexican. Alice Toklas wanted them to put a little one on wires little like the real Pépé but they said it had to be a little girl. Basket did not mind he might perhaps if he saw him. As yet they have not yet done any of mine without music to help them. They could though and it would be interesting but no one has yet. I always had a feeling that Maurice Grosser might but then he wants to be a painter and that is a pity and besides anyway probably nobody would let him.

But to come back to my seeing the opera Four Saints In Three Acts and knowing what plays are.

One of the things that happened at the end of the nineteenth century was that nobody knew the difference between a novel and a play and now the movies have helped them not to know but although there is none there really is and I know there is and that is the reason I write plays and not novels. An autobiography is not a novel no indeed it is not a novel.

The play began, we were on time and the play began but it was too far away but it did begin. I liked looking at it and I liked hearing. Mrs Goodspeed had thought we might be too far away and so she had gotten us seats nearer. We took these later and there we were nearer. That was when the second act began. It looked very lovely and the movement was everything they moved and did nothing, that is what a saint or a doughboy should do they should do nothing. they should move some and they did move some and they did nothing it was very satisfying.

Later on when I saw them playing football they did the same thing they moved some and they did nothing after all it is that that is most interesting. But that was later now we were still in Chicago.

After it was over we went behind and I signed photographs for each one of them and Saint Theresa was very lovely. Later on much later on when we were leaving America some one asked for me on the telephone and when I said who is it, a voice answered Saint Theresa, and that was my farewell to America, it was she and a delightful voice and she was Saint Theresa for herself and for us. She explained that to me they all did they all said all the words were such natural words to say.

So we flew back again to New York, Carl was not then with us but it was all right, flying was now a natural thing for us to be doing.

So we came back to New York and home to the hotel it was the Algonquin and now perhaps it is his son because it is the same name the one whose wife has been killed in the bathroom I hope it is not his son. George the head-waiter who was a Greek and a charming one one might have known him without going to America but Mrs. Case who said when Alice Toklas lost her little book with all the dates for lecturing in it, Carl had told her she had better have several copies and anyway she never did have any other well anyway it was gone and she was very troubled and fussed and Mrs. Case said why are you fussed it will come back again, it did, we never are here, and they never were there and we never were there and the little book came back again.

In New York that time Alfred Harcourt asked us to come and week end with them and to go and see the Yale Dartmouth football game.

Two things are always the same the dance and war. One might say anything is the same but the dance and war are particularly the same because one can see them. That is what they are for that any one living then can look at them. And games do do both they do the dance and war bull-fighting and football playing, it is the dance and war anything anybody can see by looking is the dance and war. That is the reason that plays are that, they are the thing anybody can see by looking. Other things are what goes on without everybody seeing, that is why novels are not plays well anyway.

That is the reason why the only plays that are plays from the nineteenth century are Gilbert and Sullivan. In America they want to make everything something anybody can see by looking. That is very interesting, that is the reason there are no fences in between no walls to hide anything no curtains to cover anything and the cinema that can make anything be anything anybody can see by looking. That is the way it is. Well anyway we liked going with Harcourt to see the football game. First we drove all through New England not all through later on we drove through a great deal more of it but it was our first driving through it in a motor-car.

I was fascinated with the way everybody did what they should. When I first began driving a car myself in Chicago and in California I was surprised at the slowness of the driving, in France you drive much faster, you are supposed not to have accidents but you drive as fast as you like and in America you drive very slowly forty-five miles an hour is slow, and when lights tell you to stop they all stop and they never pass each other going up a hill or around a curve and yet so many get hurt. It was a puzzle to me.

I was first struck with all this that first day.

In France you drive fifty-five or sixty miles an hour all the time, I am a very cautious driver from the standpoint of my French friends but I often do and why not, not very often does anybody get killed and in America everybody obeying the law and everybody driving slowly a great many get killed it was a puzzle to me.

And then there were all those wooden houses they were not a puzzle to me they were a continuous pleasure to me.

That driving so slowly in America is something. During the war Clemenceau remarked that one of the things that was most striking was the way the nations were not at all as they were supposed to be, the Englishman was noted for his calm and the English soldiers tended more to be hysterical than any other one, the

196

Americans were supposed to be so quick and they were so slow, the French were supposed to be so gay and they were so solemn. A young French soldier who was one of those who taught the American soldiers how to use the French mitrailleuse told me that to his surprise the Americans understood very quickly the mechanics of the gun but their physical reaction in action was very slow very much slower than the French one, consequently it took more Americans to do anything than it did Frenchmen and so of course it was done less quickly. He also told a story of when he posted the Americans as sentry, he told them that when they heard a sound like quack quack it was not a duck it was a German and he said he told them this and they always understood and then when it was the German they did not disappear quickly enough and the German got them.

Well anyway when we were there at the ball-ground everything was orderly and we went in. I had not been inside a stadium since the days of bull-fighting in Spain before and during the war, and getting in while a crowd is getting in is always exciting in an outside place more than in an inside place besides there are so many more of them. We were seated on the Dartmouth side because Harcourt is a Dartmouth man. All I knew about Dartmouth was that Bravig Imbs had written a book called The Professor's Wife and he had told us about Dartmouth then. Later on they asked us to come but by that time it was too late and it could not be arranged but we did see them playing football not very well it must be said not very well.

But the preparation was interesting that they did well. The players were longer and thinner than I remembered them, both sides were, they did not seem to have such bulky clothing on them, they seem to move more. But there are two things about football that anybody can like. They live by numbers, numbers are everything to them and their preparation is like any savage dancing, they do what red Indians do when they are dancing and their movement is angular like the red Indians move. When they lean over and when they are on their hands and feet and when they are squatting they are like an Indian dance. The Russians squat and jump too but it looks different, art is inevitable everybody is as their air and land is everybody is as their food and weather is and the Americans and the red Indians had the same so how could they not be the same how could they not, the country is large but somehow it is the same if it were not somehow the same it would not remain our country and that would be a shame. I like it as it is.

As I say it was not a very exciting game and those around us came to know that I was there, a very little boy came from somewhere and he asked me to write my name, I did. And then from everywhere came programs and would I write my name and then there was a man he was very drunk and his wife was coaxing him along I suppose it was his wife and anyway she was coaxing him along and he said he had to see me he just had to see me and I just had to see him, I did see him and he did see me, and then his wife kept coaxing him and slowly he went away. Alfred Harcourt had not seen it all before and he said we had better go before there was any more but there never was anything that was a bother and so we went and drove back again and again through all that country that was the country I had known.

And we were always in New York and I was always walking and I liked best Seventh Avenue, I bought a stylograph there for a dollar, it is a good one, I bought an American clock that was not so good but the stylo is an excellent one. I talked over the radio once, they never seem to want to pay you for doing that unless it is advertising, that seemed to us a very strange thing, so I talked once naturally nobody wanted to pay me for advertising, there is something very funny about that. I have been thinking a lot about it lately. In France before there was a republic all France's great writers were members of the Academy, since the republic not one. Before there was a republic all the great buildings were built by the great architects all the great painters painted the ruling people since the republic not one. It is a very funny thing.

We came to talk about that day before yesterday Jean Saint Pierre and I. Jean is the eldest son of the notary at Belley who did everything for us when we needed him, and now he is dead and has left a large family behind him and Jean is the eldest one he is now twenty-two. He has passed his law examinations and is now deciding to remain in the army instead of going on with the law, he does not know yet but he thinks so, and this is the first time we have seen him in Paris and we were glad to see him, he was on his way from La Fleche to Belley. And we talked a great deal in the little time we saw him. We always talk about a generation and what that generation is doing, he says every generation that is every two years is completely a different thing now everything is so confused and his youngest brother seventeen years old is a complete enigma to him. I told him about my worry about republics. He said yes, he said his mother was what is common in France a passionate republican and she too was beginning to have doubts and still why doubt anything, a republic is certain to end in a dictatorship and a kingdom and a kingdom is sure to end in a republic and again and again. Why said Jean should one doubt anything one generation and there is one every two years sees the world very differently, those who began the depression have a different point of view than those who began when the depression was really going on. The Abbé Dimnet told me when we went over together on the Champlain you are going over to America now after thirty years and it will be interesting but oh said he oh you should have seen them when they were rich. Well anyway they might not have listened so much to me when they were rich and are they rich now this I do not know.

So we went on being in New York and Carl Van Vechten gave us a Negro party all the Negro intellectuals that he could get together. I know they do not want you to say Negro but I do want

199

to say Negro. I dislike it when instead of saying Jew they say Hebrew or Israelite or Semite, I do not like it and why should a Negro want to be called colored. Why should he want to lose being a Negro to become a common thing with a Chinaman or a Japanese or a Hindu or an islander or anything any of them can be called colored, a Negro is a Negro and he ought to like to be called one if he is one, he may not want to be one that is all right but as long as he cannot change that why should he mind the real name of them. Ulysses Grant says in his memoirs all he learned when he was at school was that a noun is the name of anything, he did not really learn it but he heard it said so often that he almost came to believe it. I have stated that a noun to me is a stupid thing, if you know a thing and its name why bother about it but you have to know its name to talk about it. Well its name is Negro if it is a Negro and Jew if it is a Jew and both of them are nice strong solid names and so let us keep them.

The only Negro that interested me at this party whom I had not met before, Saint Theresa of course I had met before, the only one was a high school teacher a very intelligent fellow and I liked meeting him. He told me he taught in a high school and how he happened to say it I do not know but he told me he was teaching white children. I was surprised. Oh yes, he said they had obtained that, according to their time and training and their standing they were sent where there was a vacancy just like any one. I was surprised.

Those living there in America are not as often surprised as I am because after all there they are. However I was a little bothered. We never went to Harlem that is we went through it very often whenever I spoke at Columbia and the university extension and that was quite often and I must say it gave me an uncomfortable feeling that America was like that everywhere. On every avenue anywhere there were Negro children and they were playing then anywhere in any part of New York as if it were natural that they should be where they were playing and it was natural that they should be there. Now that there is no more emigration of emigrants into America white American families must be always getting smaller and the Negro families are they as they always did getting bigger. Are they, well anyway if so perhaps it is funny. It may come to happen to be funny.

And in the meantime the vice-president of the University of Chicago said that he was doing the inviting and that everything would be arranged as we wanted it to be arranged and so our month of New York was almost over. Yes it was.

And then we took a plane again to Chicago. By that time it was winter.

We saw it was winter from the windows of the Drake Hotel. I had not seen winter for many years and Alice Toklas had never seen it. We liked it.

And then we met Thornton Wilder. We might have known him long ago. Would that have been as nice as knowing him now. This I do not know.

There is always some one that one is seeing more than any other one. Thornton Wilder began. We settled down to ten days in Chicago, we did not know then that we were coming back again.

The central part is a beautiful city. They told us that the modern high buildings had been invented in Chicago and not in New York. That is interesting. It is interesting that it should have been done where there was plenty of land to build on and not in New York where it is narrow and so must be high of necessity. Choice is always more pleasing than anything necessary.

I had no idea that they would throw such a beautiful dark gray light on the city at night but they do. I mean the lights do. The lighting of the buildings in Chicago is very interesting and then I liked the advertisement for dancing that they had at the end of the beginning of everything they had a room and figures dancing solemnly dancing and in the daytime it was the daytime and at night it was nightime and I never tired of seeing them, the sombre gray light on the buildings and the simple solemn mechanical figures dancing, there were other things I liked but I liked that the most.

Chicago may have thought of it first but New York has made it higher much higher. It was the Rockefeller Center building that pleased me the most and they were building the third piece of it when we left New York so quietly so thinly and so rapidly, and when we came back it was already so much higher that it did not take a minute to end it quickly.

It is not delicate it is not slender it is not thin but it is something that does make existence a non-existent real thing. Alice Toklas said it is not the way they go into the air but the way they come out of the ground that is the thing. European buildings sit on the ground but American ones come out of the ground. And then of course there is the air. And that air is everywhere, everywhere in America, there is no sky, there is air and that makes religion and wandering and architecture.

When I used to try to explain America to Frenchmen of course before I had gone over this time, I used to tell them you see there is no sky over there there is only air, when you look up at the tall buildings at that time I left America the Flatiron was the tallest one and now it is not one at all it is just a house like any house but at that time it was the tallest one and I said you see you look up and you see the cornice way on top clear in the air, but now in the new ones there is no cornice up there and that is right because why end anything, well anyway I always explained everything in America by this thing, the lack of passion that they call repression and gangsters, and savagery, and everybody being nice, and everybody not thinking because they had to drink and keep moving, in Europe when they drink they sit still but not in America no not in America and that is because there is no sky, there is no lid on top of them and so they move around or stand still and do not say anything. That makes that American language that says everything in two words and mostly in words of one syllable two words of one syllable and that makes all the conversation. That is the reason they like long books novels and things of a thousand pages it is to calm themselves from the need of two words and those words of one syllable that say everything.

However we were in Chicago and it was winter and we liked looking at it from the Drake's window and I liked walking in it and it was cold and the wind was blowing and almost every day I walked down to the center of the city where there was a fruit and vegetable store where I bought little red colored Italian pears I think they called them Ferrara and I seemed to be the only one that liked to eat them they kept them to make fruit baskets look pretty but I did like to eat them and they were surprised when every day almost I came down and bought five or six of them. Everybody continued to know me and that continued to be a pleasure. It was windy and it was cold but I did stop and we did talk and one day I stopped and talked to two of them. They said they could not hear me lecture because I did not lecture where they could come to hear me but they could stop and talk to me and I said that pleased me better and they said it did them too. One of them was carrying something. I always ask anybody who is carrying anything what they are carrying. I like to ask them and I like to know and this was a satchel of a funny shape and so naturally I asked him. Marionettes he said oh I said, do you make them oh yes he said and what do you with them, well he said I earn my living carving furniture but I do this besides and I play them, I know Punch and Judy and nothing more I said, and he said but there are lots of them being made in Paris and I said yes I know and I know some people who always go but I never have been I said, and then we said it was nice meeting and I went on and they went on and I never asked them their name, I usually do but I did not, I like to know the name and occupation and what their father did or does and where they were born about any one. After all occupation and your name and where you were born and what your father's business was is a thing to know about any one, at least it is for me.

It was over a year later we were back in Bilignin and I had a letter from Donald Vestal, that was the year of knowing Donalds I knew three, and I had never known a Donald before. In the St. Nicholas when I was a child there had been a nice story of a Donald and Dorothy who had been twins and had been almost drowned in the sea and there was some complication and it was all found out by a bit of black shawl when they tasted it tasting of the sea, and Donald had saved his sister once by shooting a mad dog and in California where dogs never went mad it was very romantic to know about mad dogs, well anyway that was the only Donald with whom I had been familiar and now there were three, one might say four only the fourth I did not know very well. Donald Sutherland at Princeton who had written and sent me manuscripts before I came over and I asked for him after the Princeton lecture and he was young and very good-looking and had gray hair and was very nervous when I asked for him after the lecture, and then there was Donald Klopfer the partner of Bennett Cerf and he was tall and pleasant and a little not very happy but every one was happy enough and then Harcourt's partner was also Donald Brace and now there was Donald Vestal and I had a letter from him asking me to write him a marionette play. I did. I was writing all about identity and dogs I always write about dogs why not they are always with me and identity and that is always with me, there is me myself and there is identity my identity and so I wrote a marionette play for Donald Vestal about identity. We wrote to each other several times.

He was the first one to tell me about artists working for the government. In France they are on the dole like anybody but they do what they please, but there they were doing what they were suggested to do, here the minute the government pays them to do anything they are not on the dole. To be sure in France they do not like to teach in America they do. So it was natural that in France artists like anybody if they have no means of support go on the dole but on the dole they achieve their own anything and do anything with that thing while in America even if they are artists somebody will teach them and they are taught, and being taught they must either be that or teaching and so it was natural that once they decided to put artists on the dole that they would organize that they should be taught. Donald Vestal as he was able to do what he did would naturally be teaching that would be natural enough. He wrote to me all about this and then he wrote to me that they were going to play the play in Michigan at Detroit, of course those that did the good work were not being taught they were really not even on the dole but anyway they did play the play and he sent me photos of it and they are rather touching, there are two Gertrude Steins and they are rather touching, and they played it twice and Donald Vestal wrote me about their being moved and about his having become known in doing this with me and it pleased me. Before that there had been the presidential election and once he wrote to me and said that he was doing what he was doing and he was ready to let the president do the thinking for him. Why not, if not why not.

Generally speaking when a population gets large they cannot do their own thinking that is they cannot feel that they are doing it and as they do not feel that they are doing it naturally well naturally organization is what they do and if they do do that, then being organized there is no thinking to be done. So then everybody has to begin again as if no organization could be done but not yet no not yet and not every one no not every one and hardly any one yes hardly any one.

So we went on spending our two weeks in Chicago, the Hutchinses asking us to dinner. Bobsy and Barney Goodspeed were to be there and Thornton Wilder.

We went to dinner it was a good dinner. We were at dinner but Hutchins the president of Chicago University was not there later he came in with Mortimer Adler.

Hutchins was tired and we all sat down again together and then he began talking about what he had been doing. He and Adler were having special classes and in them they were talking over all the ideas that had been important in the world's history. Every week they took a new idea and the man who had written it and the class read it and then they had a conversation about it.

What are the ideas that are important I asked him. Here said he is the list of them I took the list and looked it over. Ah I said I notice that none of the books read at any time by them was originally written in English, was that intentional I asked him. No he said but in English there have really been no ideas expressed. Then I gather that to you there are no ideas which are not sociological or government ideas. Well are they he said, well yes I said. Government is the least interesting thing in human life, creation and the expression of that creation is a damn sight more interesting, yes I know and I began to get excited yes I know, naturally you are teachers and teaching is your occupation and naturally what you call ideas are easy to teach and so you are convinced that they are the only ideas but the real ideas are not the relation of human beings as groups but a human being to himself inside him and that is an idea that is more interesting than humanity in groups, after all the minute that there are a lot of them they do not do it for themselves but somebody does it for them and that is a darn sight less interesting. Then Adler began and I have forgotten what the detail of it was but we were saying violent things to each other and I was telling him that anybody could tell by looking that he was a man who would be singularly unsusceptible to ideas that are created within oneself that he would take to either inside or outside regulation but not to creation, and Hutchins was saying well if you can improve upon what we are doing I challenge you to do it take our class next week and I said of course I will and then Adler said something and I was standing next to him and violently telling him and everybody was excited and the maid came and said Madame the police. Adler went a little white and we all stopped and then burst out laughing. Fanny Butcher had arranged that Alice Toklas and I should go off that evening in the homicidal squad car and they had come and there they were waiting. Well we all said good night and we went off with the policemen.

It was a rainy evening. They were big men and we were tucked in with them and we went off with them.

We drove around, we had just missed one homicide it was the only one that happened that evening and it had not been interesting it had been a family affair and everybody could understand everything. The sergeant said he was afraid not much would happen, it was raining and when it rained nobody moved around and if nobody moved around there could not be any homicide unless it was a family affair as this one had been and that was not interesting some day he said when it is a really nice night I will let you know and then you will see something but we did like that night when nothing was happening and we did not stay long enough in Chicago to have a nice night. It was very interesting, it was the night they caught Baby Face and they were having messages all the time about that and it was twenty-five miles away so it was pleasantly interesting but not except that it was the first time we had heard the radio in a police car not too exciting. And then we rode around and around in all that part of Chicago where there were so many houses and then they took us into the Negro ones, and in one we got out with them, there were lots that is several Negroes coming around in a way and each one had a little bottle and after all what did it matter. nobody said anything and then we

207

went into one of the houses and it might have been a Southern one it might have been one of those in Baltimore where when I was a medical student we went to deliver a little Negro baby. There were ten or twelve there and others in other rooms men and women, all orderly enough one in a corner cooking, some in bed some just doing nothing and anyway it was all orderly enough and the sergeant said he was looking for a one-eyed man and of course there was one and that these ladies were looking for a purse that had been stolen and of course they knew that there had not been but it made them just uneasy enough so that the relief made us all have a pleasant feeling and they told me where they came from each one of them mostly from somewhere in the South one was a Canadian and now they were here and anyway they had no plans about anything and not any of them were there more than enough and so we left them. And then we went on and went to some places where there were Chinamen but not very many of them, we just stayed in there long enough to leave them and then when we were going around again I asked the sergeant did he know of course he knew in Chicago but did he know when he was in another city did he know which ones were the bad men in a town or could he be mistaken. Well he said yes he could be mistaken in a town where he had never been living, perhaps not but he might be he said after all you are a writer and you think about people a lot but after all often you are mistaken but no that does not matter, no I said that does not matter, no he said after all you are always looking so you had to be mistaken but all the same and you know that yourself all right although you are always more or less mistaken you do know the difference all the same between one man and another one and I said yes, and he said the one the only one thing that has always worried me was an old Negro who was killed right near that Chinese corner. It happened a couple of years ago. He was an old Negro not very old but old, he worked a little every day he just made enough money to keep him, he never had any money on him, he had nobody nobody knew him only as everybody knew him, nobody had any kind of feeling about him and one night not very late just at that corner no it was quite early in the evening somebody shot him and nobody heard anything nobody knew anything nobody saw him or anything, he was shot down dead nobody touched him, there was no reason why there was any shooting at that corner, he was just shot on that corner and although there were people eating around there nobody happened just to have been looking or to have been hearing anything or to have been anywhere there when they shot him. He was of no importance and so nobody was put on the job of finding out about him and that is the only time I ever knew anybody shot and no reason for anything and as he was of no importance I will never know why anybody shot him. I said it worried him and he said yes it did, it did come back to him.

We went on riding and it was getting later in the evening toward the morning and then we stopped again and we went inside somewhere with him and there we saw a walking marathon.

There is a difference between waking and sleeping and most generally one does know the difference between waking and sleeping not always but almost always one does know the difference between waking and sleeping but here there was nothing neither waking nor sleeping, they were all young ones and they were moving as their bodies were drooping. They had been six weeks without sleeping and some no longer had another one with them they were moving and drooping alone but when there were two of them one was more clinging than moving and the other one was supporting and moving. There was plenty of light and a little noise.

The sergeant and we were standing and the manager of the place came up and said would we like them to be photographed with us but we would not have liked them to be photographed with us or we to be photographed with them.

Jacques Viot who discovered the surrealists when they were discovering surrealism that was some time ago met me day before yesterday again. I had not seen him in between. We were talking about the cinema, he is now doing film stories for the French films and he said you have to remember in writing film stories that it is not like writing for the theatre the film audience is not an audience that is awake it is an audience that is dreaming, it is not asleep but it is always dreaming. The walking marathon was more that than any film. I have never seen it again.

We went out and by that time it was still raining it was nearing morning and the driver was sleeping but he was driving and we went on and we were to get back to where we were to be taken on the Lake Side Drive and we were going there but I said were we not going in the wrong direction because this part I knew and they said yes they did not know that part of Chicago and I said it was funny that the squad car could get lost in Chicago but I would not tell any one and we came home and we said good night to them. Sometimes I would like to go out again.

It continued to be winter and we were staying a little longer. At one lecture when I came into the hall I saw three large chairs on the platform and three sitting in them. What are they doing there I asked the young woman who was meeting us, oh they are the president vice-president and the treasurer of the club and they are reading the minutes, all right I said we will wait here until they finish, oh no she said, but I will wait I said until they have gone away, but they are sitting there, oh no I said, I will wait until they go away. They did not want to go away they wanted to stay but I would not go on until they went away and they did go away but it was rather a dreadful moment when they did go away.

There is a difference between making speeches and lecturing and that difference made all the difference to me. I might have made speeches but I was lecturing and lecturing I had to be alone to see and I was.

I find out just today and in Paris that Americans and Europeans are different. Two things happened to me today. I backed my car into another one when I was parking in front of the magasin du Louvre and my spare tire went over his fender. That was one thing. I looked at it and I talked about it to a taxi chauffeur who was waiting and then he went away, we could do nothing, Alice Toklas said that as I moved my car the cars were separating but they did not. The owner of the car came and I said I was very sorry, he said nothing and then we tried together and I said we had better take off the spare tire and I began and he went on with it and we were both working and an out of work came along and I beckoned to him and the tire was taken off and the cars separated and the tire put back, and there had been nothing difficult about anything and I said I was sorry and we all went away and that was one thing, a very little later in the day we went to get some knives that had been left to be sharpened and it was in our quarter in the rue de Rennes and I stayed in the car. I noticed two people standing and looking as if they were meeting some one or looking for some one they were American they had an anxious look and they were looking and they were tall and not young a man and woman and there was a car in front of them a Ford car an American one not a French one. I went into the knife place so as to have an excuse to come out again and look at them, I did, the woman still anxious smiled and I smiled and she said how do you do Miss Stein and I said how do you do and I said what are you doing here. We are looking for a man to drive our car because she said and he said yes my wife is nervous and as we do not know the streets well she is afraid to have me go on driving and we are just up from Nice, could we find a man to drive it. Well I said my garage is near but there is nobody there to drive the car but I'll speak to a taxi driver and I did and he knew of no place where they could find a man to drive their car and Alice Toklas came out and they were anxious and we talked and we went in and we tried to telephone and we came out again and I said let me take you somewhere and the wife said let him follow you to your garage and then you will find some one, and I said yes let us do that and she said she would take a taxi to her hotel and she did we did not see her go and he followed me in his car, and the brakes were not working and he decided to leave the car and took his baggage out and he said thank you and I said if I had been in Newark he would have done the same for me and he said yes and we said good-bye.

It made me suddenly feel that that is why shutters are open or none of them and no walls around gardens or anything the anxiousness of an American man and an American woman is all the anxiousness they have in them, well anyway they are that way, and I remembered anywhere in America you can get a man or a boy to drive your car anywhere you could want to go, I did when I was afraid to drive into the Yosemite, not that it was a difficult drive but I just felt that way.

So we stayed our two weeks in Chicago and Mrs. Goodspeed took us to the opera and to concerts, one of them was Lohengrin and the other was Salomé. It was funny going to opera again and to concerts it seemed as if Europe had not been, it was just the same as it had been. I do not say that there are not concerts and operas in Paris but that had not been what I had been living no not at all and here in Chicago it was just as it had been before there was everything.

And then the Hutchinses asked us to come and nobody was to know anything not even Thornton or Mrs. Goodspeed and we went to dinner and then I went to take over their class with them. I had gotten used to lecturing and did not think about that as a thing but here I was to be teaching and anything is a funny feeling and that was.

So we all sat around a long table and Hutchins and Adler and I presiding, at least we were not to be but there we were as if we were, well anyway I began talking.

I began to talk and they not Hutchins and Adler but the others began to talk and pretty soon we were all talking about epic poetry and what it was it was exciting we found out a good deal some of it I used in one of the four lectures I wrote for the course I came back to give them but it was all that after all in epic poetry you can have an epic because the death of the man meant the end of everything and now nothing is ending by the death of any one because something is already happening. Well we all came out and they liked it and I liked it and Hutchins said to me as he and I were walking, you did make them all talk more than we can make them and a number of them talked who never talked before and it was very nice of him to say it and he added and if you will come back I will be glad to have you do some teaching and I said I would and he said he would let me know and then I said you see why they talk to me is that I am like them I do not know the answer, you say you do not know but you do know if you did not know the answer you could not spend your life in teaching but I I really do not know, I really do not, I do not even know whether there is a question let alone having an answer for a question. To me when a thing is really interesting it is when there is no question and no answer, if there is then already the subject is not interesting and it is so, that is the reason that anything for which there is a solution is not interesting, that is the trouble with governments and Utopias and teaching, the things not that can be learnt but that can be taught are not interesting. Well anyway we went away.

It was winter and it went on being winter and we went away to places where we had never been, we went to Wisconsin and Ohio and Indiana and Minnesota and Michigan. That all was exciting one of the most exciting moments was when on a train and stopping at a station we were in Ohio and we saw it said Marion and we remembered all about the President's Daughter and it was historical and exciting but that was not the only time. We had all read the President's Daughter and in a way it is one of the best descriptions of small town life in America that has been written

and it was what was for us a real thing and when we saw Marion
written on the railway station it was one of the moments that were
perhaps only three or four that I have ever had. The first one was
Concord and Lexington and a young college boy in Berkeley California has just sent me a postal of the bridge at Concord and he
too had as everybody brought up in California has that moment
of history. Then there was the fire-place at Eton where Tom Brown
was roasted and now there was Marion in Ohio. These things do
happen, that is what it is to feel like history a place is real to you
but it is not there and then when it is really there then it is not
real any more. It is that that gives anybody a historical feeling.

Another time that was not as real as Marion but still it was something was when in Toledo they always asked me how I wanted to
be entertained and I always said I did not want to be entertained
but I like driving around and I was always ready to drive around.
In Toledo they drove us around, that is I like to be driven around
if I do not have to go inside of anything, and be shown anything
I do not much care for that and I never did it, but I do like driving and I like to sit with the chauffeur and I like seeing country
so we did that. As we were going along they told us that one of
the houses belonged to the man who made Champion spark-plugs,
that was something. All through the war I had had to insist that I
wanted for my Ford les bougies Champion pas Americains pas pas
français, because mine were the smaller and not the larger, well
anyway it was something that I said not every day during the war
but often enough because those old Fords did use up spark-plugs
and here was the house the man who made them lived in. Would
you like to go in they asked me oh yes I said and we went in, of
course the man was not there he was naturally busy elsewhere but
his wife was and she was charming and I told her all about the
Champion spark-plugs and my feeling for them and she said she
would tell her husband. She did tell him and they used to make a
tiny one in silver as a watch charm but alas there was the depres-

214

sion and now they made them of steel and they gave me one and I keep it in my jewel box but I would rather it had been a silver one.

So we left Chicago and it was winter and we went to Madison, Wisconsin. Before I left America I had visited almost thirty universities and I began to really only like that, there were lots more of them where I would have liked to have gone we only got to know about some of them after we had left where they were but it would be fun to go to every one of them all over the United States, I sometimes think it would be fun to talk to students in every university all over the world, it would be interesting and they would like it as well as I would because of course they would like it, and certainly I liked the thirty I did visit. One that I liked most was this one at Madison. It was cold at Madison and snow and ice and not easy walking which I mind because I like walking and they took us to a university house where we ate and slept and where they all came in and out, it was like our first arriving everybody was there and after that we liked being received by a man and a girl and a car and going in and out everywhere. Soon among those in and out I found was one that had been at the medical school with me Dorothy Reade and I said could we be alone and she said yes but we were not because by that time Wright the architect he lived near there was there and with him was a Russian and anyway would we come with them but by that time we thought we would like to eat something and be quiet before lecturing and we would meet them all in the evening after lecturing but by that time he had gone away and anyway well they gave us a very good dinner up in the room and outside it was cold and the lakes were colder, I liked looking out of the window at everything. I had walked a little but it was difficult walking.

We had a good talk afterwards there were two or three there who knew a lot about words one of them a reddish headed professor, and then we went to bed and we got up and it had not snowed but there was certainly more snow and it was whiter and Dorothy Reade took us to the flying field, I never knew her very well and I did not know her then very well and she was the same as she had been and then we flew away in a plane.

Did we or did we not fly over the Mississippi then going to Minneapolis and St. Paul, I do not really know but if it was not then it was some other time where the Mississippi was a little river. It was a shock to me that it could be that that it could be a little river and even then later in New Orleans I never quite recovered that it had been a little river when it had first been shown to us. I had passed over it once in going to California that was long before I left America but it had been at night and I had not seen it and when I first saw it it had been a little river. One of the things in flying over America is the lot of water, there is a lot of land of course there is a lot of land but there is a lot of water. Everywhere of course where there is land there is a lot of water, in France in motoring you are always crossing bridges but then the water is a small lot of water but in America particularly when later we flew over the valley of the Mississippi there was a great deal of water, on the whole I was surprised that relatively there were many less mountains than there was water. Of course really the most impressive water to fly over is where there is no water and that is over the region before Salt Lake City, there it is the bottom of the ocean and when you have once seen the bottom of the ocean without any water as one sees it there it is a little foolish that the ocean should have water, it would be so much more interesting to look at if it had no water. Rivers are different, rivers are more interesting with water than without water. Well anyway.

We went to Minneapolis. It was still winter but not as winter as it had been in Wisconsin.

It was at this time that my real interest in reporters began.

Up to this time of course I had talked to lots of them but there was also always something happening and we went out and we went in except for Jo Alsop there had been just so many faces and that was all of them.

But now that we were traveling and not being entertained because I like a quiet life and do not like to go out to dinner and above all not to a reception certainly not when I am not to know any one, the social life I preferred in traveling was the life with reporters and I did enjoy them.

I think it was in St. Paul that it happened. Now in traveling I did sometimes look at a newspaper after all here they were a size to hold, they were something like the Paris New York Herald not quite as few pages as that but few enough to be encouraging. So in St. Paul I had spoken in the evening and when I went downstairs in the hotel I saw a different colored newspaper than I had been accustomed to seeing perhaps it was in Toledo well anyway it had a color and I noticed it and there I was and I read it, the reporter had reported my talk as if it were a wrestling match and it was very well written and of course any author would I noticed that every paragraph or so he introduced one of the best sentences I had written and it came in well. It pleased me I like good writing and then we went out and we were to have lunch and then leave which we did. At lunch the one who had arranged the lecture came up and said something, I said I was much taken with the way my lecture was written up, what she said, yes I said, it was about the best writing about myself I have read, but she said everybody is furious because it reflects so on the taste of this city not at all I said he writes well and what is more he understood what I said which is to me a pleasant thing and does not often happen that is not by reporters reporting, well she said there is his editor over there, everybody has been complaining to him so that he was going to fire the young fellow who did it, he had asked especially to do it and this is the way he did it, of course he asked I said because he knew he would understand and he did, I'll go she said immediately and tell his editor and tell him what you said, I said I am sorry we are leaving I would like to have seen him and then as we were leaving she said I told the reporter and he had tears in his eyes and he said you saved his life and I said I hope he will go on.

I got very much interested in reporters. Reporters are mostly young college men who are interested in writing and naturally I was interested in talking with them. I always knew that of course they would say what it was the habit for newspapers to say I said and yet I did like talking with them. Once it may have been in Cleveland or Indianapolis, I was talking there were two or three of them and a photographer with them and I said you know it is funny but the photographer is the one of the lot of you who looks as if he were intelligent and was listening now why is that, you do I said to the photographer you do understand what I am talking about don't you. Of course I do he said you see I can listen to what you say because I don't have to remember what you are saying, they can't listen because they have got to remember.

I found that very interesting and of course it is so, of course nobody can listen if they have to remember what they are hearing and that is the trouble with newspapers and teaching with government and history. The lecture I wrote for the Chicago University has to do with this thing and the difference between original writing and anything which is a remembered thing and a great deal that I wrote in the Geographical History of America which is about identity and the lecture I wrote for Oxford and Cambridge about What Are Masterpieces And Why Are There So Few Of Them all have something to do with this and so thank you the photographer who said this thing.

I liked the photographers, there is one who came in and said he was sent to do a layout of me. A layout, I said yes he said what is that I said oh he said it is four or five pictures of you doing anything. All right I said what do you want me to do. Why he said there is your airplane bag suppose you unpack it, oh I said Miss Toklas always does that oh no I could not do that, well he said there is the telephone suppose you telephone well I said yes but I never do Miss Toklas always does that, well he said what can you do, well I said I can put my hat on and take my hat off and I can put my coat on and I can take it off and I like water I can drink a glass of water all right he said do that so I did that and he photographed while I did that and the next morning there was the layout and I had done it.

There was a photographer that was much later in New Orleans and we spent a long time he telling me how he followed Huey Long photographing him and all he knew about him and how they had almost killed him those who were protecting Huey Long and had mistaken him but now Huey Long is dead and it does not make any difference to any one.

Each one of these hotels was a real hotel to me and the life in them so many people seemed to be sharing something and meeting in numbers and we we were not lost in them each one of them was not like any other one of them. I remember the one in Indianapolis that was a strange one a very strange one one ate pretty well in any one of them but not in the Indianapolis one not very well it was as large the rooms as the furniture in them and the furniture was as heavy in its color as the hangings, mostly in the hotels even later in the Southern ones everything was well not new but new enough but not in that one. Indianapolis was exciting, somehow it was different than Ohio and Illinois later on I could see that in a way it had to do with St. Louis. The size of everything in Indianapolis was different from anything in Ohio or Illinois or Wisconsin or Minnesota entirely a different size, I was tremendously interested in each state I wish well I wish I could know everything about each one. There is Ohio, Louis Bromfield comes from Ohio, they are rich and they are generous and they are innocent and they are prosperous yes they are. But not Indianapolis. I have known a good many from Indiana.

I lectured in the evening the audience was of men and women

the men were able-looking might have been judges and lawyers and they were interested and interesting. The next morning we went to the Foster Museum, everything he had ever done was there a good many in original and all in facsimile and records of all the songs could be made to sing and two secretaries to show everything and the purse that was on him when he was dead and the founder of the museum. It was in a building in a garden. They were moving it to another city where they could build a museum that would look more like a church and then we left and went to see an Indian collection collected by the son of the man who had founded the Foster Museum. Indiana Indianapolis and Indians. He showed us how they were slicing in thin slices the Indian mounds I suppose they have to slice them if they want to know what is inside in them and of course they do want to know what is in them and each one might be different from the one they had had open. Well anyway Indianapolis had not been in any way a disappointment.

It was Alexander Woollcott who had told us about the Foster Museum. We had met him in New York at a lunch Bennett Cerf gave to have all of us meet all of us and at table we were talking and I said something in contradiction and Alexander Woollcott said Miss Stein you have not been in New York long enough to know that I am never contradicted. We liked being together because we both had poodles and mine we have both seen mine I have not seen his, Woollcott was over last winter and Basket was beautifully washed and shaved to receive him, as he was coming for lunch Monday Basket had to be bathed on Saturday and so for two days we would let Basket not do anything hardly attend to his normal functions because it was raining and the white must not become gray because Basket is the most beautiful white poodle his is not a white one. He is going to write a book about poodles and he asked me to write him a lovely letter about Basket and I did a very lovely one. We liked having Alexander Woollcott here we took him to the ordination of the bishop of Monte Carlo which happened at Notre Dame he is Bernard Faÿ's uncle this is the second one the second uncle to become a bishop and in benediction Woollcott sent us the largest and the loveliest flowers that Paris has ever given any one. He says he likes to because for many years he always wanted to and now he does. We also liked talking about Mildred Aldrich he had known her and he took us to lunch at Katharine Cornell's and we did once have the best lemon pie there that was ever made anywhere. I always remember the husband of Katharine Cornell and the Hauptmann trial. Everybody was going there we did not, I like to read detective stories but really not see them, to know what they are but not to sit with them at least I have never sat perhaps I would like it well anyway I did not.

The husband of Katharine Cornell had gone every day and then he did not go any more, and he said the reason why was that he could not go any more because the day before coming back in the train Mrs. Hauptmann was there in front of him and she said to some one I wonder if it is going to snow or if there is going to be any skating. The naturalness of her saying this thing to some one suddenly made it that he could not go again and he did not go again.

So we had met Alexander Woollcott and he had told us to go to the Foster Museum.

I was much interested in passing over Ohio and Indiana. I was much interested in the Ohio country there where it was made of ground that came up to a bit of wood and the farm house in between and then falling down into a piece of meadow. It was interesting that the houses and the barns were well painted in Ohio and over the border in Indiana they were built differently and not on a wooded rising and they were not well painted as they were in Ohio. I know how the houses being built and the taking care of them changes in France from one province to another and there the same was happening from Ohio to Indiana. Afterwards I asked and they told me that many of these farm houses had no electricity that surprised me, in France any farm house or barn has electricity but then in France they live in villages and in America they do not it would be harder to supply every one of those farm houses with electricity but did it not say sometimes that every farm house in America has its telephone and if it has its telephone and radio then it must have its electricity. Well anyway.

When we were in St. Paul we went to Minneapolis and there I met another doctor whom I had known in the Medical School she and her husband both of them, he Ulrich had been known in those days of the Medical School as the friend of women, well anyway it was not very exciting meeting them again. And then some one told us that Sherwood Anderson was somewhere around. Ah if he was we would see him certainly we would would some one find him and some one did.

He had a sister-in-law who was married to a doctor in Fall River, Minnesota and Sherwood was traveling around to write what he thought everybody felt about farming that is the farmers. And so we were to meet at his brother-in-law's. It was winter it certainly was winter and the brother-in-law called for us to drive us out and he put a shovel in and we said what is that for and he said we would see what it was for and we did. They did not shovel us out but they shoveled somebody else out. We had a very pleasant time together. A very good Virginia dinner and a very pleasant evening altogether. They had a rug there made by an old woman in Virginia we liked so much and Sherwood said he would send us one and he did I think it was the same one and we have it in Bilignin and everybody especially French people admire it every time they see it, the pale colors are so American and the river and the house and the simple harmony of it and the taste in it, they all are astonished that they never have seen anything like that before done in America. Lord Berners who has written the music for the ballet pantomime which is to be given in March in London is also going to do the decors and he made a drawing of this carpet and is going to use it as the back drop of the stage, the name of the play is They Must Be Wedded To Their Wife but as the title is too long for advertising we call it A Wedding Bouquet and so we were to fly from St. Paul to Chicago and there catch a plane specially stopped for us to Iowa City. This was the only plane we did not like as a plane, the first one did not go at all there was something the matter with the engine and the second plane well it went but perhaps there was something the matter with the engine and then before we came to Chicago certainly we would know Chicago it was beginning to come down. It was a lovely star-lit evening and the plane was commencing to come down. Alice Toklas began to say what are they doing we must get to Chicago to catch the plane for Iowa City and she called the second pilot and she told him. No he said we can't get to Chicago we are coming right down in Milwaukee and there if you want you can get the train for Chicago but said Alice Toklas indignantly why do you start a plane if it cannot go where it is supposed to go. The plane can go all right he said but no plane can go tonight to Chicago. Why not said Alice Toklas it is a lovely night, may be so he said but lady he said wouldn't you rather be even in Milwaukee than in your coffin.

We landed in Milwaukee and we took a train a sort of electric street car to Chicago. I was interested in the passengers there and in the way they read the newspaper. They kind of read their newspaper but it was not really very interesting but when they got to the part about the Quintuplets and how the doctor took care of them then they folded their paper so that they only had that spot and then they settled down to solidly reading. It was interesting to me that that was really the only thing in the paper that was really real to them.

So then we did get into Chicago and there was a blizzard in Chicago a terrible blizzard in Chicago and we could not find Mrs. Goodspeed's chauffeur and it was pretty hard to get to the Drake Hotel and he was right no plane could get into Chicago and you never can tell and we did not get to Iowa City. I would like to have seen Iowa. Carl and Cook come from Iowa, you are brilliant and subtle if you come from Iowa and really strange and you live as you live and you are always very well taken care of if you come from Iowa. Cook used to tell us about the way the little Presbyterian community of Independence Iowa turned into a wonderful place when the trotting races took place, and of course Maud S. and when I was little everybody knew the horse Maud S. came from there. Well anyway we never did see Iowa.

So we went to Michigan it was a large plane the largest in which we had been.

The life of the hotels there was so much that is they did so much in the hotels.

In Detroit we did not like it in the hotel it was one of the big ones, we did not like any of the rooms they showed us and in the rooms we were to be in we did not know who had come in and out while we were coming in and some one asked Alice Toklas a question and it was a funny one and we did not like it. We were to stay three days but we only stayed one and Jo Brewer telephoned to us and we were glad to see him and the two cars with the staff from Olivet College came and they took us away with them and that was a pleasure. I had walked around a good deal and the place had been foreign that is it was foreign and they called out at every corner through a megaphone where to go and how to go and it was not a pleasant voice it was a policeman and it all might have been anywhere well but not there, I kind of liked it there were back streets that might have been French that is the things they did in them but they were American and therefore they were frightening as French things are not frightening and so after having always driven a Ford car I never have driven any other one there in its home I did not see them at home. This can happen. The food was good which it was not at Olivet not so bad as Vassar but not good but we had a very good time at Olivet.

224

It was the first little college we had seen all the rest had been universities and gradually we knew all about colleges and junior colleges and I suppose there will be more kinds and degrees of colleges before we ever get back again but Olivet was the first one that was really a country village and they were boys and girls it sounded like something very pleasant and it looked like something very pleasant and it was something very pleasant.

We had known Brewer as an Oxford man a friend of Harold Acton, Acton is now a Chinaman, he has been teaching in China a long time and I imagine he really does now really look and feel like a Chinaman some people can and do and he will and does and can.

Brewer then became a publisher and he published Useful Knowledge for me all the poetry and prose I had at that time done describing America, and then he liked doing everything as well and anyway publishing is like gambling or anything if you do not make money you can lose it and when you lose too much of it you cannot lose any more of it. Well anyway they made Brewer president of Olivet and he was very serious about it any American can be serious when he is serious about it and almost any American can be serious about it, some English people can be serious about what they are serious about but more Americans can be and are and Joe Brewer is and was he is serious about being president of Olivet.

They were all pleasing and we liked to be with them, we all spent an evening talking and I had to sign my name for all of them and then I asked them all to sign all their names for me. I like names and there were quite a lot of them. And then they all that is the two cars with some of the staff in them drove us to Ann Arbor where I was to lecture. It was nice and cold but not like Wisconsin awfully cold. It was just cold. The country was less American it was more English and French well anyway it was more like anywhere it was less American, the horizon was less American and the houses were interesting and it was there I first saw the shaving advertisements that delighted me one little piece on one board and then further on two more words and then further on two more words a whole lively poem. I wish I could remember more of them, they were all lively and pleasing and they all had to do with shaving like the one when we were young and pleased us about Lo the poor Indian whose untutored mind shaves off his whiskers and disappoints the wind, lots of those that they did two words at a time were better than that I wish I could remember them I liked them so much.

And so we arrived at Ann Arbor. It was not at all like Olivet, I had no idea it would be such an enormous place with so many students in it. All I really knew about Ann Arbor was that it was there that Avery Hopwood had left his money to found awards for those who were at the university and wanted to write in an original way. Poor Avery he had always wanted to write a great novel he did write something but they destroyed it, probably it was nothing but confusion at least so he said when I used to ask him about it and the man in the English Department who had charge of it asked me what advice could I give him about it. They did not know quite very well how to distribute the prizes.

The only suggestion I could make them would be that it would be rather amusing if they did with writers the way the Independent salon had done with painters. Suppose they let any one who wanted to write something write it and publish a huge volume of it every year not taking out anything and just see what it would be that they would be printing. But we do do that he said we only take out what is manifestly not worth anything, ah yes I said but that is just it, who is to judge of that manifestly not worth anything. No the thing should be without jury and without reward which was the motto of the first salon d'independence, no one was a judge of what was or was not manifestly worth anything. It would have been rather fun if they had done it, I would have liked to read such a volume, but the minute anybody has judged of any of it anybody

226

might just as well judge of all of it. Of course they have never done it. I do wish they had, it would have been a nice way to please Avery.

And then we went off in a plane back to Ohio.

We liked Columbus Ohio, it had a nice climate and it was a pleasant country round about and it had a restaurant where the ladies entertained each other and where they made very good dishes the kind we had read about but good and we were met by a young student, Jean Reeder and a young man with her and they were just like the commère and the compère in a review it was all satisfactory and natural and refreshing. Alice Toklas wanted to come back to live there. She wants to come back to live not everywhere but in Avila and in New York and New Orleans and California, I preferred Chicago and Texas but I did not want to come back to live there. I like Paris and I like six months in the country but I like Paris. Everybody says it is not very nice now but I like Paris and I like to live there. Just today I saw on the quay three colored prints made in 1840, one of Baltimore one of New Orleans and one of Sacramento. They were twenty-five francs a piece and I did not buy them but I liked looking at them. I like to live in Paris.

We did like Columbus Ohio. It would seem that a great many years ago a professor of English of the University of Ohio in Columbus came to see me and it had been a pleasure to him and to me. We exchanged a few letters and that was long ago.

He had taught all his classes to read me and now he was dead, I had not known about this and he was seconded not in his professorship but in his feeling about my work by Sam Steward who had been in Columbus but was now in Helena Montana and would we go there, we never did get there and later he was in the University of the State of Washington and they threw him out because he wrote a book called Angels On The Bough which is a very interesting book. It has something in it that makes literature. I do not know quite what but there it is. That is one of the things that

227

is so perplexing, why do books that are books that do everything why do they not make literature, I do often worry about that, anyway the Bulletin of the American Association of University Professors realize this and now he is teaching in the Loyola University of Chicago who also know this thing.

Well anyway we have never met but he is interesting.

Another thing that interested me in the city of Columbus was the museum, everywhere we went they would talk to me about painting, American painting, I looked at it all I looked at it everywhere it was not interesting, that is to say it was all right but if you considered it from the standpoint of the Louvre it was not interesting and for me I can look at or read anything but if I have to decide about it then I have to think of it from the standpoint of masterpieces, I am sorry but I do naturally think that something is a masterpiece that is to say as long as there is anything there will be that thing and if not then it is something else. There was no painting like that in America there just was not, there was architecture there was writing but there was no painting no painting like that. The painting was like any learnt painting, it was good painting enough not awfully good painting as painting but good painting enough and I liked to look at it I like to look at anything but that was all there was to that. They like to build museums, and they build they really like to build anything and why not. But in the Columbus museum I came into a room and it was a pleasant one. It was all cubist and good Picassos and Juan Gris and others but really good ones. There had never been anything like that either in choice or quality or like that in any other museum. How did that happen I asked and they told me. There was an old man in the town I think he was seventy so they told me and he had never owned a picture, he was a business man or a professional man and he lived in Columbus, Ohio. He went to New York quite often and there he once saw a cubist picture. He found it interesting he had never been interested in any other kind of painting. He bought

228

one and another one and he bought very lovely ones and he bought a roomful and when he died he was by that time eighty something he left them to the museum with money enough to build a room for them.

Well we went on to Cleveland and that was pleasant too and it was the first American city where the streets were messy they said there was a reason but I do not remember the reason but I remember the streets were messy. We did not stay in the town they said we would be better in a hotel outside the city, well anyway there were pleasant people one of them and she said she wanted a distraction and I said why not improvise on the piano I do. And she said what do you do and I said you never want to use anything but white keys black keys are too harmonious and you never want to do a chord chords are too emotional, you want to use white keys and play two hands together but not bother which direction either hand takes not at all you want to make it like a design and always looking and you will have a good time. She said she would try but any one perhaps not every one can do it and enjoy it I do.

Well anyway we took the airplane to go to Washington that is to go to Baltimore.

It was nice that way we went over Pittsburgh Allegheny where I was born, I was born and if I wanted to have it be anything it really was not. Jay Laughlin lived there and Mildred Weston Kiddie's wife and perhaps that meant more. Anyway the river winds and I can remember my mother said that it was very dirty and everything was black in a few hours naturally we were dressed in white as babies and children but it did not look black any more not as we went over it and the sky was blue and the air was clear. And the mountains separating it from Washington was the straightest line of mountains I ever saw, with first just a little green and then a little black and then snow on top and then a little black and then a little green and a straight line as far as they could be seen and then we were over Virginia and the Potomac and the Potomac was something that gave me that feeling and then we came down in Washington. Some reporters were there. Are you going to see the President they asked me. That is up to the President I answered them. But anyway we went from one station to another to go to Baltimore and we went to Baltimore. Baltimore is where all my people come from, Washington was dusty as it always had been and we went to Baltimore, and at every station I knew the name of everything and the woods looked as I remembered them they did.

If not then you have to remember where your father was born and your mother. Some do not. In a way I do not. My mother was born in Baltimore and my father had been married to her there that was in 1864 and my brother Michael was born the year after but not there. We were all born in Pittsburgh or in Allegheny but naturally it was in Baltimore where we were born longer and that was because after all everybody has to come from somewhere, nobody thinks about that enough now to be a bother but sometimes they think about it enough to be a pleasure and sometimes not. I always remember the member of the Sûreté the French police when we were getting our papers to visit the hospitals and to go everywhere during the war. He came to see us and we went into the matter of where we were born and where our parents were born and where our grandparents were born and then he said and what is the difference any way. Nowadays nobody really is going to feel one way because their father or their mother certainly not their grandfather or their grandmother were born in one country rather·than another. For instance he said a grandparent might have been born in Belgium and how was anybody going to know on which side Belgium was going to be, one usually said he meditatively likes the country in which they have always lived not always but usually he said. Well anyway my grandfather my mother's father was not born in Baltimore but he was born very long ago he was born in 1800 so I have been told and before he was twenty he had come to

Baltimore and after that he was always there. I do not know whether I remember him but I did see him when I was about five. How can you tell what with photographs and hearing whether you remember seeing yes or no. Alice Toklas says yes well anyway. So Baltimore was that thing. My father's family did not come there as soon they came just before the civil war, and they wandered they were not always there, and they were not all of them there, a number of them but not all of them as my mother's family had been and so my mother's family who were people who were always there did not consider my father's family as quite equal to them, my father's family all were rich men my mother's family were not not any of them but that is the way they felt about everything. I used always to say to French people who lived in the provinces that I perfectly understood their family life and their feelings of differences and what happened to every one because that was the way they lived in Baltimore. They still do nothing really can stop any one living and feeling as they do in Baltimore. This time I did not see my relations that is only the cousin where I was staying and then just before leaving, my aunt Fanny who was now fairly eighty and my uncle Eph who was a sculptor and he too was almost eighty and they were just as they had been, they had just separated one part of the family from another part of the family and they had installed themselves in a different apartment, they had before that had a home together and they were just as determined and just as interested in it as they ever had been. I do describe them well in The Making of Americans all of them and the grandfather who was an old man. He had been a tanner and had lived in an old house and there he had had his wife who had been born in Baltimore and his eleven children. The Making of Americans tells all about them. We stayed not in Baltimore but at Pikesville and we spent Christmas there. They made us hang up our stockings and they filled them and they put in some of those square little books that they sell in the ten cent stores and I delighted in them. I do like the square books that they sell in the ten cent stores, the shape of them is a complete thing and what is inside them. It is that and Lascaux said it when I explained to him that is the romantic thing about America that they do the best designing and use the best material in the cheapest thing, the square books and the old Ford car. I always remember Lascaux the French painter, it was he who having always lived in an isolated country and coming to Paris thought the automobiles going around the Arc de Triomphe were a carousel and it only slowly dawned on him that they were always different cars not the same ones and it was he who as a child thought the most romantic thing in the world would be to have a stove, they had always had an open fire and then later he had a radiator and he never did have a stove which would have been a romantic thing.

I was once very interested in Belley they had a train at the yearly fair they call in that country the vogue and this train ran around a circle and went in and out a tunnel and all the women and the children were so excited they had all been in automobiles that was not exciting and airplanes were not exciting even if they had not been in them they were not romantic to them but trains going in and out of tunnels that was a romantic thing. It made me think a lot about what is romance. Automobiles are not romantic but trains are perhaps automobiles with trailers are romantic perhaps yes, some wars are romantic others are not, some places are romantic others are not, I think a lot about that. Well anyway Lascaux did think that the cheapest thing being made of the costliest material was romantic. It was romantic to him and it is, that the cheapest thing is made with the most care and the highest-paid creators are those that make that thing. It is romantic. Perhaps Hollywood too is that thing.

Well anyway we went to Washington to stay for a week there.

Washington there always is the Potomac and Virginia which is over there. That can make anybody remember that as an American. I am always telling Bernard Faÿ and any other Frenchman that if they did not know the America that made the Civil War they do not know about America, and always sometimes America will be that thing. It is not only pioneering, their going on and on to the end and then when they had nothing more to find they had then to come back again. I am always explaining to French people that Europeans do not know anything about disillusion, Americans have to have so much optimism because they do know what it is to have disillusion, the land goes away from them, the water goes away from them they go away from everything and it is all of it so endless and yet they have all been from one end to the other end of it. Yes they have all been. I was interested when I asked the students in the colleges where they came from to find that very many of them go as far away as they can from where they come from. Why I said do you just put your finger on the map as far away as you can and say you will go to college there. Well not exactly they said and they did not really have to because they naturally would be going there where it was as far away as it had been. And yet where can they go. It is the same with making money, any American should and could think of himself as a potentially rich man and that they had been but now now mostly there is not as much chance of changing as there is for a European not any more they are more likely to be an employee than anything and that does make a difference does it make less or more disillusion does it make less or more wandering or does it make the same very likely I think it makes the same.

And so roads are the important thing and what is on them.

Wherever I went the roads and what is on them were not the same as they had been thirty years before when I left America, not in Washington not anywhere and that is what makes the country different, the rest is as it was but the roads and what is on them not. I thought about that a lot in Washington because then for about a week I was not doing anything but thinking about that thing.

And that is why when you look at it it does not look at all the same, the houses what difference do houses make but the roads and what is on them. One of the first times I ever was in an automobile was in Washington and when it went up a very little hill it did not go very well and all the little boys kept yelling git a horse.

As I said in Capital Capitals and it sings so well

Fourth Capital	They play horses
Fourth Capital	We have all forgotten what horses are
Third Capital	We have all forgotten what horses there are
Second Capital	We have all forgotten where there are horses
First Capital	We have all forgotten about horses.

Capital this and Capital that.

Well that is the way the capital was, I wrote it about French capitals but Washington was just the same only it did look different and not at all the same.

We were staying with some one and we were all asked to tea at the White House and we went. I had never been before.

We were the only ones asked to tea, we went upstairs not downstairs and in a passageway we had tea a passageway which was a hall. Mrs. Roosevelt was there and gave us tea, she talked about something and we sat next to some one. Then later two men came through from somewhere going to somewhere, one quite an old one and the other one younger, Mrs. Roosevelt asked them if they would have some tea they said no and they stood and I asked some one who was next to me who are they and she said it was Mr. Howe and I had heard of him and then they went on away and Mrs. Roosevelt said yes they were all writing the message to Congress that was going to be given next day and they were all writing it and each one and any one was changing it and then we went away.

Ellen Lamotte said let us go to Virginia for New Year's evening and so she drove us down in her Ford car. We liked that we only stayed the night but we liked that it was on the James River and there was just a little snow, later on we were there again but just then we liked that.

I had been to Richmond long before and Harper's Ferry and the battle of Gettysburg long before, I have just found the two volumes of Grant's Memoirs on the quays and have just bought them to read again. I always liked the way Grant said that he knew what the other general would do because after all they had been to school at West Point together and the Mexican War together and the others acted like generals but he acted like one who knew just what the general opposite to him would do because that one had always been like that in West Point and after all what can anybody change to, they have to be what they are and they are and so Grant always knew what to do.

The thing I always want to tell Frenchmen and it does impress them is the way Grant let the southern soldiers all keep their horses and their guns, they would need them in going back to farming and so it was natural that they should keep them. That is what made it all not a war but natural, everybody else made it a war but Grant made it natural. I always want to collaborate with some one about General Grant, I have written about him in Four In America, as if he might have been Hiram Grant instead of Ulysses Grant and what a difference that would have made. Lloyd Lewis liked what I said about him and so now I want to collaborate with him about General Grant.

So we drove through Fredericksburg where Ellen Lamotte had been to school and through the rest of Virginia down to Richmond and the James River. Later on we went again to lecture and that time I did everything but this time we only ate spoon bread and little tender loins of pork and hot bread on the James River. I was very excited naturally I was and although I had always known everything about the Civil War I could not believe it when I saw it but it was all there that McClellan had gotten to within seven miles of Richmond it was unbelievable, to get within seven miles and to go away again, I had never really believed that it was so until I saw it there where it said it. Unbelievable that it was so. I can still see the stone that says it and know it was not invented but I cannot really yet believe that it is so. After all how can any one get there and go away but Grant knew that McClellan had always been that way. After all everybody being as they are makes it be what they are and of course they are it is exciting that they are what they are. We came back again to Washington, we went to Baltimore to lecture and it was a foggy night and they drove us over and the white line separating the middle of the road was all that could be seen. And then we had an oyster supper, and then we went back again and the railroad stations in Washington were just as I remembered them and then we went back to New York and to go on.

We liked to go back to New York and home to the hotel, the Rockefeller Center building the third part had gone up a lot it was almost done, it was cold in New York but you could still walk and they were all glad to see us as we walked as glad as they had been and that was a pleasure we were not sure they would be as pleased as they had been but they were. We changed our clothes again that is to say we left some things and took other things and we went away.

We went to New England and we stayed in Springfield Massachusetts and we went everywhere from there. We stayed there because the Kiddie was there, he was one of the editors of the Springfield Union and Mrs. Wesson, Smith and Wesson when we were in California as children we always had a revolver which was a Smith and Wesson, it is funny about names of course you know somebody has them but when you see one of them who has one of the names it always gives one a funny feeling of nothing being real at all. Grant did learn at school or at least he heard it very often that a noun is the name of anything and of course it is but then in a way it is the most troublesome of anything, if it is a name it should mean just that thing it should mean a revolver and not a person but it would not mean a revolver if it had not already meant a person. Well well.

I did not know that New England had become like Switzerland where there were schools and colleges and hotels and houses. It was that. Everywhere there were schools boys' schools girls' schools and colleges and houses, of course there were some woods and some mountains we went over and through some of them and there was the Atlantic Ocean but otherwise there were schools and colleges and everybody went to school in them. There were hotels too and it was in these hotels men were drunk in them we had not seen men drunk much anywhere else. We had expected to but we had not. When I was at Radcliffe as a student I naturally knew a great many New England women, naturally I did and of course I read Howells, he is very interesting one can read him again not perhaps as good as Trollope but pretty good and any one can read him again. He too knew that New Englanders had a fear of drinking, they also knew about it in Louisa Alcott I always remembered it in Rose In Bloom and how they worried about offering any one a drink and even about communion wine, any one in that way might suddenly find that they had a taste for drink and I slowly realized that New Englanders might. In California we had all had wine to drink like any Latin and drinking wine can make you drunk but not so very likely. The French with the Americanization of Europe have taken to what in California they used to call hard liquor instead of wine and water. They used to put water in their wine now they drink less quantity but no water in their wine and they drink hard liquor. Well I did realize in New England that that to me mysterious thing they used to talk about a taste for liquor did indeed matter. In New York and in the Middle Western country it had not seemed to matter. Another thing we saw for the first time and that in Springfield was the driving around and around to pick up somebody who had been left to do some shopping. That seemed a very funny thing to do. It was like the thing Lascaux thought when as a country boy he came to Paris and he thought the automobiles going around the Arc de Triomphe were a carousel. When they did that the first time in Springfield because we had left Mrs. Wesson and Alice Toklas to do some shopping I thought it was like that driving around and around the block because there was no way to wait and so to pick them up. It felt very funny that. I saw of course there was nothing else to do but it did seem a funny way to do. I was interested in everything we did and we did that. And confiding your automobile to any door-keeper or any one to take away for you that was very uncertain and not at all European, I commenced then in Springfield becoming more intimate with everything American.

We went everywhere in the automobile and once we were stuck in the snow but not quite. That is not when we were going to lecture but going visiting. We met Jo Alsop's mother there and I promised to send stamps to two boys there, and I collected them for quite a while but we had no way of knowing who they were so I sent them to Kitty Buss. She collects them. Carl Van Vechten says if there was no other reason for wanting the Roosevelt administration it would be because of all the new stamps such nice stamps they are always making but I myself like very much better the advertisements the French government put on their stamps, Blédine la Seconde Mamman and Blédine pour bébé and Pétrole Hahn contre la chute des cheveux and the Layettes Tetra, I send these faithfully to everybody and nobody has ever mentioned them except Clare de Gruchy with whom Alice Toklas went to school, nobody else has ever mentioned them, do they not notice them or does it not please them or do they think that stamps should have their own individual being, well anyway I do continue to put them on the letters I write and I write a great many of them. I like to write them.

So we went on lecturing at colleges and even in schools in New England, and I found out all the troubles they have with chains on the tires. It is surprising that there has not been found anything better to do about them, they always break and when there is no snow they skid and when there is there is no way to take them off without a good deal of trouble and then there are little cheap ones which are easy to put on but unlike other cheap things in America they break so easily they cannot really be made of the best material. Perhaps it is like weather there is really no way to regulate them, I was interested in everything. I lectured in men's colleges and in women's colleges, the men's I liked best was Wesleyan. It was Hitchcock that arranged that. I had known him in Paris and not liked him, he was a friend of Virgil Thomson and I had once seen him rather wonderfully on the rue de Rennes, but over there I did like him, he was very pleasant and he arranged everything and after the lecture I liked talking to the Wesleyan men. We talked about and that has always been a puzzle to me why American men think that success is everything when they know that eighty percent of them are not going to succeed more than to just keep going and why if they are not why they do not keep on being interested in the things that interested them when they were college men and why American men different from English men do not get more interesting as they get older. We talked about that a lot at Wesleyan. Then I liked Mount Holyoke, I liked that the best of the women's colleges in New England, we talked there mostly about the theatre and as they were really interested it was interesting. Afterwards it seemed rather strange to me that the two colleges which were really made to make missionaries were more interesting than those that had been made to make culture and the other professions. It made me wonder a lot about what it is to be American.

What schools and colleges do to any one is one of the things that is bothering. It was thirty years before but the universities had not changed each one of them put a certain stamp on those who went to them or did those who were going to be that way go to that one. But schools do it too and very often there is no choice but there is the parents' choice. Just yesterday we were all talking and they were talking about something, there were some Chinamen there and Americans and so the talking was political and they were talking about the character of Roosevelt and I said something and the American said no that would not be possible no one who had been to school at Saint Mark's could be such a one.

After all a school is a school. We went to the Choate school it was interesting.

It was the first time I had ever seen such a school. When I was brought up in East Oakland we all went to public school but at that time as the population was not large anybody could go to school with anybody. If you went to a private school that was because you were defective in some way or came from South America or something. Nothing able-bodied and ordinary-minded went anywhere except to a public school and a public high school. Alice Toklas says in San Francisco it was different, all the little girls she knew went to private school, well anyway anybody can know that what happened to them happened to every one. So I had known nothing of private schools and now I was knowing. Not everybody but a great many these days in America go to private schools. There was a time and perhaps there still is when I did think that America had become very much like England was when it was Victorian. I had thought that before I went over after that I was not so certain that it was so much like England when England was Victorian.

But the private schools were supposed to be forming what in England were called the governing classes only in America did they govern well perhaps they do now after all. From Roosevelt to

Roosevelt there might have come to be the governing classes but really and truly they are not, they have really come to be the employees. I was interested.

I went to the Choate school and they were charming to me. The boys from twelve to sixteen listened really listened to everything I had to say and I talked to them about whether one's contemporaries were really contemporary. And then later the next morning we had a talk about that. I had been much struck by the Choate school literary magazine which did have extraordinary good writing in it, and now the Utica High School has sent me a Gertrude Stein number and again it is striking how well they are writing. It is a bother.

Once long ago René Crevel and I talked about education. I said that French boys believed in the teaching of their teachers. American boys did not. Later on I talked with François d'Aiguy about this. He said French boys who went to the lycées which are controlled by the government did believe in what the teachers believed, and therefore they never did revolt, but boys who went to what in France they call a boite, a box that is to the religious schools, the Catholic schools, they did not have to believe what the teachers believe, they could and did believe in Catholicism but they did not have to believe what the teacher believed and so they did have some intellectual freedom. I said to the Choate teachers I wonder if the boys can ever come to be themselves because you are all so reasonable and so sweet to them that inevitably they are convinced too soon. Is not that the trouble with American education that if they are to be convinced at all they are convinced too soon is it not the trouble with any republican education. Other than republican education does not convince them so most of them do not have any conviction and the few who have are not convinced too soon. Education does not do something but a certain kind of woman either goes to or comes out of Smith or Bryn Mawr or Radcliffe or Vassar or Wellesley. Anybody can almost know just what is all their life after going to happen to them and it almost does, Oxford and Cambridge make them different the same, and Yale and Harvard or Berkeley and Palo Alto, even having different presidents in succession does not seem to affect anything, it can hardly be food and climate as they are all pretty near together, what is it perhaps it is food and climate perhaps it is because even near together can be a good distance apart, and the food was different, they ate very differently in one of these colleges from the other one they certainly do and did. We ate in each one of them and so we know, the climate did not seem so different but perhaps it was more different than it seemed.

No they had not changed not any one of them I might have gone to school with the ones where I did go to school, that is Radcliffe the others were as they had been, it was easy to see and know that they were as they had been.

Well what had I been. Of course after all there was the nineteenth century and there is the twentieth century, that is undeniable and I began then when evolution was still exciting very exciting. I just found on the quays Darwin's Descent of Man and I have just given it to Louis Bromfield who had never read it. After all to him Darwin was not so near as he had been when I began knowing everything.

Science meant everything and any one who had an active mind could complete mechanics and evolution, philosophy was not interesting, it like religion was satisfaction in a solution but science meant that a solution was a way to a problem. As Carl said of Mabel Luhan, a marriage for her is but a springboard to a higher life. That was what science was every solution was an opening to another problem and then William James came that is I came to him and he said science is not a solution and not a problem it is a statement of the observation of things observed and perhaps therefore not interesting perhaps therefore only abjectly true.

There was of course science and evolution and there were of

course the fact that stars were worlds and that space had no limitation and still if civilizations always came to be dead of course they
had to come to be dead since the earth had no more size than it
had how could other civilizations come if those that were did not
come to be dead but if they did come to be dead then one was just
as good as another one and so was science and progress interesting
that is was it exciting but after all there was evolution and James'
the Will to Live and I I had always been afraid always would be
afraid but after all was that what it was to be not refusing to be
dead although after all every one was refusing to be dead.

After all one is brought up not a Christian but in Christian
thinking and I can remember being very excited when I first read
the Old Testament to see that they never spoke of a future life,
there was a God there was eternity but there was no future life
and I found how naturally that worried me, that there is no limit
to space and yet one is living in a limited space and inside oneself
there is no sense of time but actually one is always living in time,
and there is the will to live but really when one is completely wise
that is when one is a genius the things that make you a genius
make you live but have nothing to do with being living that is
with the struggle for existence. Really genius that is the existing
without any internal recognition of time has nothing to do with
the will to live, and yet they use it like that. And so naturally science is not interesting since it is the statement of observation and
the laws of science are like all laws they are paper laws, as the Chinese call them, they make believe that they do something so as to
keep every one from knowing that they are not going on living.
But after all I was a natural believer in republics a natural believer
in science a natural believer in progress and I began to write. After
all I was a natural believer just as the present generation are natural believers in Soviets and proletarian literature and social laws
and everything although really it does not really make them be living any more than science and progress and democracies did me.

This is what I mean. After all if you ask a question unless not even then when you are very little is the answer interesting, if there is an answer why listen to it if you can ask another question, listening to an answer makes you know that time is existing but asking a question makes you think that perhaps it does not.

And so we left New England behind us and went back to New York and there we arranged to go to Chicago University later, I was to give four lectures and a week of conferences and a week of meeting individual students, two weeks in all.

And then we left for Washington and for all points South. Carl went with us to Richmond, we were quite excited we were going to North and South Carolina and New Orleans and Alabama and Saint Louis. We were very excited.

We were going to Richmond. We were going to the University of Virginia and William and Mary and the University of Richmond and then later we found out about Sweet Briar and we went there. We were going to see Virginia. After all that can mean anything or something to any American. I had been in Norfolk Virginia and in Hampton fairly often we used to go to New York from Baltimore by water and then we did used to go to Old Point Comfort sometimes from Baltimore but Richmond I had seen once in coming back from Norfolk when the hurricane outside would not let the boat go on, and we had to come back again to Baltimore and we had to change trains in Richmond but now we were really going to be there and we were. We went by train. The first thing that there was to see in going all the way through Virginia I always in a train all the time look out of the window the first thing to see was that there did not seem to be any inhabitants in Virginia. It was the only place in America where there were no houses no people to see, there were hills and woods and red earth out of which they were made and there were no houses and no people to see. Of course when they fought there it had been called the Wilderness, the campaign in the Wilderness but I had no realization that almost all Virginia was that, after all the novels make it sound inhabited, the stories of it make it sound inhabited but there was of course the days and days of fighting in the Wilderness and I had never thought of that. And then they asked me what I thought of Virginia and I said I thought it was uninhabited, and they all of them wrote about that did I mean spirits of others or did I mean something else and I meant nothing but that that it was uninhabited.

The rest of America had been very much inhabited much more than I expected, roads and country were inhabited the country looked and was inhabited but not in Virginia no not Virginia. Later on when we were driving from one university to the other and we went through all the miles of uninhabited Virginia Mrs. Muncie said to me when I said that to her, oh yes she said my father says that in Virginia he is an interesting man my father and he says he sits and lets the pine trees grow.

We were in Richmond not so Southern as I had expected and not so Virginian, the houses were like those in the middle-western towns with trees and squares in them but not as Richmond as I had expected. There was the site of Libby prison the building is in the museum in Chicago and there was Poe's home and there was plenty of open space but it was not as Southern and it did not look like an old city not as I had expected to have seen it, it was not really as Southern as Baltimore or even Philadelphia of course it was but it was not the way that I had expected and there did not seem to be many old houses in it as there were in New England cities and any way I was not disappointed it was a nice place to walk in and the hotel had baby alligators in it and we liked everything.

I walked around a good deal in Richmond, as I was walking they would come up to me in an automobile anybody and ask me if they could take me anywhere but I said I liked walking and I went on walking and there were a great many statues everywhere and naturally I did look at all of them. Once I saw one of them that at a distance did not look like a confederate war one but when I went closer yes it was one. And then I went back to the hotel. I always found the hotel again although I sometimes worried lest I would not find it but then somebody would know what hotel it was it was always the best one and any one would help me get back to it. That is one of the things that was different. I had taken it for granted that every room in any hotel would have a radio in it and that the radio would be going every minute and that even if the one in our rooms was not going we would hear all the others. Not at all mostly there was no radio in the room and if you wanted one you were supposed to ask for it of course we did not want one and in the hotels where there was one it was one that only sent out the crooning that they were doing in the dining room that seemed to be the only thing that ever came out of them. Of course we had never owned one, and practically I had never listened to one, not because there are not lots of them in France of course there are there but naturally if you are doing what I am doing you want quiet in the home and nothing very modern, anybody can understand that. So I went on walking around Richmond and seeing the statues there are a great many of them, and I meditated as I always had meditated about the Civil War. It was one of the interesting wars in the world the Civil War, the French revolutionary fighting before Napoleon took charge of it had been the first one of one crowd against another crowd of people just that, and the Civil War was completely that. The 1914–1918 war was bigger and had different arms but eventually it added nothing to what had been imagined in the Civil War and naturally I always thought about that. And here I was in Richmond and I had always thought about General Lee and I did think about that. I had always thought not thought but felt that Lee was a man who knew that the South could not win of course he knew that thing how could a man who was destined by General Scott to succeed him in command of the American armies who knew that war was dependent upon arms and resources and who knew all that how could he not know that the South could not win and he did know it of that I am completely certain, he did know it, he acted he always acted like a man leading a country in defeat, he always knew it but and that is why I think him a weak man he did not have the courage to say it, if he had had that courage well perhaps there would have been not just then and so not likely later that Civil War but if there had not been would America have been as interesting. Very likely not very likely not. But the man who could knowing it lead his people to defeat it well any way I could never feel that any one could make a hero of him. I could not. I said this one day down in Charleston, I was talking to some man who had a Southern wife and a Southern father-in-law, who was an important Southern newspaper editor and he said that is interesting because my father-in-law one day it was a rainy Sunday and some body said something about Lee and my father-in-law said yes he was a great man a great great man and we all love him and I sometimes think that if he had been here of a rainy Sunday well yes I would not want him here all day of a rainy Sunday.

No, leading his fellow citizens to defeat did not excite him it did not exalt him it did not depress him, he did it because he could not say no to it and that does not make him interesting all day of a rainy Sunday.

So I was interested in being in Richmond and in Virginia and I was interested in hearing what they were all saying and I was interested, after all there never will be anything more interesting in America than that Civil War never.

And so we went to the University of Virginia, Charlottesville and I had a good time there, Jefferson did make a place that is a pleasure there, if you can have enough columns and they are all over then a place is interesting, Washington used to be like that, columns are always interesting and there never were as many of them anywhere as there were there at the University of Virginia, so many of them and where you could see all of them. They took us all around to see everything and they gave us good food everywhere and in the hotel and just opposite was the Court House and there they were standing and leaning there of course they were all there, and they were there. And of course Poe had been to the University and I was speaking to the Raven Society and of course I had always liked Poe I liked his explanation of the Raven and I liked his None can sing so wildly well and best of all I like because that is Bilignin in the greenest of our valleys by good angels tenant-ted, at least that is the way I always say it, I am never corrected when I say it wrong at least I never change the saying of it, and then just the morning of leaving the president of the Raven Society gave me his key to Poe's room in the University where they have their meetings, it is a Yale key with Raven on one side and Virginia on the other, and of course it is just a Yale key and perhaps he gives it to every one but I do not think so, I think he just gave it to me and I always carry it in the bill folder I bought on Fifth Avenue and with the permission to drive that I got in California. That was very funny. They said I had to have one so I went with some one to get it and they asked some twenty questions and nothing had anything to do with how you drive or with machines, it all had to do with your health and your mother's and father's health and with what you would do if anything happened and what the rules of the road are, well I answered them all and they were mostly right after all those things are just ordinary common sense and I said afterward but Alice Toklas who cannot drive at all could have answered all these questions just as well I suppose they take it so for granted that everybody can drive they would no more think of asking you about the actual making the car go than they would think of asking you how you make your legs go when you walk. That you can make the car go they take for granted,

248

that you make it go and stop and turn around they take for granted. So those are the things I carry in my pocket, the Raven key and the permission to drive in California.

We went to William and Mary and it was there that I began to talk to them talk to them about everything. I told them what was the use of their being young if they had the same opinions as all of them who were eighty and a hundred then what was the use. Somebody has to have an individual feeling and it might be a Californian or a Virginian. It was a Californian, I can call myself a Californian because I was there from six to seventeen and a Virginian might have an individual feeling, California and Virginia have at one time had a feeling that they were not part just being American, when Alice Toklas a Californian and Pat Bruce a Virginian used to talk about what was American I always said that Richmond and San Francisco did not make anybody know what was American, it was just Virginia and California and is California that now no not now and Virginia well I told them that there was no use in being young if they had the same way of thinking as if they had the opinions and they did have them and the same point of view and they did have them of what Virginia had been. What was the use. And that is all there is about it, it looks as if it might commence and it never does begin and like General Lee they lead themselves to a predestined defeat and knowing it, if they did not know it then it would be a forlorn hope but they know it and so what is the use of their being young, there is none.

It was lovely at William and Mary, even the parts that had been done over, of course the parts that had been done over by Rockefeller were done over, but if they are not there and you want them there they have to be done over, and somebody a great many do want them there. You put new where the old was and old where the new was and that makes restoration and perhaps some time hardly anybody can tell but not just now not now at all but we liked it all. Then they drove us to Yorktown and that was not so

249

exciting as Richmond had been, it was lovely rolling country and it was a little winter yet but it was almost spring. Then we went back to Richmond again.

Then we heard of Sweet Briar.

When we were going to Richmond at some station we saw a great many very good-looking girls and the same kind of young men, the young men were from the University of Virginia that we knew but we knew that there were no women there and then we heard about Sweet Briar. Later two professors and one of their wives came to Richmond to take us to Sweet Briar, one of their automobiles did not go very well it had been so well prepared that it did not go, he was a Spaniard and that might be even so, but any way we did get there and then later they took us not these but some others as far as Chapel Hill.

Sweet Briar was charming, it had box hedges and it was charming. We stayed there a night and a day. Naturally the Northern girls came South but once there they might as well have come from there, it was charming, and I talked a long time to one of them and I met all of them and we liked everything, spring had almost come.

The one I talked to was neither North nor South, they had always been in the army and in that way any one can marry any one who comes from there or anywhere. She too was Virginian that is to say she believed what they had believed when Virginians were Virginians. They believed that they saw the tree when the tree had been replaced by a building, seeing the tree might be interesting, if it could be made interesting but for this generation seeing it as a tree when it has been replaced by a building and that building not made of wood can be not being interesting. Well it does not make much difference, some creation has to be made in any generation, and since it is not made by a Virginian then it is not made by a Virginia even if a thing is not there it can be pleasant and Virginia was it was very pleasant.

After all every century has to be made by somebody being something and it is difficult to do it again and anyway when it is done it is done and having been done it does not make any time to begin again. When I began writing I was always writing about beginning again and again. In The Making of Americans I was making a continuous present a continuous beginning again and again, the way they do in making automobiles or anything, each one has to be begun, but now everything having been begun nothing had to be begun again.

Now I am writing about what is which is being existing. I am not interested in their going on anyway we were driven from Virginia to North Carolina. Every state was exciting. The part of Virginia next to North Carolina was more inhabited, as North Carolina was, there were farms and people on them and there were no more hills and woods covering them. They told me that North Carolina was not like Virginia and South Carolina and it was not.

There we first saw cotton growing that is to say we saw the stalks where it had grown the summer before, it was the first farming we had seen since we had been in the South, the fields were small and the country was simple and pleasant and then we came to Chapel Hill. I had never heard of Chapel Hill but it is important, lots of places that the name was not known not to me were and here they had the best collection of Spanish books anywhere in the world and lots of students from everywhere in the world and a nice town and a pleasant spring. It was spring then. Of course I often have not heard of it even if it is well known but there are lots of places in America that have enormous collections of something very often the best anywhere and they are not well known at least well yes not well known, and beside Chapel Hill was the first state university in America and I had never heard of it and did not know that it was so of North Carolina. However there it was and we liked it. Duke's College was near too and that was made by tobacco, Lucky Strikes and Camels, the better cigarette that we had met when the

251

doughboys first came over and they had made the Duke fortune and they built this university and now there was the depression and they did not have very much money and so Chapel Hill was the better. So they said and we believed them.

We liked Chapel Hill we liked the hotel, you ate well, we liked the professors and the men and women and I liked walking and then there was a place a sort of tower and it had newly planted box hedges around it and it looked like a water tower but it was not a water tower and when I went inside to read what was cut into it, it said that it was erected by a family the name was given and that was all that there was to it. No war no peace no anything, there was a family and it had a name there was a tower and there were lots of box hedges around it and they were small now but some time they would be larger. That was at Chapel Hill.

Then we were to go to Charleston one of the professors said they would take us to Cheraw and some one from Charleston said they would call for us at Cheraw and we did not know where Cheraw was but we liked it and it rained. We went to Cheraw it rained all the way through North Carolina and then we lunched at Cheraw. Cheraw looked as it should, it was a planter's hotel, it rained but it looked as it should and we ate very well. There they called for us and it rained and we went on to Charleston, and it was a very different state from the state of North Carolina. It was South Carolina.

It rained all day and all the way and the houses on each side of the road were interesting, there were school houses with white children and school houses with Negro children, there were little ones and there were lots of them surprisingly tall but that would be natural in South Carolina, the houses the ones where Negroes were living had a fire burning which showed as if the house was burning it was on the floor but we thought it was probably in a kind of a well as the houses were built on little stilts to keep them off the ground and let the chickens and things live under and then later we forgot to ask any one in what the fire was built that seemed like a bonfire inside in the building it could not have been built on the floor because the earth was not the flooring, well anyway anybody down there knows about the fires and we forgot to ask them and we did not think of it again. And then we went over the road that goes through the swamps and we saw for the first time the moss hanging from the trees, the moss is not really moss but streamers very pretty in the hand but dirty in the trees, and it is spreading, it is going all the way to California and with it the mocking bird is traveling. After all trailers must take anything that wants to go wherever it feels comfortable for growing, nothing can stop them. The moss hanging does look dirty, we are accustomed here in France to the mistletoe which makes a round ball everywhere in almost every tree, but there it is streaming and it looks as if it had been left behind by a flood that went over everything and all the way and then in Charleston we knew that a flood like that is not an invention.

We finally were in Charleston and the hotel had the best food of any food we had yet eaten and then we were invited to see the swamp gardens and they gave us lunch beforehand and that was the best lunch of all the lunches we have ever eaten, we can still tell everything we ate and what it was that made it better than anything else that we had ever eaten.

The swamp garden was wet we were in a boat and it was raining, it was a quiet flood and the trees had the habit of it but as we had not it was wet and we did not have to remember it. There are things like the illustrations of Dante in America, there were the walking sleepers in the Chicago marathon and there are the trees in the swamp garden in Charleston. Perhaps America will have that something having neither earth nor hell nor heaven, I would like anything they did that made them, thank you very much for everything and of course every one is very welcome.

We met DuBois Heyward there in Charleston, and we liked

him. Porgy is a good story later in Texas it was amusing, he is a gentle man DuBois Heyward like his Porgy. We left Charleston and flew to Atlanta Georgia and took a train there for Birmingham, Alabama. I like all these names, Birmingham in England and Birmingham in Alabama, Birmingham in Alabama was a manufacturing town very much of a one a name does do something if it does anything.

In flying from Charleston to Atlanta we did know that there was a great deal of water and the fields were made against the water and that made them like the painting they call it abstract painting but there is no abstraction it is exactly like the fields with ploughing against the natural way the land is lying so that the furrows will not fill with all the water there is there to fill them. I liked looking down at them I did I did like it I liked looking down at everything or out at everything I liked looking at everything and there it all was and it was really there but it was hard to believe that it was all really there. Anybody born there can only know that about something but not about that thing but even so if any one has been away then it is all as not real as anything. We landed in Atlanta Georgia and were driven to a railroad station, I had never before been in Georgia and we went through Georgia. There on the road I read buy your flour meal and meat in Georgia. And I knew that that was interesting. Was it prose or was it poetry I knew that it was interesting, buy your flour meal and meat in Georgia.

What is the use of a country if you have a state, little by little they lose it and get it. I was brought up to believe in the North.

During the 1914–1918 war we had talked to so many Americans, but there in America we never met any of them, any of them that we had met during the war of course it is a big country and even if anybody does know you after all there are a great many who do not talk to you, a great many write to you but there are a great many who do not more do not than do it seems not but it is true.

There was the Kiddie of course he had come to be again and then there had been Duncan. Duncan had meant so much to us in Nîmes. Alice Toklas when we were going to Alabama tried to hear of him again, he had been in Alabama the last we had heard of him and he was in Alabama he was in Birmingham. They discovered him, he had not known about himself in the Autobiography when they discovered him. It might have been exciting. It was funny we knew all about them but we did not know what they were going to do, we thought we did but we did not, we did not think the Kiddie would become a school teacher and then an editor we thought he was to become a dignified business man, and we thought Duncan would become an energetic something and he did not, he became a failure as a decorator, now we would never have thought about that as he was naturally the organizer of everything for the officers and for his company, and the only time he ever mentioned anything was when he said looking at the flag that is the rose color my mother does my room over when I come home from anywhere. We might have thought of it but we did not, Americans when they are twenty-one are always organizers I suppose those that really organize later do not organize then, they use up their organizing energy and then well then then they become a failure, after all to be older is to be older, we did see Duncan and his mother and his sisters and his wife and his children. One little boy read a great deal young American boys do read a great deal they read anything that they can get that is printed, lots of young American boys are like that they were like that when I was a little girl and it is surprising with radios and everything that they are still like that, not surprising because really being alone with reading is more intense than hearing anything, anybody really can know that and anybody when they are very young really can know that, Duncan's little boy did and I liked it that he did, I always like it that nothing is so intense as being alone with a book.

So we went away from Birmingham, they came over in a band

from the University near by to listen to me and if we had had time we would have gone over but we did not have time, just lately one of them who is writing about Southern authors asked me if I had said what one of them said I said, I said of course I do not remember but if they said I said what they said I said very likely I did because in general Americans are accurate when they say you said what you said, French are much less accurate about what you said. So we went away from Birmingham by airplane to New Orleans and we went over the water this time not land water but sea water and came to the large hotel in New Orleans, it seemed very political I do not suppose it was but so it seemed. Sherwood Anderson was in New Orleans and that was a pleasure and he brought us to the hotel twenty-five oranges for twenty-five cents and they were very sweet oranges and we ate them all together and it was a pleasure.

It was a pleasure it was warm like summer and Sherwood was there and he had his car and we went about together and we ate in restaurants together and we met the man who wrote Green Pastures, in New York the one who had put it on the stage came and talked to us one day at the restaurant at the Algonquin and we went about with Miss Henderson we had known her in Paris she and her family had always been in New Orleans and she took us to see her friends in the old houses where all their portraits had been painted by the same painters as the contemporary French had been and the only one who has made New Orleans feel as New Orleans was then is Thornton Wilder in his little play called The French Queens, we liked being in New Orleans, after all we had lived for thirty years in France and after all Alice Toklas says not but still there it is after all.

It was like a provincial town in Southern France not the hotel and of course there were a great many more Negroes everywhere but the Negroes were like French Negroes and not like American ones, they did not have it on their mind being one, they naturally were in New Orleans and it was not of any importance to any one, French Negroes take being French as a natural thing, the French believe in family and in occupation which makes class but being a Frenchman covers everything and a French Negro has the same thing, it seemed to us that the New Orleans Negroes were more French than American. I lectured at Tulane University and the head of the English department drove us around and we liked everything he told about his father-in-law founding the society of the century-old live oaks, it is the oaks themselves that are the society not the people that own them, and that excited Alice Toklas very much because she was sure that in California there were lots of them and he said perhaps but the oaks like any chosen one have to have their papers to prove their birth and age and everything has to be in order. We liked all we heard about Louisiana and we wanted to come back and go all around everywhere there and it was a little late for the azaleas and camelias but we saw some and we saw the little hill they built in the park to prove they had one so that New Orleans children would know a hill when they saw one and Sherwood was indignant when I complained of the Mississippi River and that I had seen it where it was not a very broad one and he took us all along it and said it is an enormous one and I said well and he said well can't you see that it is a mile deep as well as a mile wide and I said that Mark Twain's Life On The Mississippi had made it so real to me and the Saint Nicholas when I was a little girl and there was a story of a flood and I had liked that and now well there was something the matter I could not quite get used to it not looking quite as enormous as I had always seen it when I read about it and he said come again and see it and sometimes it is like that if you come again and see it you will be astonished that you did not know how wide and deep it was and looked and anyway we liked being in New Orleans.

The hotel did look like a political hotel it looked as if everybody in it had something to do with politics, the only other hotel we had seen that looked like that was at Lansing the capital of Michigan where the big hotel opposite had just burned down, it looked like one of those political hotels the one in which we were there and ate very well and everybody in it looked like the photographs in any American book which is the life of a man important in politics. It was very funny the other day for the first time I went to the French Chamber of Deputies. You always have to do a thing for the first time and after all these years I went to the Chamber of Deputies, we know the librarian now, he lives in the country near Bilignin, and so he gave us cards to go and so we went. Herriot was there raised up on high and he sat and he looked like the American statesmen of 1870-1880 and it was funny he was the size and the clothes and the being awake and asleep and the cuffs and the men coming over and talking to him and being President of the Chamber of a republic makes them alike Frenchmen or Americans, they are just like that.

It was there at the hotel that the press photographer told me all about his life photographing Huey Long, of course we did not see him, he might have been there but he was not and now he is dead and that is all there is to him.

We left New Orleans in an airplane it was not a very big one and we were to fly to Saint Louis but the airplane did die at least it only got as far as Memphis, Tennessee and we now know that when they did not go on any further it really did not matter there was a reason for it and why bother. We used to want to know the reason but now we just got out and went on some other way. Memphis, Tennessee was exciting. Every where we stopped was exciting. We went to the hotel there.

I had always known about Memphis, Tennessee and it looked like Memphis, Tennessee, it looked just as it should, Memphis, Tennessee, all except the hotel, the hotel was a good hotel we did eat very well. And there seemed to be so much social life there, very many girls and very many men and they all seemed to be there as if there was no other anywhere all the life they lived they lived there. We left there and took the train for Saint Louis. I liked that train ride, the conductor told me all about the kind of people that lived all along there. Tennessee and Arkansas of course I liked to look out at Tennessee and at Arkansas, there were farms small farms all along there. He said foreigners who settled down there made a better living than those who came from there and then we arrived at Saint Louis. We ate very very well there. I was interested in Saint Louis, and it was enormous the houses and the gardens and every way everything looked, everything looked enormous in Saint Louis. We enjoyed it there. Perhaps Sherwood was right and it was the Mississippi but the Mississippi had not done that elsewhere. Anyway they did what we wanted. They asked us what we would like to do and I said I would like to see all the places Winston Churchill had mentioned in The Crisis. They were very nice about it only it was difficult to do because naturally they should have but they really did not know a lot about what Winston Churchill mentioned in The Crisis. The Crisis was a best seller when I read it and naturally I remembered it, it is funny I never get over being puzzled about it, best sellers are well written and they are moving and of course in the nineteenth century best sellers were things that go on being but the difference between one that is and one that is not writing that goes on being read, you do know the difference that is to say I know the difference when I can or cannot read it not that that has anything to do with it either, I can read things and be held by them and they are nothing that will go on being read and I do know the difference of course I know the difference but to describe the difference, it is not possible to describe the difference, I tried to in the lecture I gave last winter in Oxford and Cambridge What Are Masterpieces And Why Are There So Few Of Them, it is the same thing that knowing inside in one that one is a genius, what difference is there inside in one from the others inside in

259

them who are not one, what is the difference, there is a difference what is the difference, oh yes it seems easy enough to say it and even if you know it although inside in yourself you do not know but there is one if there is one. Anthony Trollope and Dickens and Thackeray were best sellers in the nineteenth century in the twentieth century best sellers mostly are not that thing, The Crisis was not that thing although I can read it again and again, oh yes it all has to do that inside in you you are separated away from connection and at the same time you do not think about that thing, well anyway I did describe it in a way in What Are Master-Pieces And Why Are There So Few Of Them.

When I came to Saint Louis I wanted to see all the places mentioned by Winston Churchill in The Crisis but they mostly could not find them, we found the Mississippi River and almost where they went to it, and some of the homes and then we gave it up and went on to see something that they could find and that I had not really known was there and that was the house of Ulysses Grant.

It was a cabin and it had once been lived in, when you read Grant's memoirs it does not quite sound as if that was the sort of place that he lived in. I have just been reading it but there seems to be no doubt about it that was the house he did live in. And then we drove back again and I asked them how could people when now they could not have so many servants how could they live in those big houses that were everywhere in Saint Louis, in London now almost every one has given up living in those big houses but they said yes in Saint Louis yes they did still in Saint Louis live in those houses yes they did, some families did not to be sure families are big families in Saint Louis, they did a great many did still live in these big houses. And we ate very well in Saint Louis and then we flew to Chicago because in Chicago I was for the first time to teach that is not to teach but to be regularly with students around me. Of course I talk a great deal and naturally if you talk well anyway there always are some who are there when I am talking and I was a little nervous about this teaching but it really turned out to be just the same as it always had been, I talked a great deal and they talked some and it really was not any different than if I had been here at home. A few were quite a few more were there but as I had found the difference between three and twenty or five and forty once there is that difference it does not really seem to matter. That is what makes governments what they are.

Thornton Wilder gave us his apartment it had two bedrooms and a sitting room dining room with a little kitchen and it had a nice way to see the Midway which was snowy and I liked to see it and I hired myself a drive yourself car a Ford car and it was surprisingly cheap to do this and I was to write four lectures and Alice Toklas was to keep house in Chicago and it was all to be very pleasant and it was.

The most exciting thing was the drive yourself car.

I had been driven a great deal since I was in America and now I was to drive myself. In Illinois there was no examination you just had to find the place to hire the car and we found it. There are so many cars in America so of course they could hire me one. It was some little distance away the place where we found it under the elevated and then in a street that was a little dreary and I said to the man but this garage is too far away, when I come home in the evening I would not want to come all this way to put it away. Why he said where are you living, in a little street off the Midway I said, well he said, well I said, well he said what is the matter with it, why nothing I said it is a nice quiet street, a friend has loaned us an apartment, well he said, what is it, well I said, yes he said, and I said you mean I can leave it there all night I said and he said why not and I said but dont I have to leave a light, why isn't the street lighted he said why yes very well lighted and he said well and I said all right. And we did we left it there all and every night. One morning when I woke up I always looked out to see if the car was still there but it had been snowing all night and the car was there and it was all covered with snow, I said to Alice Toklas what shall we do and she said she would telephone to the garage. She did. They said well what is it, and we said the car was covered with snow, well they said wouldn't it go and we said how could we tell if it was covered with snow and they said isn't there a janitor there and we said oh yes, well they said he could brush it off and we called him and he did and then we went off. Everything in America is just as easy as that.

It was a puzzle all the stolen cars so they said and yet nobody seemed to think about it you just left them in the street. We liked it.

When I was going to the lecture room one day one of the tires of the car had flattened, one of the boys said if you will give me your key and tell me the name of your garage I will have it ready for you and when I came out of course it was ready for me, once when we had gone into Chicago I always called it going into Chicago from the University once when we had gone in to do some shopping and we were lunching, a tire was flat and so I gave my key to the door-man and told him and told him to tell the garage I wished they would change the tire this time and when we came out there was a new car and with it newer tires and I said but that is not mine oh no said the door-man they took the other away and they left you this one and I never saw the other one again naturally not I had this one. I liked everything.

We did get lost in the park and at first we did get lost with the road signs. That is one of the things that is very interesting, the different way different countries tell you how to go along. In France it is all done by drawing in America mostly by words and most of them words of one syllable. No left U turns, that took me some time so much so that I did one. The policeman said where do you think you are going, I said I was turning, I guess you are a stranger he said and I said I was one and he said well go on but you will most likely get killed before you leave town.

Thornton had arranged everything, chosen those who were to come all the time and those who were to come part of the time, and it was all interesting. I gave four lectures which I had just written which were about organization and inside and outside because of course it is troublesome, here we are all living and we have to like something like it enough so that it is something and so I wrote about newspapers being dull reading because they repeat every day the news of that day and they have to print it as if it were just happening and it always had happened some time ago at least some hours ago and after all a thing is interesting that you see happening or that has happened long enough back so that it has an existence which is romanticism it having happened so long ago that though it is there it is really not happening here. Well anyway the great point is that it really holds your attention. Living every day does but then that is not enough to satisfy any one now because every one knows that every day has no future to it as it used to have in the emotion of every one living. When you knew that if you lived every day you would go on living then living every day was a complete occupation, but hardly any one is really convinced now that if they live every day that they will go on living, something is very likely to happen, it of course was always true that something was likely to happen to change everything only now everybody knows about everything and so living every day is not as occupying, that is the reason they like Briggs' Mr. and Mrs. because that almost looks like every day living. I said so much about everything I always have said a great deal about everything there was of course the thousand pages of The Making of Americans that I had written when I began writing. I was then and ever since filled with the fact that there are so many millions always living and each one is his own self inside him.

I talked with them all almost every afternoon the things I would naturally have been writing. There is a bother about that you get more familiar with a thing when you say it than when you write it, when you say it you repeat it when you write it you never do because when you write it is in you and when you say it they hear you. After two weeks I wondered if I heard what I said or if I only heard them hearing what I said. When I write I write and when I talk I talk and the two are not one, no not for any one and when they come near being one, then the inside is not inside and the outside is not outside and I like the inside to be inside and the outside to be outside, it makes it more necessary to be one.

It was the first time I had been with a number of students all together since I left Radcliffe and did the experiments there on automatic writing and had about twenty Radcliffe and twenty Harvard students to experiment on. Then I concluded that there is no such thing as automatic writing among the people as one knows them. There has been a lot said about those experiments in automatic writing and I might as well tell it all over again.

To begin with.

When I was at Radcliffe I was of course very interested in psychology. I was interested in biology and I was interested in psychology and philosophy and history, that was all natural enough, I came out of the nineteenth century you had to be interested in evolution and biology, I liked thinking so I had to be interested in philosophy and I liked looking at every one and talking and listening so I had to be interested in history and psychology, I did not like anything abnormal or frightening so I did not care for histology or medicine and I do not like what is not what people are doing so chemistry and physiology did not attract me, and astronomy and mathematics were too far away and again too frightening, I read everything that was natural enough and not a thing to be studied, I knew what writing was and if you read it and could read it you knew it so there was no use having any one teach you anything about it, I suppose about all these things I have not changed much.

James and Münsterberg were interested in me and so although I was an undergraduate indeed one who had not yet passed the entrance examinations they said I could come to the seminar in psychology and I liked that.

We were quite a funny lot, Sidis was there who afterwards had the son who passed everything when he was a little boy and then did nothing, McDougall a man afterwards well known who worked on conversion, William James was interested in that in connection with his Varieties of Religious Experience and Thorndyke who was busy incubating chickens and what they did then and a man named Leon Solomons who came from California and who was an intimate friend of mine, there were a number more but these were the ones I remember. Münsterberg had just come from Berlin and was interested in experimental psychology and William James liked thinking and talking and wondering about what any one was doing and we all of us worked with both of them. Sidis was interested in studying sub-conscious reactions but being a Russian he naturally expected us to do things and we did not do them. He would have a table covered with a cloth and one of us sat in front of it and then when he pulled off the cover there was a pistol underneath it, I remember I naturally did nothing after all why should any one do anything when they see a pistol around and there is no danger of anybody shooting. We all of us were somewhat discouraging to all of us. I remember one man complained when he was not given a good mark in the course he said after all he had been as good a subject as he could be he had done everything they had expected him to do and what more could he do. Leon Solomons and I were to work together, he was a graduate student taking his doctorate in psychology, we first were to do some thing connected with a tuning fork but as neither one of us had a very good ear for music that is for notes that was given up, and then it was suggested that we should do experiments in fatigue, and William James added a planchette, he liked a planchette, we made one of a piece of wood

265

and strings and then we were to try each other, I think it was I who preferred trying somebody else, after the months in the laboratory I had lost confidence in ourselves as subjects for experimentation, however Solomons tried me and I tried him one sat with the hand on the planchette and the other did not exactly guide it but started it, anyway he had us produce writing and then I was to experiment with students who had nothing to do with the study of psychology, any of them could come and they were to come the same ones before their examination and then afterwards, this piece of the work I did alone. Here I had no results there was no automatic writing, there were some circles and sometimes a vague letter but never any word or anything that could be called writing, there were about forty of them finally chosen at random and there were none who wrote anything. I was much interested because I gradually found out what was what in The Making of Americans I called the bottom nature of each one of them and I was very much interested in the way they had their nature in them and sitting there while their arm was in the planchette and hardly vaguely talking, it was interesting to me to see how I came to feel that I could come sometime to describe every kind there is of men and women and the bottom nature of them and the way it was mixed up with the other natures in them, I kept notes of each one of them and watched the difference between being active and being tired, the way it made some go faster and some go slower and I finally felt and which in The Making of Americans I began to do that one could make diagrams and describe every individual man and woman who ever was or is or will be living and then after I did so much of it The Making of Americans I decided that since it could be done what was the use of doing it, and anyway you always have to stop doing something sometime.

So this was my part of the experiments that were reported in the Psychological Review, Solomons reported what he called his and my automatic writing but I did not think that we either of us had been doing automatic writing, we always knew what we were doing how could we not when every minute in the laboratory we were doing what we were watching others doing, that was our training, but as he wrote the article after all I was an undergraduate and not a professional and as I am always very docile, and all the ideas had been his all that had been mine were the definitions of the characters of the men and women whom I had seen naturally it was as if I had written that I did that automatic writing. I did not think it was automatic I do not think so now, I do not think any university student is likely certainly not under observation is likely to be able to do genuinely automatic writing, I do not think so, that is under normal conditions, where there is no hypnotism or anything of that kind.

So that is the story of the article about automatic writing upon which has been based a great deal of theory about my writing. No, writing should be very exact and one must realize what there is inside in one and then in some way it comes into words and the more exactly the words fit the emotion the more beautiful the words that is what does happen and anybody who knows anything knows that thing.

One afternoon they the students there in Chicago asked me about automatic writing and I told them.

I liked all of them, Thornton had chosen them not those only who were interested in literature, but those interested in philosophy and history and anything, which made it much more varied and interesting. The head of the English Department at Princeton when he selected the men to come and meet me after the lecture asked every one who had been reading my work before I came to America, naturally he said they will all read at it now but you will want to meet those who were interested before you came over, and there were again the same mixture those interested in writing were not the majority.

So I did enjoy everything, there were three of them who were always insisting on proletarian literature and I used to tease them a good deal and then one day all three of them came with their heads shaved and I asked them why and they said they just had their hair shaved off them and I said summer has not come and they said they had anticipated something, there were three others who made poetry together, one of them had a charming rabbit expression and he wrote long poems and I liked them, he and the two others were inventing meters to go with sounds but I have never since heard anything of them, one interested in history had a very good way of having things pour out of him, nor do I know what has become of him, the only one of them all whom I have continued to hear from is Wendell Wilcox. He is one of the four young men whose writing just then was interesting, and all four of them were not very young they were all nearer thirty than twenty. It does change the age that is young, once in Paris it was twenty-six, then it was twenty-two, then it was nineteen and now it is between thirty and forty. They tell about a new young man, how old is he you say and they say he is thirty. In America too the most interesting young men just then were nearer thirty, Wendell Wilcox, Max White, Sam Steward and Paul Drus.

Max White was the first one of them about a year before I went to America he sent me some short stories about Spain, he had written an introduction I read that introduction and did not care for the introduction, then one day I picked it up again and read the stories one by one and I liked them and I wrote to him and told him and he wrote to me and he went on writing and I went on answering and then when we were to go to America he said we would not know him but he would be there to see us come in. We saw him quite often in New York and he was writing novels and I got some to look at them but not to take them and then he wanted the Guggenheim Prize and wanted me to write for him and I told him he probably had not much chance but my liking him certainly would not help and he sweetly said he would rather not get it backed by me than have it with some one else back of him and that was very nice of him and of course they did not give it to him. Now his first novel has been published and it is interesting and we like him, he does something that his newer crowd do do he makes a very clear line coming out of his writing, not heavy as the last generation were doing, but clear and as if everything was there not in the air but in being clearly there. That was Max White and he was one and then there was Paul Drus. Paul Drus is a Pole and is in Los Angeles and he sells photo-engravings and he writes a simple romantic story which has no romance in it because it is intended to be simply a story as he sees it and he prints each one of these on a little hand-press and sends it to me and I like to read them, lately he has not written one, I have never seen him I did not know about him when I was over there, he writes to me and I write to him, perhaps he will not write any more of these little stories which would be a pity because I liked them. Then there is Sam Steward. Sam Steward I have never seen, he had sent me a little book it was not what I liked it had more fancy than imagination and so I told him and now he has written another one Angels On The Bough and that is a good one, that too is clear and has in it more than clarity, he and Max White both succeed in saying something more than they say, their clear line creates something, it gave me pleasure, they took away his job from him at the University of the State of Washington on account of his book but now he has another one in the Loyola University of Chicago. We are expecting him this summer I think that he is interesting. Wendell Wilcox is not in their tradition, he has a feeling for meaning that is not beyond what the words are saying and of course that does make more brilliant writing and that is what he is doing.

So there were the young men thirty years old the young men that were interesting and then of course best of all there was Lloyd Lewis and being American. He has written the book which as he says is the history of a dead man and after all an American should do that, from Mark Twain on the American writer is the only one who has been able to write about a dead man as if he is a dead man. Detective fiction does do it now but then they have to think of it as a corpse but the American can think of a dead man as all dead and make him exist as a really dead one. There was that of course in the Old Testament but since then until the Americans wrote it was never done again. Lloyd Lewis in his Myths After Lincoln did this thing, Lincoln was dead and to be a dead man is that thing and Lloyd Lewis can do it, Mark Twain was the first one who did it. Perhaps it is because America is so little inhabitable that there have been so many animals simply dead there killed of course but simply dead there.

We saw a good deal of Lloyd Lewis those two weeks in Chicago and it was America that he really saw whatever else he saw. When we went to Pinafore, he leaned over when the little midshipman was there and whispered to me and it was thrillingly, that was the costume that when Farragut was young he wore. Pinafore was a nice thing but Farragut was more thrilling.

I am always wanting to collaborate with some one I wanted to collaborate with Sherwood Anderson in a history of Grant I wanted to collaborate with Louis Bromfield in a detective story and now I want to collaborate with Lloyd Lewis in a history of Grant. They are all very polite and enthusiastic about it but the collaboration does never take place. I suppose I like the word collaboration and I have a kind of imagination of how it could take place. Well anyway.

All this time we were living in the apartment Thornton had given us in Drexel Avenue and Alice Toklas praised the way the milk was there in the morning and she had never seen the milkman bring it in, she did catch him one morning slipping it in the hole in the wall that made it possible to do this thing and he was a little sheepish these things are not supposed to be seen, not like in France where nothing comes out without everything to do with its coming in. She liked it all the things to roast in everything that went by itself, the excellent meat that came to be most excellently roasted, the vegetables that were fresh and the cook books that told everything. She has fifteen of them, Mrs. Hahner at Marshall Fields kept giving her another one and now Mrs. Hahner has not forgotten for this year she sent another one The Country Kitchen and this one did excite me as much as it did Alice Toklas, we like to think about the American kitchen. On the whole we did eat well, some places much better than others but on the whole we did eat well and well.

So we liked it all and of course we saw every one and among others Mary Garden came. It was a pleasure to meet her, Virgil Thomson had wanted her for Saint Theresa and we had talked about it and her but we neither of us knew her and anyway neither of us is really enterprising and so nothing happened then, this was several years before it was given.

It was pleasant meeting her we liked her and she liked us and we met again in California and had a pleasant time together.

And so Chicago was almost over and we were going further this time it was Texas we had never been there naturally not but now we were. Sherwood had told us a good deal about it that pleased us. There was the valley his description of that was delicious. He said the valley of the Rio Grande spoken of by all Texans as the valley is perfectly flat miles of flat land just of the same flatness on either side and yet just at one moment begins the valley, only a Texan has the feeling he knows when it is just ordinary flat land and when it is a valley, it is not like the separation between the states because that is ruled lines on a map no this was more delicate you just felt that and any Texan could feel that but not any other one. We liked it and alas we never saw it we never had a chance to get to the valley we ate the fruit it made there is so much way-side fruit in America, so much way-side so much way-side and we liked all that way-side, but we did not see the valley. And then

Sherwood told about how the Middle Western farmers came down for a little winter fishing in the South of Texas and how they called each other by their states, Sherwood was Virginia and he told how they talked and what they said and we wanted to have a Ford car and wander all over, we will wander all over.

But first we left for Texas. We flew from Chicago to Dallas, Texas, we were staying with Miss Ela Hockaday at the Hockaday School I like that name. There we ate too well almost too well the corn meal sticks and all the rest was very filling and the cook came from Louisiana and Louisiana cooking in Texas is almost the best.

We had a good time in Dallas I began almost to like Texas the best, but we did like so many places the best. Dallas is a pretty town the houses different from elsewhere, and we were interested in everything, of course it was early and the flowers were every-where but they told us in the summer it was not easy gardening, one woman told us that she had at last decided not to keep a hos-pital for flowers any more, in some places you have to keep dahlias in the oven in some places you have to keep them in the refriger-ator and in Texas in the summer there really seems almost nothing to do with them. We understood that very well in Bilignin we had tried to grow flowers that would not naturally grow there, I sup-pose it is quite natural to want to grow flowers that will not natu-rally grow there.

The girls at Miss Hockaday's school were very interesting, as we were staying there we got to know them. They did understand what I had written, and that was a pleasure to me and to them a very great pleasure. There was a nice story about Then and When.

One afternoon they were all together and I asked them to ask questions, their teacher said they had told her they had been puz-zled by the portrait of When and that one of the girls had asked her to have me tell her. The portrait of When is in Fourteen Anon-ymous Portraits in Portraits and Prayers and I said to the teacher if she would find it I would read it, and I read it out loud to them

272

and I said but I do not quite see why you had any trouble in understanding that and I turned toward the girl and she seemed very troubled and that was all. The next day she came to me and she said of course anybody could understand the portrait of When no it was the portrait of Then and she had not wanted to say because of course they all did know the difference between When and Then. Ah I said the portrait of Then is more troublesome but still it is a portrait of Then. I liked it that they felt that way about it, there is the portrait of When and there is a portrait of Then. I liked them.

Since we left America we had not seen or heard anything of any Hockaday, they had sent us charming things to the boat when we went away but since then no word from any of them, and then just a few months ago a dozen of them came and we were delighted to have them, the Geographical History of America was just out and I read it to them I always like reading to Hockaday girls. It was funny about reading, I had never read anything aloud much, except all the letters of Queen Victoria to Alice Toklas when we were in Majorca at the beginning of the war and I had never thought of myself as reading and I had never read anything I had written and then when they asked me it seemed very strange to me and then somehow I came to like it, it sounds very interesting as I read it, quite so to me.

And so we liked Dallas Texas.

Once when I was walking I saw a car with Hockaday girls and a young man they asked me to come in I did and sat next to the young man I always like to sit beside the chauffeur naturally as I have always driven and rarely ever been driven it is natural enough to prefer to be in front besides it always is pleasanter to be there. I was interested in his car it had an automatic gear shift anyway he was an agent for it and we talked of going to Austin, Texas, to the University and he said would I like him to drive us it would be a pleasure to him and I said it would be a pleasure to us. So we finally left Dallas and he and a young Hockaday girl and one of the teachers and Alice Toklas and I drove down to Austin, Texas. It was a pleasant drive and I was still interested in his car because there was nothing in front to be a bother as there is in every car and I was wondering would I have one to go back to Paris and then later I tried it in San Francisco and on the hills the change of gear is cautious, it does it slow and really I did not think it would do in the Ain, that is where we are in summer and there are hills and mountains there. But anyway going to Austin was perfect, Texas is a level surface and I liked the way they ploughed and always against the natural lay of the land and it was only after Austin that we began to see the wild flowers and the Texas cattle. Of course anybody who has always read Wild Western stories and I have read a great many of them knows all about the Texas cattle it was very exciting. But first there was Austin. When we got there we had dinner altogether and the young Hockaday girl said she had telephoned to a girl to ask her to come to dinner, she had said come I am here with Gertrude Stein and her friend had said Oh yeah, over the telephone.

After Austin we went on, some one from Houston sent their car to call for us at Austin and take us to Houston it had a Negro chauffeur and as I always sit in front we talked a lot together. We talked about the Negroes as they were in Texas. He said except as before the law they had nothing at all to complain of. I said what did he mean. Well he said any Negro has as good a chance as any white man or woman to get education to go in for a profession to earn a living to be taken care of to do whatever any man or woman wants to do in any ordinary way of living, only if by any chance he does something and the white man is against him and it comes up into court why then of course it is another thing then he does not get the same justice as a white man. What do you mean exactly I said to him explain it to me. Well he said if a white man gets drunk or something or anyway goes into the Negro quarter and he does something and a Negro hits him or anything well then the Negro cannot get justice if it comes to be a thing that they have to go to court on. But I said if Negroes can go into any profession. Yes he said but that is just where the trouble comes in, now a Negro when he is in a profession he is not conscientious like a white man. Now what do you mean I asked him. Well he said now take doctoring. A Negro he gets to be a doctor just as good a doctor as a white man and then he begins practicing, now anybody falling sick he calls him, well sometimes he comes and sometimes he don't come you just can't count on him, now a white doctor any kind of white doctor no matter how poor you are or anything or if you are a colored or a white man it does not make any difference to him, perhaps he just as well had rather not come but if you call him and ask him to come he will always come. We all began having the colored doctor when he first began and then we found that if it did not suit him not all of them but a good many of them did not come and so we all went back to white men for doctoring. Do you think later they will change about this I asked him, I don't know he said I don't see how they can, they can't really come to think that it really is necessary to always come when anybody calls them and a white man even a very rich white man or a very important white man if he is a doctor will always come when you call him to come when you think you need him.

I liked talking and listening to him he was a very nice man and he took us pleasantly to Houston and we saw lots of wild flowers mostly blue ones and we saw the flat land and we saw the cattle not so many of them it had been a bad year for cattle as there had been too much cold weather and too much dry weather and as they do not in any way protect them they all died not all of them but a lot of them still it was a pleasure to see them and even see some cowboys and one cowgirl go toward them. It was a nice day and we came to Houston and went to a hotel where they gave us so many rooms we could look out in every direction and it was near a park and it was a lovely spring.

I liked the women who came that evening one was eighty years old and had been driven all the way from Galveston and was going back again and she said she had read the things written by me for many years and said she had no more trouble understanding them than the young ones did, she said you see it is the middle-aged people that have no feeling, they are not young enough and not old enough to have any understanding. She was very charming and she gave me a great deal of pleasure.

Later when we were back here again some one wrote me that in the South they criticized a Texas author because he made Texas farm women quote Gertrude Stein's writings, and they said that was silly and the Texas farm women said not at all they had gone many miles to hear her and they could read her with pleasure, I did have that feeling with them they were what the Middle West used to be and New England before them and what Virginia remembered having been but did not remember it as that thing, there was Virginia in the Texas men and women but they were active and the country was active and they all had what was the Civil War American, I liked them.

Then we flew to Oklahoma, of course we had been over the bad lands, they come in nicely in every Western story and I never did think that I would ever see them certainly not fly over them, and they were just as bad as they had been called with nothing growing and a very strange color and not hills or flat land either they certainly were bad lands and they made reading the stories more real than ever. I like Western stories of Texas bad lands.

When I first heard about Oklahoma I always thought it was in the northwest, until I really saw it and saw it so close to Texas did I really believe that it is where it does exist. Oklahoma City with its towers that is its skyscrapers coming right up out of the flat oil country was as exciting as when going to Alsace just after the armistice we first saw the Strasbourg Cathedral. They do come up wonderfully out of that flat country and it was exciting and seeing the oil wells and the funny shapes they made the round things as well as the Eiffel Tower ones gave me a feeling like I have in going to Marseilles and seeing the chimneys come out of the earth and there are no houses or anything near them, it always is a strange-looking country that produces that kind of thing, of course Alice Toklas' father had once almost had an oil well they dug and dug but naturally the oil did not gush, naturally not these things never do happen to any one one knows, if it could happen to them you would not be very likely to know them most naturally not. We did later see in California some small oil fields and the slow movement of the oil wells make it perfectly all right that in America the pre-historic beasts moved slowly. America is funny that way everything is quick but really everybody does move slowly, and the movement of the oil well that slow movement very well that slow movement is the country and it makes it prehistoric and large shapes and moving slowly very very slowly so slowly that they do almost stand still. I do think Americans are slow minded, it seems quick but they are slow minded yes they are.

The City of Oklahoma pleased me, I liked the stores there were very good stores there and good clothes in them and the men were very big men and they were all very different from the Texans, not a bit at all like the Texans, not a bit. And then we left Oklahoma in a dust storm, a real one. The airplane went right up through one and came out on top, it was like when we were above the clouds only such dirty ones and the sunset on top on top of this colored dust storm underneath was not exciting, it was discourag-ing, and then we came down at Fort Worth.

At Fort Worth we did strike a bad hotel very well at Fort Worth it was not a good hotel. There was another one perhaps at least they said yes it should have been the other one they had flowers for us at the other one but we had been taken to this one and it was not a good one, we could not eat the mutton chops and there was nothing else we could eat and they tried again and we could not eat them. Next day we found a nice place where we could and did eat everything but by that time Miss Hockaday had driven over and showed us but before that was over we had gone to hear Porgy. This is the story of that.

They asked us to dinner to go later and hear the play Porgy done by the little theatre, there was a white little theatre and now a Princeton man had come down and started a Negro one and they asked us, the actors were amateur but they said it was interesting, it was being given in the little theatre that the whites had started and now they all said this was very interesting. We went to dinner. On one side of me was this young fellow and on the other side a bigger blond one, I did not know the name of either one of them.

We talked together the young man who was running the little theatre, and we talked of Four Saints and of Pinafore and Negroes as actors, and we liked each other and then we talked of airplanes, then the young man on the other side came into the conversation he spent all his time in airplanes so he and I began to talk about airplanes and then he said my mother wrote to me that she had met you I think in New York. Who is your mother and he said she was Mrs. Franklin Roosevelt, oh I said in that case we met in Washington not in New York. I wanted to ask you he said I have wanted to ask you what you would advise for a man in my situation, I have he said always had the publicity of being the son of my father and it is very troubling, not for so long I said after all you are well over twenty so I imagine and your father has only been President for two years so considerable of your life has been spent in a normal state of not being very well known, no he said you do not understand, it has always been like that, now what can I do about it, forget it I said, after all here has been a chance to forget it if it was a worry to him because I had not known it, but that did not seem to be really what he wanted, besides I said you can do nothing about it so why worry about it, yes I know he said and in almost a year my father is going to be the most unpopular man in America, well I said in that case forgetting it will be easier, not at all he said it will be that much worse they will remember it and I will not like it. There did not seem to be anything to be done about it and then the dinner was over.

They asked us then to go on to the theatre. The young man running the theatre asked me to go with him and see the actors while they were making up. I went with him it was a little room and they were all there and we said how do you do to each other and I told them I had just been with their author in Charleston and what a nice man he was and I would write to him and tell him that I had seen them playing Porgy. The man who was being made up to be the white man said to me the mutton chops today were pretty tough weren't they, and I said yes they were they certainly were but how did you know and he said because I was the one who waited on you. We then went to the play, the man who played Porgy did it so well any Negro actors act anything so naturally that it is natural that it should be done very well and why not since they might be any one as they are never any other one that is with Negroes a natural thing, with many of them with most of them, publicity does not hurt them because they can be what anything makes them and it does not make anything else of them because they are the thing they are then. So it is not acting it is being for them, and they have no time sense to be a trouble to them.

And then we left for California very early in the morning. It was strange our going to California where we both had come from. But we did leave for California early in an airplane. Just now a great many are getting killed in the airplanes but when we were there they told us that major accidents never happened and certainly they did not happen to us, we liked wherever we went in an airplane. We left Fort Worth fairly early in the morning and went over more level Texas and then over the desert land then through a gap in the mountains down into Los Angeles. Then we were in California where we had both come from. I had not been born there but I had been raised there, but Alice Toklas had been both born and raised there and her mother had just by accident not been born there but had always lived there so here we were back again in California, and we were to begin at Pasadena. As we landed at Los Angeles there were of course a lot to see us there and among them a representative of the Warner Brothers and would we come to their cinema place to see them. They invited us later to lunch with them but we never did go there or to any other one of them. When we first arrived in New York I did make an actuality of reading the Pigeons On The Grass and taking off my glasses and putting them on again while I was doing that thing, and it was given in the cinema theatres everywhere and everbody said everybody liked it but we had not gone. So finally Pathé asked us when they heard we had not gone to come and see it all alone. We went to their place and there it was and when I saw myself almost as large and moving around and talking I did not like it particularly the talking, it gave me a very funny feeling and I did not like that funny feeling. I suppose if I had seen it often it would have been like anything you can get used to anything if it happens often but that time I certainly did not like it and so when the Warners asked us to come and lunch we did not go.

We went to Pasadena and it was very comfortable and we were in California. The first thing we did was to hire a drive yourself car, and that was a pleasure, a brand new Ford car they gave me a much better one than they had given me in Chicago, this was a really new one and we had it all the way to San Francisco and then there they took charge of it and like everything else over there it was no bother. Over here life is much more occupying doing anything any day or in any way is very occupying because there is so much to attend to so that it will go on but over there nothing was a bother, that is what is called efficiency, it has one trouble with it and that is that it leaves everybody so much time and if you have so much time you have to fill it and to fill so much time is a bother. Over here you have no time to fill everything you do is such a bother. Well like it or not everybody has to do something to fill the time. After all human beings have to live dogs too so as not to know that time is passing, that is the whole business of living to go on so they will not know that time is passing, that is why they get drunk that is why they like to go to war, during a war there is the most complete absence of the sense that time is passing a year of war lasts so much longer than any other year. After all that is what life is and that is the reason there is no Utopia, little or big young or old dog or man everybody wants every minute so filled that they are not conscious of that minute passing. It's just as well they do not think about it you have to be a genius to live in it and know it to exist in it and and express it to accept it and deny it by creating it, anyway here we were in California. Here we were in Pasadena and the dry river bed was below us, we had not seen this for many years and it was a pleasure seeing it, it was very pleasant and we were enjoying it. Here we were back again where we had come from not Pasadena Los Angeles but California.

After the lecture at Pasadena Saroyan came to say how do you do. When I first came to New York he had written to me and when I broadcasted the one and only time when I got back to the hotel there was a charming telegram from Saroyan saying he had just heard me. That was a pleasure. It was sweet of him. Then I was disappointed when I found out that he had not made up the title A Daring Young Man On The Flying Trapeze, I could have known everybody else did but there it is I do know lots but there are lots of things I do not know. My brother and I when we were young liked to make definitions and one we made was what is a lot, and we decided that a lot is a place surrounded by a fence. I suppose there are lots that are not but anyway that is what a lot is by definition, only then we used to find things surrounded by a fence that were not lots, we used to say is China a lot because China is surrounded by a fence. Well anyway in a way a lot is a place surrounded by a fence or not and I do know a lot but I did not know that Saroyan had not invented that. Anyway when I was about sixteen I did decide and it was very exciting that all knowledge was not my province and all that had been Californian, all that decision, that is it had been made when I was a Californian and anyway I did not know that Saroyan had not made up the title and when I found out that he had not it was disappointing.

When I wrote my first story when I was at Radcliffe I called it Red Deeps out of George Eliot, one does do that, and since well since not, it is a bad habit, American writers have it, unless they make it the taken title to be a sounding board to send back the sound that they are to make inside, that would not be too bad, not that anyway it makes any difference anything is anything and anything that is anything is that satisfaction. Let us be pleasant.

Well anyway I liked Saroyan not very much but I liked him and then later we met again not really met again. After the lecture after we were back again at the hotel two young men came and we walked up and down and then they sent me two red roses without any name and then after we came back to Paris one of them wrote and I answered and then he wrote again.

We were to go to dinner at Beverly Hills which is the same as Hollywood this I have said we were to meet Dashiell Hammett and Charlie Chaplin and Anita Loos and her husband and Mamoulian who was directing everything and we did. Of course I liked Charlie Chaplin he is a gentle person like any Spanish gypsy bull-fighter he is very like my favorite one Gallo who could not kill a bull but he could make him move better than any one ever could and he himself not having any grace in person could move one as no one else ever did, and Charlie Chaplin was like Gallo. Gypsies are intelligent I do not think Charlie Chaplin is one perhaps not but he might have been, anyway we naturally talked about the cinema, and he explained something. He said naturally it was disappointing, he had known the silent films and in that they could do something that the theatre had not done they could change the rhythm but if you had a voice accompanying naturally after that you could never change the rhythm you were always held by the rhythm that the voice gave them. We talked a little about the Four Saints and what my idea had been, I said that what was most exciting was when nothing was happening, I said that saints should naturally do nothing if you were a saint that was enough and a saint existing was everything, if you made them do anything then there was nothing to it they were just like any one so I wanted to write a drama where no one did anything where there was no action and I had and it was the Four Saints and it was exciting, he said yes he could understand that, I said the films would become like the newspapers just a daily habit and not at all exciting or interesting, after all the business of an artist is to be really exciting and he is only exciting, when nothing is happening, if anything happens then it is like any other one, after all Hamlet Shakespeare's most interesting play has really nothing happening except that they live and die but it is not that that is interesting and I said I was sure that it is true that an interesting thing is when there is nothing happening, I said that the moon excited dogs because it did nothing, lights coming and going do not excite them and now that they have seen so many of them the poor things can no longer see the moon and so no lights can excite them, well we did not say all this but that is what we meant, he wanted the sentiment of movement invented by himself and I wanted the sentiment of doing nothing invented by myself, anyway we both liked talking but each one had to stop to be polite and let the other one say something. After dinner they all gathered around me and asked me what I thought of the cinema, I told them what I had been telling Charlie Chaplin, it seemed to worry them but almost anything could worry them and at last I found out what was bothering them they wanted to know how I had succeeded in getting so much publicity, I said by having a small audience, I said if you have a big audience you have no publicity, this did seem to worry them and naturally it would worry them they wanted the publicity and the big audience, and really to have the biggest publicity you have to have a small one, yes all right the biggest publicity comes from the realest poetry and the realest poetry has a small audience not a big one, but it is really exciting and therefore it has the biggest publicity, all right that is it. Well after a little while we left, it had been an amusing evening.

And then we in our Ford car left for our California, this had been California of course but not our California the California we had come from and we drove off the next morning to go traveling for ten days and no lecturing just traveling, we had a good time.

We went first into the San Joaquin Valley, naturally this was interesting because Alice Toklas' pioneer grandfather had owned all his land there and Fresno and all about was exciting, after all if that is where you were and the names of it are that it is exciting. We tacked back and forward across the valley and we did like all we saw we liked smelling the oranges and the kind of nuts and fruits that had not been there I had never been there before but she had been there and the way they cut the tops of the trees to make a straight line as if they had been cut with a razor and the fig trees fig trees smell best of all and we went forward and back until we got a little higher and saw the California poppies growing which we had not seen growing wild since we had been in California, they were like they were and it gave me a shock to see them there, it began to be funny and to make me uneasy. Then we went up a little higher and then although it was still wintry we thought that we would go into the Yosemite, we had neither of us ever been there, that I had not been there was not astonishing, we had tended to go north not south from Oakland when we were children but that Alice Toklas had not been there was more surprising, her cousins who lived then in the San Joaquin Valley used to drive every year into the valley as they called the Yosemite the others were rivers but not valleys, and so we decided to go into the valley, I wanted to see the big trees I had never seen them and anyway we decided we would go into the valley, it was spring but it was a very cold one, there was rain and there was lots of snow yet and again.

We tried one road that led to big trees but it was raining and snowing and the road looked none too good and precipitous besides perhaps not but I felt that and so we went back again and finally got to Merced, there the sun was shining it was muddy but the sun was shining and the town of Merced looked like the kind of California I knew just a little country town and we ate something there and decided to go on. I am always afraid of precipices and I could not believe that in going into the Yosemite there would not be lots of them, they had told us not but naturally I did not believe them they said the road was not dangerous, of course the road is not dangerous roads rarely are but it is what you see when you don't see anything except the sky that gives you that funny feeling and makes what I call precipitous. No matter how wide the road and how large the curve it can be precipitous to me. So at Merced we wanted to go on but I thought I would feel better if somebody else was along and driving, so we asked was there any one, in France of course there would not have been any one but in Merced of course there was there was a boy at school who sooner or later would have to go home and his home was in the valley so he said he did not mind missing school that afternoon if we gave him a dollar and of course we did not mind and although he was very young he could drive anybody any where in America can. A good many can here in France but not so young as in America, in France they can all ride a bicycle any one can do that and go up any hill and never get off everybody has his specialty.

So we were driven into the valley and there was no precipice, how they made the road as it is and going always higher and never at any time in any place to feel as if you were jumping off and never necessary to change your speed it was a wonder. Later they told us perhaps it is so that you could go all the way from California to New York and at no time is there a grade which makes changing speeds necessary, the road is made in such a way and of course there are some precipitous spots but they all said certainly not and after the Yosemite Valley road I was almost ready to believe them.

The roads in America were lovely, they move along alone the big ones the way the railroad tracks used to move with really no connection with the country. Of course in a way that is natural enough as I always like to tell a Frenchman and he listens but he does not believe the railroad did not follow the towns made by the road but it made a road followed by the towns and the country, there were no towns and no roads therefore no country until the railroad came along, and the new big roads in America still make you feel that way, air lines they call some of them and they are they have nothing really to do with the towns and the country. The only thing that worried me not so much in California but still even there is the soft shoulder of the road as they called it, that the cement road had no finish to it as it has in France which keeps it from being a danger, I suppose the roads are too long to make that possible but still it is a pity, the smaller roads are too narrow as they have a soft shoulder, some day they will make them a little wider and finish the edge of them with a little edge to it, then they will be pleasanter for driving certainly in rain and anyway. However we did like driving on the American roads and the boy brought us safely into Yosemite.

It was high there and cold and we arrived a little late but the director of the valley offered to take us to see the big trees and we went. I liked that. The thing that was most exciting about them was that they had no roots did anybody want anything to be more interesting than that that the oldest and the solidest and the biggest tree that could be grown had no foundation, there it was sitting and the wind did not blow it over it sat so well. It was very exciting. Very beautiful and very exciting.

We spent the night at the hotel, it was a very comfortable hotel and we ate very well nobody was there and it was a pleasant thing, we enjoyed everything, in the evening we went out walking and saw the wild animals which were not wild because nobody and no animals kill them an animal even if it acts wild is not wild if it can die a natural death, we saw them in the distance not very near, the air was good and we liked everything there were of course Indians there and they were proud of them but it was not very interesting, after all Indians know more about not being wild when they are not wild than animals do.

The next morning I was not afraid and I drove ourselves out from the valley and we went and saw all the wild flowers some more and trees some more and then we went to Monterey. That was too where Alice Toklas had always been for a vacation but I never had been but I knew all about it anyway. There were more people there. The director of the hotel gave us a good lunch not there but at the annex and the coast looked like all the ordinary nineteenth-century school of California painting, just like it there was no use looking at it it was just like it just as the Loire River looks like all the nineteenth the mediocre nineteenth-century painting in France, but at the annex they gave us a soup made of abalone shell fish and that was excellent, better than anything else. Then he wanted to know what celebrities I wanted to meet, any celebrity can choose whom he wants to meet and that is a pleasure and he mentioned several and I said no, no, but I had heard that one was there that to me would be a pleasure and that was the author of Merton of The Movies about the best description of America that has ever been done. Leon Wilson had a home somewhere and the director telephoned to him and asked him if he wanted to meet me as I wanted to meet him. He said yes with pleasure. So we went and it was a pleasure.

Merton of The Movies is the best book about twentieth-century American youth that has yet been done. I always give it to every one to read who reads English and always have done ever since I first read it when it was first done.

Wilson was just like the kind of man who should have written the best American story about a young American man, he is gentle and American and mysterious without a mystery and tired without fatigue and it all was a pleasure, he gave me all the books he had written and I liked having met him.

He had written the first book about the road and trailers and where they camped together in the Professor and I had liked that one but the great one is Merton of The Movies there will never be a better one. So then we ate a great deal here and there on the beach and everywhere and then we left for San Francisco and Oakland there I was to be where I had come from, we went over the green rounded hills which are brown in summer with a very occasional live oak tree and otherwise empty and a fence that does not separate them but goes where the hill has come to come down, it was just like them geographically altogether the hills they had been and a great deal of them up and down we went among them and they made me feel funny, yes they were like that that is what they were and they did trouble me they made me very uncomfortable I do not know why but they did, it all made me uncomfortable it just did.

Then slowly we came into San Francisco it was frightening quite frightening driving there and on top of Nob Hill where we were to stay, of course it had not been like that and yet it was like that, Alice Toklas found it natural but for me it was a trouble yes it was, it did make me feel uncomfortable.

It was San Francisco and it was later and we were very comfortable, they gave us so many rooms that we could see something of the bay and San Francisco from each one of them and there were so many flowers we always had had them everywhere but here there were more than anywhere. In the middle there were so many more than we had ever seen and these were from Mary Garden. Gertrude Atherton was to do everything for us and she did and we had a pleasant visit, Chinatown well the young Chinamen looked more like Indo-Chinamen than the Chinamen they had been the streets were as steep as they had been but automobiles could and did go up and down them and park themselves quickly on an angle, where it looked as if they would fall off, they did not but they might have, Alice Toklas saw so many that had been at school with her and she knew each one of them when she saw them, but then she had been to a private school, I had been to a public one in Oakland and if you have been to a public one you do not seem to have as good a memory at least they did not and I did not.

We began to do everything Gertrude Atherton took us to eat the smallest oysters there are and in a quantity they are the best oysters there are. She took us to see her granddaughter who was teaching in the Dominican convent in San Raphael, we went across the bay on a ferry, that had not changed but Goat Island might just as well not have been there, anyway what was the use of my having come from Oakland it was not natural to have come from there yes write about it if I like or anything if I like but not there, there is no there there.

We liked going with Gertrude Atherton to San Raphael. She said she had spoken to the girls the year before and she had asked what they wanted her to talk about and they said Gertrude Stein that she had been astonished that they would be interested in my writing but they were. It was raining but otherwise the visit was charming. I said to the mother superior when she said that she could not understand what did that matter if the little ones could and she said but little ones always look as if they understand and I said yes but if they look it it is as pleasant as if they do it besides anyway if any one listens to it that is as much understanding as understanding is and she too listened to me so probably she did do as much understanding as any understanding could do.

stand   take   to   taking

I   you throw my

Well there we are back again that is the only cryptogram that I could ever do.

That business of understanding is awfully worrying to any American. Other peoples say they do or do not understand something but Americans do worry about understanding or not understanding something. After all you are more or less in communication and anyway if you change you go on saying it again, and after all mechanics are one thing a thing shoves something else but when it comes to be together without shoving that is just being together and saying something of course that has nothing to do with understanding. The only thing that anybody can understand is mechanics and that is what makes everybody feel that they are something when they talk about it. About every other thing nobody is of the same opinion nobody means the same thing by what they say as the other one means and only the one who is talking thinks he means what he is saying even though he knows very well that that is not what he is saying. That is the reason that everybody thinks machines are so wonderful they are only wonderful because they are the only thing that says the same thing to any and every one and therefore one can do without them, why not, after all you cannot exist without living and living is something that nobody is able to understand while you can exist without machines it has been done but machines cannot exist without you that makes machines seem to do what they do. Well anyway after anybody has had too much of anything then they can always do without them. Convents and monasteries make people gay and it was a pleasant afternoon. Some day Americans will find out something about not understanding anything but will they like it then I am wondering. So we went to San Raphael and we went to Oakland and we went

290

to Mills College in San Leandro and I asked to go with a reluctant feeling to see the Swett School where I went to school and Thirteenth Avenue and Twenty-fifth Street where we lived which I described in The Making of Americans. Ah Thirteenth Avenue was the same it was shabby and over-grown the houses were certainly some of them those that had been and there were not bigger buildings and they were neglected and, lots of grass and bushes growing yes it might have been the Thirteenth Avenue when I had been. Not of course the house, the house the big house and the big garden and the eucalyptus trees and the rose hedge naturally were not any longer existing, what was the use, if I had been I then my little dog would know me but if I had not been I then that place would not be the place that I could see, I did not like the feeling, who has to be themselves inside them, not any one and what is the use of having been if you are to be going on being and if not why is it different and if it is different why not. I did not like anything that was happening. Later much later all that went to make the Geographical History Of America that I wrote, what is the use of being a little boy if you are going to grow up to be a man. Well some do and some do not.

If I remember what I remember then why do I remember that. I did remember that but it did look like that and so I did not remember that and if it did not look like that then I did not remember that. What was the use.

Anyway we went out to San Leandro where we used to ride on a tandem bicycle in the dust. Of course now there is no dust. But Mills College did seem dusty enough to be a memory of dust not that it really was then but in the summer there might be dust. Every year they have a poet offered to them and that year I was the one we had a pleasant evening and then we went home on the ferry that evening well anyway I had been in Oakland again.

We went to Berkeley and they had invited me I think it was the Phi Beta Kappa to lunch, and during the lunch there were a lot of them there everybody asked a question not everybody but a good many, they thought I answered them very well the only thing I remember is their asking why I do not write as I talk and I said to them if they had invited Keats for lunch and they asked him an ordinary question would they expect him to answer with the Ode to the Nightingale. It is funny everybody knows but of course everybody knows that writing poetry that writing anything is a private matter and of course if you do it in private then it is not what you do in public. We used to say when we were children if you do it in private you will do it in public and we did not then say if you do it in public you will do it in private. Well anyway when you say what you do say you say it in public but when you write what you do write you write it in private if not you do not write it, that is what writing is, and in private you are you and in public you are in public and everybody knows that, just read Briggs' Mr. and Mrs. everybody knows that but when they ask questions well then they are neither public nor private they are just fatheaded yes yes. That is what Virgil Thomson says yes yes. What is the use of asking questions, either you know your answer or you do not, mostly you do know your answer and certainly any question has no answer so why question the answer or answer the question. Of course you have to, because that is natural it is in fencing what you call a riposte and if you are stronger than the other one is left dead but after all he might just as well not be dead. Just today it was happening young Chester Arthur, not so young, it did happen that my uncle made the monument for the tomb of his grandfather but that had nothing to do with the matter we were talking about the future of America, and anyway it is a pleasant thing to answer well to questioning, naturally I do answer well because after all if I do not talk too much or too long I do say what is there to be seen but of course if I do talk too much or too long then it gets to be arguing and that is not interesting, because after all what is said is not meant and what is meant is not said in arguing, anything that is read is understood that is it is felt otherwise they would not go on reading but anything heard is not felt because nobody naturally no body can stop listening and therefore writing is the thing. Well anyway we had been in Berkeley. And now a young fellow from Berkeley Bobby Haas writes to me and he tells me he has collected everything that has been printed that I have written and he will give it to the University and anyway I like being told anything, anybody does but I like best to be told this thing.

We then went with Mary Garden to see the Crocker family and the Crocker garden. One of the first pictures that I had ever seen was The Man with the Hoe by Millet and my brother and I had seen this and bought a photograph of it and we took it home and my older brother after solemnly looking said, it is a hell of a hoe and it had belonged to the Crocker family and they still had it, and we did see it, we went there and of course in between several times in between we had gone to look at the Pacific Ocean, it was the Pacific Ocean and it made the same noise that the Pacific Ocean had made it undoubtedly was the Pacific Ocean, about the Cliff House there was a difference of opinion I said that there had been a bridge a little weak bridge out to the seal rocks out certainly to one and certainly then to another one of them and Alice Toklas said that there never had been one. Well anyway when we came back from the seeing The Man with the Hoe by Millet we did just happen to see happened to be there when the first big airplane was flying off to Honolulu, it had a lot of little planes around it and we were very pleased to have seen it. I would like to go around the world in an airplane, I never did want to do anything and now I want to do that thing.

At Menlo Park we met some one and he said he had a home in the Napa Valley. Saint Helena is where we used to take the stage coach to go up into the mountains into the Etna Springs where we used to swim in mineral water and go down into the quicksilver mines and where the Chinamen were working and where the overseer could swear fifteen minutes without repeating himself and where we knew the madrone and the manzanita and where my brother and I had walked at least we had intended to walk but every one gave us a lift from St. Helena to Etna it was where a great deal that I could remember did happen, and he said would we like to go there and we said yes. We did but I did not remember I just did not remember how could I remember after all I could not remember anything. But anyway we had bought fresh crabs in San Francisco and we ate them and then we drove back again. And so we took the airplane to go back to Chicago we stopped at Omaha and really we did not stop in Chicago only for the night and then we went on back to New York.

On the airplane leaving there was a young man he was from Stanford University and I had spoken twice there, and he wrote questions on a piece of paper and I wrote him back the answers, he had been at college he was at college with Will Rogers' son and he wanted to know why Will Rogers was not literature, and then he wanted to know what was and then he wanted to know what I meant by the difference between writing and speaking and we spent all the time handing papers forward and back, perhaps he has kept them and so he knows what I answered him, I naturally do not, but it was interesting it always is interesting to answer anything.

I liked going over the Salt Lake region the best, it was like going over the bottom of the ocean without any water in it and I was very satisfied with it after all it is nice to know the difference between the ocean with water and the ocean without water in it. After all it is a satisfaction to know that an ocean is interesting even if there is no water in it. That is what I like about America it is interesting even if there is no water in the ocean of it, as some one whom Alice Toklas used to know used to say Lizzie you do know Lizzie what I mean.

294

But it was what I liked and then the barrier at the end of it and then the ranges the high ranges for the cattle they always tell about that in the stories of the cowboys and then gradually getting down lower, there was not much grass there but then after all America is just as interesting with no water or too much water or no ocean or no grass there that is what I like about America, and then we stopped at Omaha, I walked around in Omaha it was late at night but it was a pleasure I liked being in Omaha but I did like being everywhere everywhere where I was I never very much wanted to be any other place than there, and then the night in Chicago and then New York. The Rockefeller Center building was finished it all was a pleasure and that was a pleasure and they all seemed as pleased to see me as they had been, Alice Toklas said they now said there goes Miss Stein before they had said there goes Gertrude Stein well anyway having them say it was still a pleasure and then everything was all over and we got on the Champlain to go back to Paris again.

Before we went on the Champlain I asked Bennett Cerf about my writing, I always want what I have written to be printed and it has not always happened no not mostly happened and now I timidly said something to him, he said it is very simple whatever you decide each year you want printed you tell me and I will publish that thing, just like that I said, just like that, he said, you do the deciding, and so we happily very happily went on to the Champlain.

CHAPTER V

Back again

It was all over and we were going back again, of course it was all going on being there there where we had been even if we were not there and it was as if we had not been. After all we had been. On the Champlain it was not exciting, we were still celebrated of course but we were soon across the ocean and back again, there was one nice American who told Alice Toklas that she was going to have a career that would soon be beginning, and that I would go on succeeding, we wondered what the career of Alice Toklas was going to be and when it was to begin and then it almost began she decided to write a cook book and if she did the career would begin and she will but she has not yet had time, naturally enough who can and of course this she would not let me do for her and with reason. Georges Maratier has found for her some cook books of the first and of the second empire and down in the country Madame Giraud has given her the written recipes of her mother and her grandmother and she says she must also do some work at the Bibliothèque Nationale and besides that there is the book of Monsieur Tendret who tells about how to make the essence that makes the sauces everything and which is the whole of everything, the barnyard and the dairy, and it is all very exciting and when she gets it written the career the American on the Champlain predicted will begin. Well anyway we were on the Champlain and we were coming back again, just as we came near to Havre the Normandie on its trial trip came out and ran around us several times, she could go fast because we were going the way the Champlain goes ordinarily and the Normandie ran all around us several times without any trouble. She was a pleasure and it was a nice day as we came nearer and then there we were back again in France. Of course but that we had expected was that everything looked little and littler than it had looked. Come back to anything is always a bother you have to get used to seeing it as it looks all over again until it looks as it did which it does at last.

And then we came on to the shore and then into the train and then through to Paris. The cities we saw worried me, after all European cities the old parts have beautiful architecture but the new parts that is everything for almost a hundred years have not and as gradually European cities are having a larger and larger part new and as the new parts in America are more beautiful than the new parts in Europe perhaps the American cities are more beautiful than the European. Interesting if true.

We came in to Paris and there it was and there they were and Trac was there and it was a pleasure to see him to be sure he would of course not be with us long, but he was there and it was a pleasure.

And then we had to see the place 27 rue de Fleurus we had always had as home and then we had to gather in Basket and Pépé and then we left for Bilignin, it was to begin again being as we always had been although of course it was not the same thing.

Settled down in Bilignin I became worried about identity and remembered the Mother Goose, I am I because my little dog knows me and I was not sure but that that only proved the dog was he and not that I was I.

To get this trouble out of my system I began to write the Geographical History of America or the Relation Of Human Nature To The Human Mind and I meditated as I had not done for a very long time not since I was a little one about the contradiction of being on this earth with the space limiting and knowing about the stars in an unlimited space that is that nobody could find out if it was limiting or limited, and now these meditations did not frighten me as they did when I was young, so that was that much done.

I meditated a good deal about how to yourself you were yourself at any moment that you were there to you inside you but that any moment back you could only remember yourself you could not feel yourself and I therefore began to think that insofar as you were yourself to yourself there was no feeling of time inside you you only had the sense of time when you remembered yourself and so I said what is the use of being a little boy if you are to be a man what is the use. Of course in The Making Of Americans I had already had that when I used to say that every one is to themselves a young grown man or woman they are never to themselves inside them a very young or a very old one. And so I began to be more and more absorbed in the question of the feeling of past and present and future inside in one and naturally that led me later to meditate more even than I had in the lectures I had written for Chicago on the subject of history and newspapers and politics.

I have been talking a lot just now to Chester Arthur as to what is the political history of America, there is no reason why I should have told it all to him not even the reason that my uncle made the monument of his grandfather's tomb it is more likely that like Seabrooke he knows how to make you feel like telling why you are what you are and I did I told him, you tell others it that is because you are naturally one who is talking but you tell him as you tell Seabrooke because they make you feel full inside you of why you are what you are and so you tell them all there is to tell.

It was a mixed summer we began with something else and ended up as we usually do with an Indo-Chinaman. Then we had the French army, Frenchmen do their military service and then they have to come again in five years or so and do a month or so and then again ten years after they have been they have to do twenty days and of course they have to be put somewhere and some one decided to put them this summer in Belley and its neighborhood so in Bilignin with its twenty-eight families we had five hundred of them. Frenchmen are never put into tents that is unless there is nothing else that can be done they must always have a roof over them, any kind of a roof is better than none and so we had about twenty-five in the barn and they bothered Basket and Pépé naturally and they bothered us some not very much but still some. After all they were drunk a good deal after all they cannot discipline reservists they can only keep them walking and however much they walk they must stop sometime and naturally if they stop they must occupy the time and the only way to occupy the time is by drinking that is natural enough and as they had not seen each other for a number of years and unless there was to be a war they would probably never see each other again they naturally had to drink together all the time they were not walking, Frenchmen like Americans are never rude or impolite even then, so it was a bother but not really bothersome and then they did sing songs and one of them had an accordion and an accordion is always a pleasure. After they left the Abdys came.

In English novels a baronet is always villainous or peculiar, and sometimes both, I have in my life known two baronets and they are not at all villainous, they are gentle and sweet but they are peculiar, Bertie Abdy is one and Francis Rose the other one, I came to know them about the same time but not together no naturally not together. They are each of them peculiar and so naturally I did not know them together.

Francis Rose is a painter he does a great many things and he has a great many ways of doing a great many things but he is a painter and from his earliest childhood he painted not like a child but like a painter and he has painted like a painter ever since. Bertie Abdy is not a painter I have made him in my play Listen To Me, he is the Sweet William who had his genius and who looked for his Lillian. He has his genius, his genius is in being that thing, in having his genius and looking for his Lillian, he dislikes with a violence that is disconcerting all modern art and all Americans, and to prove that the exception proves the rule he is very fond of me and he is going to print for me the two hundred Stanzas of Meditation I have written and he has tried four different printers already but printing like everything is something of which there is more bad than good of that he is perfectly certain. Later when we were in Cornwall together his wife Diana, kneeled upon the eye of the big chalk horse there to wish what there is to wish for and so I have told in the play Listen To Me, I wrote that one after we had been in Cornwall but first they came to Bilignin, we had known them well in Saint-Germain, indeed it was in telling Bertie Abdy in answer to questioning all there was to tell of Paris as it had been that I first put it together as it later was written in The Autobiography of Alice B. Toklas, he too is one to whom you tell what you have told to any one but telling it to him makes it be something that has come alive again. So they were with us in Bilignin and we had a very happy time. They suggested that the next winter I should lecture at Cambridge and Oxford again and they arranged it and we did go over that winter.

After they left Thornton Wilder and Bob Davis came and the Geographical History that I was writing went on. Bob Davis was a philosopher basing himself on Vienna, Vienna is a nice place I was there from eight months old to three years and we all walked and talked together. I always did like the word commentaries, Caesar's commentaries I did not care for the Caesar part as much as I did for the commentaries part and I wanted Thornton to make the commentaries, he did make them he even did write them but when it came to printing the Geographical History Of America Or The Relation Of Human Nature To The Human Mind he would only print an introduction, it was a disappointment and so I told him. So we went up the hills and down again there are lots of hills around Bilignin and we talked about the relation of human nature to the human mind and Thornton pleasantly eagerly and in a way said everything, he has something that is like the letters Lewis Carroll wrote he writes the same kind and he has the same serious beliefs and precision. Woollcott should not have any difficulty in understanding the author of Alice in Wonderland after all there is his and our Thornton Wilder. Then I worry about Thornton I have made him my literary executor will he get weak and let any one he admires and believes in some, he does in me but that is not the same thing of course not, well anyway here and now it is said that he is not to let his left hand know what his right hand is doing and his left hand does lead him where he is led. I am not leading him I am confiding in him and that is what we did in going up and down the hills near Bilignin and he loved Pépé because as he said Pépé passed and existed from one caress to another.

We talked about time about the passage of time about the dogs and what they did and was it the same as we did, and of course I was clear, Alice Toklas says and very often mistaken but anyway I am clear I am a good American, I am slow-minded and quickly clear in expression, I am certain that I see everything that is seen and in between I stand around but I do not wait, no American can wait he can stand around and do nothing but he can not wait, that is why he is not like Milton who served by standing and waiting, Americans can neither serve nor wait, they can stand and sit down and get up and walk around but they can neither serve nor wait. These were the things we talked about going up and down and Bob Davis sometimes said something, of course he was not articulate like Thornton nor articulate like I am but every now and then and we always listened to him naturally we listened to him always listened to him when he said something. And so it was a pleasant time there in Bilignin a very pleasant time.

And then they went away toward Vienna and I went on with The Geographical History. It was a pleasant summer all our neighbors wanted to know all about what we had done and how we had done it and we came to know more and more of them, the younger generation around there like to give surprise parties, I do not know whether the French always did but it is not very likely that they learned it in America, in France everybody knows everybody in the house and outside knows that the surprise party is to be given, in America as I remember somebody knew but not the person to be surprised, well anyway I suppose there is a way of finding out who first had surprise parties France or America but anyway it was amusing to meet everybody and Alice Toklas made American cakes and cookies and they all liked it naturally. So we did have a pleasant summer, we ended up naturally with having a Chinaman as a cook and then when we came back to Paris we had an Austrian. I suppose it was natural that just then it should be an Austrian and Thornton was there to read his references which were in German and he cooked beautifully Austrian and it was all very natural that we should like it.

Thornton does not like Paris. He says he does not and he is right he does not. It is funny about Paris I like it. It is supposed that everybody likes it but there are a great many who do not.

But Thornton and I liked walking around even so, and we walked around the last evening, he was going away to America the next day and I walked home with him and he walked home with me and we talked about writing and telling anything and I said I had done things I had really written poetry and I had really written plays and I had really written thinking and I had really written sentences and paragraphs but I said I had not simply told anything and I wanted to do that thing must do it. I would simply say what was happening which is what is narration, and I must do it as I knew it was what I had to do. Yes said Thornton.

And now I almost think I have the first autobiography was not that, it was a description and a creation of something that having happened was in a way happening not again but as it had been which is history which is newspaper which is illustration but is not a simple narrative of what is happening not as if it had happened not as if it is happening but as if it is existing simply that thing. And now in this book I have done it if I have done it. Anyway Othmar cooked us Austrian cooking and he pleased us telling us Austrian stories and how Austrian he was and how Hitler had come from the same part of the country that he had come from and that Hitler was just like Othmar himself he was a crazy Austrian, and we would have gone on eating Austrian cooking, and Othmar was engaged to a little Austrian who used to come here and sit with him and help him and Othmar said she was an angel and he put her picture next to that of the Virgin and then then he began to cry there was another woman he was not engaged to her but she intended to marry him and she put an advertisement in the paper for him and he was afraid that if he did what she told him she would marry him and if he did not do what she told him he was afraid and so he would do what she told him and so he began to drink a little more so that he could leave the house and not see her and then he cried a good deal more and what happened to the nice Austrian who used to sit with him we do not know and we never saw Othmar again.

And so that winter we had a pleasant time and I wrote a number of things about people in Bilignin, a little narrative of each one of them and college papers printed them and then finally the Atlantic Monthly printed one, that was a pleasure again.

And so we had a pleasant time and then Diana Abdy wrote that we were to go to England to stay with Lord Berners near Oxford and then later go to them in Cornwall. Daisy Fellowes said do stay with Gerald Berners you will find that it is very comfortable the only house in England where the corridors where the halls are warm. Of course we went we always like to go. I wrote two lectures, one for Oxford and Cambridge and a second one for Oxford to be given at the French club. A tall count came to see us one evening and asked me if I would. Of course I said yes, he was very pleased about it. Later he invited us to dinner and then to see him later in his rooms and I said that I could make no arrangements he should ask Lord Berners and Lord Berners wrote to me and said there are seven of us but that does not seem to be too much for the hospitable count, so everything was arranged and we flew to England our first flight in Europe and everything is new if you do it the first time or do it very often anyway we did do it for the first time. It was a thin green country France, and then there was the channel it was foggy but we liked seeing it and then England was not a thin green but a very dark and solid one, I never can get over the pleasure that everything being the same each thing is completely different from every other one, it is a pleasure it might be a pain but it is a pleasure. We liked being in London again. When we went to Oxford with Lord Berners it did not seem to be quite the same Oxford that it had been, of course there always had been a great many Hindus and a great many pale yellow-haired men and many small men I suppose there always had been but there did seem to be a good many more of them. That was in the first audience the one for the English Club and then we did dine with the count, there were a good many more than seven of us and it was a very good dinner and I do not drink wine but they all said it was very good wine and we hoped that the French foreign office was paying for it because the hospitable count did not seem to be a very rich one. That evening the audience was quite a little darker and taller and I talked about France and England and America and how you could tell one from the other of them. They asked questions and argued a great deal after and then finally we were all leaving, as I went out there were about seven very tall ones at least they all seemed to be big ones and as I passed the first one said I am an American thank you, and the second one said thank you I am an American and the third one said you made them take it thank you I am an American, and then two together said we liked your talking up to them we are Canadians thank you and I shook hands with them and they all said it had been a pleasure and it had. Later when I went to Cambridge it was a very interesting audience, years before I had liked the Oxford audience better than the Cambridge but this year the Cambridge was more interesting than the Oxford one, perhaps they have changed again, any two years can make a generation. When I was in Cambridge the American students asked me to take tea with them just with them and I did. There was one Englishman there and I was puzzled why there should have been as the conversation was purely American. I said to him what part of England do you come from, Southampton he said, oh I said that is the reason and they all burst out laughing.

We went to Cornwall where we had never been and passed Dartmoor prison which always comes in to Edgar Wallace detective stories. So we had a good time in England and then we came back to Paris again, that was a month before we were leaving for Bilignin and I began writing this book but I was hesitating whether it was the narrative about which I had talked to Thornton.

I had begun writing and we were back in Paris and Paris was getting complicating not for us but for it, everybody was once again talking revolution, when French people are unhappy that is when they are not occupied completely occupied with the business of living which is their normal occupation their enormously occupying occupation and when for one reason or another that is not occupying them they naturally immediately talk about a revolution. What do we do we asked Georges Maratier, nothing said Georges Georges always knows everything that is going to happen really knows don't bother said Georges if I should call you up on the telephone any day and tell you go get it, then go and draw out enough money to keep you several weeks that is all, just do that, perhaps and very likely I will not tell you to but if I do telephone to you then you just do that. Nothing else said we no provisions no going away, no said Georges you just do that. So one day he did telephone and we did just do that but nothing came of it, we found out afterwards he had been right it did very nearly happen just what I do not know but it did very very nearly come to happen.

Of course in France you never know it may be anything it might be another republic or soviets not so likely red very red or rather pink often quite pink, a king not so likely but perhaps a king not very likely a Bourbon or Orleans king but barely possibly, just now more likely just a prince some prince about whom nobody is thinking, Bonaparte perhaps Georges is a Bonapartist but he does not really think it likely that it will be a Bonapartist no, he hopes so but he never really warns you that it will be so, not likely fascism, the croix de feu does not really like that, that is made up nearly entirely of veterans and veterans in France are mostly republicans orderly republicans, but as Georges says perhaps but not very likely most likely a fairly red red and then a pink red that will look like a red red and then a small reaction that will make it look as if everybody is afraid but nobody is afraid not afraid of that, no said Georges reflectively what Frenchmen are afraid of is that the franc will go to pieces too often but politics Frenchmen are never really afraid of that.

Well when we went away to Bilignin that spring there was an uneasy feeling but as Georges truly says the French are not afraid of politics after all they had one real and original revolution called the French one and since then anything else is nothing and just now there is no danger of a foreign war not to their feeling and so they talk a lot about everything but they are commencing to be more occupied with daily living completely occupied with that and so that is their normal way of being.

But just then it was not like that, the women in Bilignin were worried, Frenchwomen are not often worried, they are occupied very occupied but they are not worried. And the women of Bilignin last spring were worried. Do you think they asked us as having come fresh from Paris that I would know, do you think they said

one and another of them do you think that we are going to have a
civil war. They were worried. The men were confused and the
women were worried. The men had to vote so they were confused
the women were worried. The men admitted that in a place like
Bilignin there were three young and husky ones, who were communists that is what they called communists that is the popular
front, they were two father and son very firm ones who were croix
de feu and there were about ten that is all the rest of them who
were admittedly confused and only wanted to be let alone and
who wanted to vote with the side that is going to win not because
they are time serving but because it tires them to think about anybody governing and they hope if there is a majority that it will all
settle down and so they want to make it that there is that majority
so that it will settle down. I came more or less to the conclusion
that is the way majority voting is done, I was interested in everything and just then the Spanish civil war began and that scared
everybody really scared them, scared them because it was so near
and so frightening and also anything foreign may cause foreign
fighting and Frenchmen like fighting but they do not want a war
again not now no they know that, they all know that, and so the
Spanish civil war scared them. The women felt better than they
had felt they felt the men seeing what was happening over the
border and realizing what civil war was really like they would settle down and be just simply Frenchmen again. Well anyway that
is what happened last spring.

Gradually I began writing little things about is money money or
isn't money money. I was kind of worried about the fact that
money is always voted in round numbers so many millions billions
and when it is gathered by taxes it is always little sums or big sums
but always uneven sums, my eldest brother had always done all
that for me and now I was paying it myself he having gone to
California and I was finding it surprising, how could so many uneven sums make an even one and how could that even sum be

307

paid out again into uneven ones and not leave something the matter. Undoubtedly it does leave something the matter, so I began to think is money money or isn't money money. If the money as any one earns it and spends it is a different money from the money they vote can it ever come to be the same thing which it undoubtedly does, and yet if they did not organize it all then there would be no automobiles perhaps and I like automobiles, but anyway if you organize too much then everybody gets bored with that, if you have dim lights and you add another perhaps it makes less light to your feeling than if you only have one dim one, if you have enough of them then you are in total darkness anyway to your feeling, and so I worried about that, and wrote some more about that, after all money is money if you live together and as the world is now all covered over everybody has to live together and if you live together call it what you like it has to be money, and that is the way it is. You live on this earth and you cannot get away from it and yet there is a space where the stars are which is unlimited and that contradiction is there in every man and every woman and so nothing ever does get settled. When you have war then you want peace and when you have peace then you want war. America is funny it always thinks it wants what Europe can't have and then it always likes to come and look at what Europe does have, well as my grandfather used to remark there is a great deal to be said on both sides. One day at Bilignin I was walking and one of them on top of the hill stopped and I stopped and we were talking. It is funny I said they manage everything but the weather it is funny that they have never invented anything that does decide the weather. Oh said he you know I often think about that, I look down on the village down there and I think suppose every day we could vote what weather we were to have tomorrow. What fighting there would be what killing of one neighbor by another, we all do our work in our way, and we do not want the same weather, most things that we vote for do not really matter, you are a little more or a little less uncomfortable as the government does one thing or another but the weather oh dear he said that would be disaster.

Of course they could be organized and then even the weather would not matter but would they like it. They are being organized and it makes them sadder, well I suppose they might just as well be sadder as not. After everybody gets sad enough then they will try something else, and anyway people can not just go on being sadder or there would be no will to live.

So I wandered with Basket and Pépé and I enjoyed myself and I took to gardening and it was a great pleasure I cut all the box hedges and we have a great many and I cleared the paths more or less well, the box hedges I did very well and then the weeds came up in the garden and we had corn the Kiddie who sends it to us says now we must not give it to any fascists but why not if the fascists like it, and we liked the fascists, so I said please send us unpolitical corn, and Bennett Cerf and Jo Davidson came to see us and we called for them in Geneva and got lost getting out of Switzerland the way we always do. There are some places where you always can get lost, we have gotten the best of some of them we now can get to Senlis we used to get lost in the Bois de Vincennes going to Mildred Aldrich we never finally got so we were certain not to get lost, we used to get lost in the park in Chicago but then they do not tell you there very well they expect everybody to know and then we used to get lost going through Beaune we do not any more but I must say Bennett was astonished to the extent that we could lose ourselves in such a small country as Switzerland. Switzerland was a disappointment to me. We had been in Belley for years all the summer and we had never gone to Geneva because I was afraid of going over the mountains and then why I do not remember quite why but we had to go and to my astonishment there were no mountains to go over you just went right along among rolling hills and there you were in Geneva and then we had to go to Ferney where Voltaire lived and then right

309

across a piece of Switzerland and then to Vevey and Lausanne all the places in the English novels that they make so mountainous and it was all flat, it was a puzzle to me things never are the way they tell you, well anyway Bennett Cerf and Jo Davidson came and we had a pleasant time and Bennett liked this autobiography and I always go on but it is an excitement if they say they are just crazy about it which he did. Then later on Gerald Berners came and he played the music for the ballet in which Pépé is and for which we are going to London next Friday and it was a nice summer, and then it was over and then we came back to Paris again. Here there was Meraude Guevara and a new crowd of young painters and then everybody cheered up because of course there was Mrs. Simpson. Everybody needs being excited by the story of Mrs. Simpson at least once a year, it cheered up the gloom of organization, and the difference between sovietism and fascism and new deal and sit-down striking, Shorty Lazar a funny American who used to live in Paris long before the war and who said they called him Shorty because of his proportions and who taught a great many people painting, Shorty used to say remember every room has its gloom and the great thing to do is to find the color that will cut that gloom. Well organization has its gloom and the only thing for a long time that really cut that gloom was Mrs. Simpson and King Edward and the abdication.

Of course naturally in the meanwhile I went on writing, I had always wanted it all to be commonplace and simple anything that I am writing and then I get worried lest I have succeeded and it is too commonplace and too simple so much so that it is nothing, anybody says it is not so, it is not too commonplace and not too simple but do they know anyway I have always all the time thought it was so and hoped it was so and then worried lest it was so. I am worried again now lest it is so.

Anyway the Saturday Evening Post printed the little articles I wrote about money then and the young ones said I was reactionary and they said how could I be who had always been so well ahead of every one and I myself was not and am not certain that I am not again well ahead as ahead as I ever have been. Of course all this time I was always looking at pictures, why not except walking and driving an automobile it is what I like best after my real business which is of course writing. I like writing, it is so pleasant, to have the ink write it down on the paper as it goes on doing. Harlan Miller thought I left such a large space in between so that I could correct in between but I do not correct, I sometimes cut out a little not very often and not very much but correcting after all what is in your head comes down into your hand and if it has come down it can never come again no not again.

So I went on looking at pictures all the time and it is one of the nice things about Paris there are such a lot of pictures to be seen just casually in any street anywhere, it is not like in America where you have to look for them, here you just cannot help seeing them and I do like to see them. There is a great deal about painting going on just now, a great deal has been decided and has been put away and something has commenced something that has been dimly felt for the last twenty years but which each one of those who tried to do it killed it in doing it. The history of painting is this.

Ever since Cezanne everybody who has painted has wanted to have a feeling of movement inside the painting not a painting of a thing moving but the thing painted having inside it the existence of moving. Everybody since Cezanne has tried for that thing. That made the Matisse school so violent, and then the violence as violence does resulted in nothing, like the head-lines which do not head anything they simply replace something but they do not make anything, then there were the cubists the cubists, decided that by composition, that is by destroying the centralization they would arrive at movement being existing, then there were the surrealists they thought they could do it by invention, and then there was the Russian school that wanted to do it by space filled with nothing, Berard also was of this school, it derives from the Spaniards who naturally always think of space as being filled well filled with emptiness and suspicion.

Recently there have been a young crowd who have tried it again tried to solve the problem of space by classicism and there is a South American who says it can be done by color and Francis Rose who does it by imagination, and now Picabia again says that he has a new technique that can do it, technique can do it he says and I am not certain that he is not right, he has just done a painting where a piece of it is done, a little piece but it is done, the others make it dead when they want it to be living, Miró is trying again, they all know that they have to find the way to do it, all those so far have tried it have gone dead in not giving birth to it, I am always hoping to have it happen the picture to be alive inside in it, in that sense not to live in its frame, pictures have been imprisoned in frames, quite naturally and now when people are all all peoples are asking to be imprisoned in organization it is quite natural that pictures are trying to escape from the prison the prison of framing. For many years I have taken all pictures out of their frames, I never keep them in them, and now that I have let them out for so many years they want to get out by themselves, it is very interesting. Picabia I think will do it, I do think he will do it. Naturally I have been mixed up a lot with pictures and lately very much interested to know more about what others who have pictures think about pictures.

This year the year of the Paris exposition, they are having pictures everywhere and they asked me to be on the committee of the Petit Palais to decide what pictures should be put there. I always say yes, and having said yes Alice Toklas says I have to do it, sometimes I do not but this time I did do it. It was all very funny.

There were a great many on the committee, collectors, and critics and practically no painters naturally not and museum directors

312

and municipal counselors as the Petit Palais belongs to the city, I had never been with that kind before and we began to vote about what they wanted. Naturally I got excited I was surprised at so many things, that they would like Bonnard and Segonzac that was natural Bonnard is a good painter and Segonzac a bad one but they both are in what they call the tradition and the tradition is naturally easy enough to like so that in liking it there is no strain, that was all right but what did astonish me was that they had to accept but not with acquiescence Picasso and Braque and Derain but that they all accepted without any trouble Modigliani now why I asked every one, that was a puzzle to me, finally an under-director of museums answered me, he said it is simple Modigliani combines Italian art with Negro art and both these arts are admitted by every one and as there is nothing else in Modigliani naturally nobody takes any exception. I myself would never have thought of that explanation but it is undoubtedly the correct one. Then of course I tried to introduce Picabia but to that there was no exception he was greeted by a universal no, why not I asked them because he cannot paint, they said, but neither everybody said could Cezanne, ah they said that is a different matter. Furthermore he is too cerebral they said, ah yes I said abstract painting is all right, oh yes they said, but to be cerebral and not abstract that is wrong I said oh yes they said, I found it all very interesting. And then the voting was very interesting, it reminded me of Matisse's description long ago of how they voted the first time he was on a jury for the autumn salon. They began with the a's and everybody looked very carefully and they refused some but they accepted a great many and then the president said but gentlemen remember that the space is limited you must be more exigent and so they looked a little less long and refused a great many and that went on and then the president said but gentlemen after all we must fill the Grand Palais and you are refusing a great many and so they did not look at all long at any of them and they accepted most of them. Voting is interesting. Well anyway, they began to vote at least they said they did but actually they did not and of course I wanted a room for Juan Gris and they said yes yes and I said but you haven't voted it and they said oh yes we did and I said when oh just now they said and somebody else said oh no and they said oh yes well all I want is that they give it to him I said are you certain that they will and the director of the museum said oh yes and that is what was called unanimous voting, well anyway after all I got to like the director of the museum, it is rather nice in France he was for a long time chef du cabinet for Briand and he writes a book about Matisse and Victor Hugo and knows a great deal about everything and has really made of the Petit Palais a very interesting museum and now after all well voting is voting but now after all I am lending him two Picabia paintings to put in, I am lending lots of Picassos of course but he is going to put in two Picabia paintings, you can vote for anything but you can always add anything which is a pleasant thing, that is the reason that Stalin has just announced that there must be a democratization again of Sovietism, that is a natural thing that it is necessary so soon again.

Pictures are interesting and there are a very great many of them in France.

And so our winter went on and now it is spring, and next Friday we go to London to see The Wedding Bouquet put on. Picabia and I will perhaps do one for the exposition the play called Listen To Me, perhaps it is the son of Renoir who will put it on for us and it is all about how the world is covered all over with people and so nobody can get lost any more and the dogs do not bark at the moon any more because there are so many lights everywhere that they do not notice the moon any more.

But first we are going to London to see The Wedding Bouquet and then it will be today.

We left Paris by airplane having first provided ourselves with a

Tunisian boy for Bilignin who seems a nice one and it was a lovely day and the earth is nice to look down on in the spring, we are tied to this earth but after all that is not such a bad thing.

I love airplanes I like them even better than automobiles I like the peaceful hum and the unequal rocking and the way everything looks from them after all if you like and I do like miniature anything and things streets or houses or trees or foliage made of wood or metal for children you naturally do like airplaning, it is completely that thing, it is that itself and what you see when you are looking.

And we were in London again and it is cheerful, even the ragged ones and the used up clothes are cheerful and the new clothes are very cheerful, Paris for the first time in all these years has been depressing, if you have what you wanted and it is not what you want it is naturally not encouraging, that is what they meant when they said that it turns to dust and ashes in your mouth, and Frenchmen have always been so occupied and now they have no occupation, well anyway either they will or they won't, and as Jean Saint-Pierre says every two years makes a generation why not every two months or two minutes why not. Well anyway we are liking it here and every one we know is excited about the ballet and we met Fred Ashton, who did the making a play of the Four Saints and who is now doing it again, so they all say we have not seen it, they all say it is very sad and everybody has to laugh and that is very nice.

We met Fred Ashton. I am always asking Alice Toklas do you think he is a genius, she does have something happen when he is a genius so I always ask her is he a genius, being one it is natural that I should think a great deal about that thing in any other one.

He and I talked about a great deal on meeting, and I think he is one. More likely than any one we have seen for a long time. He was born in Peru and was for three years when a young boy in a monastery and his parents were both English but he does know what it is to be a Peruvian and that made it possible for him to do what he did with the Four Saints to make a religious procession sway and slowly disappear without moving, perhaps being a Peruvian will help him with A Wedding Bouquet.

And Constant Lambert was there the conductor of all the music of it, he had had the idea of putting in the program the descriptions of the characters as I had made them in the play, like they used to do in melodrama, the first play I ever wrote was that, Snatched From Death or The Sundered Sisters and it was nice that without knowing he had that feeling.

Alice Toklas is at present most interested in the curtains in all the English houses when we come to England that is what she finds most exciting that and everything else done by women.

We went to the country for the day and night before watching the rehearsal, I have never seen a rehearsal and it will be very exciting. In the country I went over to a village called Littleworth and passed a field full of calves, being English calves they are brought up to be by themselves separated from the cows and the bulls, in France the calves are always with the cows not often with bulls but often with oxen. Animals in different countries have different expressions just as the people in different countries differ in expression.

And then we went to the Sadlers Wells Theatre for the rehearsal I had never seen a rehearsal a dress-rehearsal, and there were so many there, not only on the stage but everywhere and they do make them do it again and I liked hearing my words and I like it being a play and I liked it being something to look at and I liked their doing it again and I like the music going on. Daisy Fellowes said everybody worked and I was the only one not working. It is quite true what is known as work is something that I cannot do it makes me nervous, I can read and write and I can wander around and I can drive an automobile and I can talk and that is almost all, doing anything else makes me nervous.

I did like the ballet. It was a play and well constructed and the drop-curtain had a bouquet that was the most lively bouquet I have ever seen painted and Pépé the dog was charming and they were all sweet and kind and English, and the characters were real even if they were French and the music and all went together and really there is no use in going to see a thing if you have not written it no use at all, anyway that is the way I feel about it. And so tomorrow is going to be the day and as they all of them have done the work I am not at all nervous not at all and we will see an English audience. England has changed it is the same but it is no longer nineteenth century, Belgrave Square is still there I like to walk around Belgrave Square, the monarchical principle does prevail, and now that there is no other such anywhere it leaves them all free from care, anything that you do that is unique you enjoy when everybody does it it is a responsibility but when you are the only one doing it there is none of course there is none. And so the English are really having a good time. Tomorrow is another day and we will go to the theatre again and see how it is done when there is an audience there. Tomorrow then.

It was tomorrow which was yesterday and it was exciting, it was the first time I had ever been present when anything of mine had been played for the first time and I was not nervous but it was exciting, it went so very well. English dancers when they dance dance with freshness and agility and they know what drama is, they like to dance and they do know what drama is, it all went so very well, each time a musician does something with the words it makes it do what they never did do, this time it made them do as if the last word had heard the next word and the next word had heard not the last word but the next word.

After all why not.

I like anything that a word can do. And words do do all they do and then they can do what they never do do.

This made listening to what I had done and what they were doing most exciting.

And then gradually it was ending and we went out and on to the stage and there where I never had been with everything in front all dark and we bowing and all of them coming and going and bowing, and then again not only bowing but coming again and then as if it was everything, it was all over and we went back to sit down.

I guess it was a great success.

I hope sometime they will do one as a play. I wonder can they.

And then we went somewhere and we met every one and I always do like to be a lion, I like it again and again, and it is a peaceful thing to be one succeeding.

And I like being in London and I like having a ballet in London and I like everything they did to the ballet in London and I like the way they liked the ballet in London and then we went back again to Paris and going back I saw the only thing I have ever seen from an airplane that was frightening, a wide layer of fog close to the water that went right down the middle of the Channel, but the large part near the shore was clear I do not know why but it was frightening and there we gathered everything together and left for Bilignin. That is a natural thing, perhaps I am not I even if my little dog knows me but anyway I like what I have and now it is today.

Index

322

Gertrude Stein refers to her work

Gertrude Stein—thoughts and views on:

GERTRUDE STEIN was born in Pennsylvania in 1874. At Radcliffe she was an outstanding student of William James in psychology, and conducted laboratory experiments with Hugo Munsterberg, which led her to study the anatomy of the brain at Johns Hopkins. In 1902 she joined her brother Leo in Paris, and lived abroad until her death in 1946. Her salon in the rue de Fleurus, over which she presided with Alice B. Toklas, became the gathering place for prominent writers and painters, among them Sherwood Anderson and Hemingway, Matisse and Picasso.

VINTAGE BELLES—LETTRES

VINTAGE BIOGRAPHY AND AUTOBIOGRAPHY

VINTAGE POLITICAL SCIENCE
AND SOCIAL CRITICISM